The Re-emergence of Fascism

THE
RE-EMERGENCE
OF
FASCISM,

DENNIS EISENBERG

South Brunswick
New York: A. S. Barnes and Company

6778
Printed in the United States of America

CONTENTS

TO UNDERSTAND what we mean by the modern fascist—the fascist of the 1960s—to understand the proliferation of neo-Nazi and right-wing extremist movements which is a feature of modern Western life, it is necessary to delve briefly into the roots of this political creed, so often called the ideology of despair and nihilism.

Basically fascism appeared on the political scene as a form of anti-socialist violence under dictatorial control. It incorporated within itself the narrowest form of nationalism. This in turn inevitably led to racialism—the social cancer of the twentieth century.

Dictators are not the invention of this age, but the way authoritarian rulers utilize force today *is* new, for the fresh horizons opened by science and technology, as well as the modern weapon of propaganda with its newly developed psychological trimmings, add a mighty dimension to the despot's fist. How the newly discovered instruments of power came to be pressed into the service of fascism is the secret of much modern history.

Socialism—the first mass secular political ideology—with its universal idealistic principles of dignity, justice and equality, arose out of the Industrial Revolution. To combat this force of socialism, or Marxism, which was to be seen in its most powerful and threatening form in the Russian Revolution, the middle and upper classes, fearing the loss of their well-established positions in society after the First World War, grasped eagerly at the salvation offered by fascism. This was seen in particular in Italy where Mussolini was projected by fascism as a 'shield against the red menace'.

It was essential for fascism to make an ideological impact, to stir the blood and the imagination of the masses, and it seized on the twin forces of nationalism and racialism, both doctrines of division with the emphasis on 'US' as opposed to 'THEM'. The doctrine of 'Our house, our town, our country', or as the Germans put it with such uncompromising thoroughness 'Ein Volk, Ein

7

Reich, Ein Fuehrer', is the exact opposite of the principle of 'love thy neighbour as thyself' preached two thousand years ago by Christ and which embodies the basic ideal behind socialism.

To facilitate the seizure of power, as the fascists did in Germany in the early 1930's, certain conditions must be present. Basically a large disgruntled strata of society—preferably belonging to the same class, with the same background and prejudices—has to be receptive to the new philosophy. Large sections of the middle class in Germany were perfect material; already ruined by inflation in the years following the Kaiser's War, the small shopkeepers and artisans faced disaster a second time during the economic crisis which stemmed from the events of 1929.

Helped by the panic and blind conservatism of fading gentlefolk, this petty *bourgeoisie* was eagerly looking for the salvation which Hitler promised. Another factor which helped the Nazis in Germany and the fascists in Italy was that the established Government in both these lands was weak. In Germany the country was still smarting under the humiliation of its defeat in the First World War, the Treaty of Versailles, and the loss of its colonies. Riding into power on these weaknesses and the mounting economic chaos, Hitler whipped up popular and frenzied support by a blatant exploitation of the 'Master Race' theory with the Jews as his scapegoat.

How useful it was to have a minority like the Jews upon whose heads the blame for the country's economic evils could so conveniently be heaped! Even the name of 'national-socialism' was carefully worked into the myth. With the word 'socialism' a picture of rosy progress, social justice and working-class interest-at-heart could be conjured up, while the Nazi leaders ensconced themselves in power and destroyed all organs of democracy in the process. The word 'national' implied cocking a snook at all 'foreigners'. Certainly no taking orders from Moscow or Wall Street—Nationalism after all was one of the basic pillars of fascist ideology.

Thus Hitler's Germany was built up with its network of Nazi propaganda spreading round the world with country after country throwing up its own believers in 'national-socialism' in one form or another. It had many friends in many lands. For example settlers of German descent who eagerly spread the new gospel in Latin America; local sympathizers in Britain who saw a common enemy; and supporters in South Africa and in many other places. All were actively engaged in spreading Nazi propaganda, organizing secret underground cells and in Europe preparing for the promised invasion by German arms.

In the countries which were overrun by the Wehrmacht, the 'fifth column' of Nazi sympathizers like Quisling in Norway soon became active traitors. After the defeat of Hitler, with Germany lying in ruins, the world waited apprehensively to see what would happen to the Nazi disciples of fascism who had brought about the most disastrous war in the history of man.

Many leading Nazis were brought to trial, but many escaped via such sympathetic lands as Spain and Portugal to the Argentine and other Latin American countries by means of carefully pre-arranged networks like the 'Odessa' (Organisation des Ressortissants de la SS), and a Roman Catholic welfare body in Vienna run by Bishop Alois Hudal, Rector of Rome's Pontifical Teutonic College.

How deeply had the propaganda churned out by the master-minds of the Hitler régime infected the young and middle-aged in the West? The answer seemed a depressing one; soon there were the same anti-semitic incidents occurring in parts of defeated Germany. Jewish cemeteries were desecrated and swastikas were painted on walls. Otto Ernst Remer, leader of the fascist Socialist Reich Party—outlawed in 1951 as unconstitutional—was treading the same path as the early Hitler, with the difference that 'World Communism' had taken the place of 'World Jewry' as the catch-phrase number one. After all there were not that many old Jewish rabbis left to be beaten up in German streets.

Then came the uncovering by the British in 1953 of the conspiracy by Dr Werner Naumann and six accomplices. Bundles of incriminating documents were found indicating that a plot to overthrow the German Federal Republic by placing Nazis in key positions was being carefully organized.

Naumann, who had been named by Hitler as the man to reconstruct a 'New Germany' was arrested, and the Minister of Justice in Bonn, Dr Thomas Dehler admitted: 'Naumann could have been a very great danger to the German state.'

The extent of the projected fascist revival in Europe which centred round this would-be Hitlerian heir was indicated by the string of visitors who had come to Germany to pay their respects. They included the British fascist leader, Sir Oswald Mosley; the daughter of Pierre Laval, who had been executed for collaboration with the Germans in France; General Ramcke, who was busy forming his own Nazi organization in Germany, and Luftwaffe air ace Colonel Ulrich Rudel.

Dr Adenauer was moved to intervene in the matter such was its seriousness. He said that Naumann, a one-time assistant to Goebbels, had been in contact with Nazis outside Germany; that financial help had come from Britain through Sir Oswald Mosley, and from Belgium through Leon Degrelle, the former Rexist leader who had sought refuge in Spain at the end of the war. Backing had also been given to Hitler's chosen successor by other sympathizers from France and from South America.

A few years later in the south of France, the movement launched by Pierre Poujade bore many resemblances to the one which Hitler had founded in Germany. It was racialist in outlook and it appealed to the same type of small-time shopkeeper who had so enthusiastically bawled out 'Heil Hitler' some twenty-five years previously.

A world-wide outbreak of swastika daubing was triggered off on Christmas Eve, 1959, by two members of the German Reich Party who painted the Nazi sign and anti-Jewish slogans on Cologne synagogue. Within days the same act was repeated in countries as far apart as Sweden and Australia. Swastikas were tarred on to the doors of Antwerp's main synagogue and simultaneously in London the words 'Juden Raus' (Jews get out) were scrawled on the walls of a Notting Hill synagogue. Similar slogans appeared in provincial cities throughout Britain. In Oslo, swastikas were painted on the walls of the Foreign Office, while in Genoa, Nazi slogans appeared on buildings and poison pen letters were sent to prominent Jews living in the city. Any doubts about the identity of the men who lay behind these activities were at least partially removed when the two members of an international fascist movement, 'The European New Order', were arrested in Italy and ordered to stand trial by the State Attorney.

In Germany itself fifteen people were arrested by the authorities for carrying out similar activities in a number of towns, and in Berlin a score of young students who were taking part in a clandestine meeting of a nationalist youth group were also taken into custody. At this gathering a black, white and red flag—the old nationalist colours—was displayed. Pinned to the group's emblem was a swastika.

People began to wonder uneasily whether there was some justification for the few lone voices who had been crying out about the revival of an international fascist organization, and who had been gathering evidence that Nazi movements had been springing up and attempting to unite their forces throughout Europe, the Middle East, South America and Africa.

The capture of Adolf Eichmann in May 1960, in Buenos Aires, gave the conscience of democratically-minded people in the West a further jolt. It was obvious that Eichmann had been helped by 'friends' in high Government places in various lands since he fled from Germany at the end of the war. The men who had shielded Eichmann, the self-confessed henchman of Himmler and Heydrich, had also been shielding other Nazi criminals—Eichmann's assistant Franz Novak for example; the doctors who were guilty of murdering tens of thousands of men, women and children, Professor Heyde and Dr Hertha Oberhauser; Dr Joseph Mengele from Auschwitz in hiding in South America and Rademacher in the Middle East. Johannas von Leers, formerly a member of Goebbels' Propaganda Ministry, was another who had first taken refuge in Latin America and then held the key post of Head of the Department for Jewish Questions in the Egyptian Propaganda Ministry until his death at the end of 1964.

The trial of Eichmann again showed the extent of co-ordinated action which exists between fascist groups in Western countries. In Australia prominent Jews received threatening letters saying that if Eichmann died, so would they.

In Washington, George Lincoln Rockwell's 'storm-troopers' demonstrated outside the White House carrying banners inscribed with the swastika and the words: 'Ike—Help free Eichmann!' The 'National States Rights Party' which operates from Birmingham, Alabama, devoted an entire issue of its publication *Thunderbolt* to the captured Nazi using such headlines as 'Eichmann Trial Giant Propaganda Hoax', 'Judea Declares War on Germany', 'Jewish Deceit at Dachau', 'The Jewish Fake Photos', or 'The Great Lie of the Six Million'. The magazine also carried illustrations which claimed to demonstrate 'Jewish atrocities'. Almost the entire contents of this particular issue of *Thunderbolt*

INTRODUCTION

were reproduced from a special printing of a journal published by
the 'British National Party'.

The long-established *Common Sense* magazine, which has a
readership of half a million in the United States, also claimed that
the 'Nazi crimes were fakes'. Published in New Jersey, *Common
Sense* maintains close contact with Nazi groups in Scandinavia
including the 'Sveriges Antijudiska Kampfoerbund', 'Fria Ord'
and 'National Tidning'.

In Italy tracts were distributed which stated: 'International
Jewry with the tacit consent of Western democracies have claimed
another victim in Eichmann, the noblest survivor of a heroic
generation which in Nuremberg consecrated their lives to the
supreme principles which would have created a new European
order. Eichmann, we pledge to remember you.'

Added the Spanish news weekly 'SP': 'The Jews invented an
Eichmann in the Argentine. They caught him in the way you net
a butterfly, then they indoctrinated him the way a clown in a
second-rate circus is taught his role as a Sunday extra.' Cried
Belgian fascists: 'The trial is a diabolical world conspiracy.'

In addition to the concerted action on Eichmann, there has
been a constant effort by fascist leaders throughout the Western
world to minimize the brutalities committed by the Nazis during
the war. For instance, the veteran Canadian fascist, Adrien
Arcand, writing in the extremist Belgian journal, *L'Europe Réelle*
in 1961 said: 'Only 600,000 Jews were killed—half of them during
the Warsaw Ghetto revolt; the rest as a result of insanitary camp
conditions caused by Allied bombing.'

Claimed editor Rodrigo Royo in 'SP': 'I am certain that there
were no gas chambers, as is claimed, for the extermination of the
Jews. I have been in German gas chambers. They were technical
installations of the army for testing the soldiers' gasmasks. All
else that has been said on the subject is sheer fabrication.'

Even as the Auschwitz trial at Frankfurt in 1964 and 1965 was
revealing the ghastly behaviour of the Nazis in concentration
camps, Colin Jordan in his party's *The National Socialist* said in
an article entitled 'The Great Lie of the 6,000,000': 'The zeal
of some Jewish propagandists to exploit the theme of extermination at Auschwitz has outrun their sense of mathematical
propriety and has indicated that they hold a very low estimate of
the intelligence of their readers.'

In fact, says Jordan, 'population statistics culled from Jewish sources can prove that no more than 300,000 people *of all races* died in Nazi concentration camps.'

It is worth quoting further from the article by Jordan for it gives an indication of the distortions pumped out by similar fascists in their journals throughout the West.

'From the moment the National Socialists came to power in Germany in 1933, Jewry—through its colossal power over the press, radio and cinema of the remainder of the globe—began the greatest campaign of vilification which the world has ever seen.

'The main target for fabricated horror stories were the concentration camps, a type of open prison inaugurated by the British during the Boer War, and adopted by Hitler as an emergency measure during his great clean-up of a corrupt and decadent Democratic Germany ripe for Communist revolution.

'Undoubtedly there were some brutalities in these prisons, as in many other prisons in many other countries. It is also true that, in the final stage of the war, starvation, disease and consequently death were prevalent on a large scale, after the tremendous Allied bombing had destroyed stocks of food and medical supplies, or, by paralysing transport, had prevented these necessities reaching some camps overcrowded by the transfer of prisoners from others evacuated because of the Soviet advance.

'What is equally true is that before the war the Jews magnified and invented brutalities to an enormous extent in order to incite Britain and other countries to make war on Germany, and that their own guilt in this respect is immense. Furthermore, at the end of the war, in order to try and discredit National Socialism for all time, the Jews inflated their propaganda to the stage of alleging mass exterminations, putting forward the greatest lie of all time to the effect that no less than 6,000,000 Jews had been killed.

'Faced recently with the signs of resurgent National Socialism, the Jews have sought to reinvigorate the diminishing potency of this great lie by propaganda trials, notably the Eichmann Trial in Israel in 1961, and now this year the Auschwitz Trial in Germany at present in progress.'

Another campaign which echoed round the West was the co-ordinated propaganda effort to free Rudolf Hess from Spandau

Prison. Said the extreme *Charivari* from France: 'Seventeen years after the war the Spandau Prison in Berlin stands as a witness to the ignominy of the Nuremberg trials.'

'Hess,' it added indignantly, 'was accused of having conspired against peace. This is utterly ridiculous. The responsibility for the outbreak of hostilities in 1939 does not rest solely with the Germans. Hess's flight to Great Britain was a measure *for* and *not against peace.* There was no peaceful settlement because the War-Lord Churchill in league with the American master Bernard Baruch, preferred blood, sweat and tears to an alliance with the Germans against Soviet Russia. Churchill was prepared to sacrifice the British Empire in order to win a useless war because Wall Street and the City of London had decided to liquidate the Berlin–Rome–Tokyo axis.'

'Rudolf Hess was an idealist, but he was an embarrassment to be eliminated. And this is precisely what happened,' said *Charivari.*

Leaflets printed in several languages were issued by the 'British National Party' under the title of *Nation Europe, Ring 42 of Coventry.* They demanded the immediate liberation of Hess, described as: 'This man, who had been judged for having made efforts to stop the Second World War in 1941, and who, twenty years later, is still in prison.'

Nation Europa, one of the major organs of international fascism published monthly from the North Bavarian town of Coburg, chipped in with: 'Rudolf Hess flew to Britain during the war on an errand of "mercy" while the German armies were halted outside Dunkirk in order to let the escape of the British Expeditionary Force salvage British prestige and leave the door open for peace.'

'German hands were stretched out but they were not clasped; they were hacked off,' says *Nation Europa* bitterly.

A similar campaign on Hess's behalf was run by the *Deutsche National Zeitung* of Munich as well as numerous other publications.

In another of its issues, *Nation Europa* claims that 'German war guilt is the greatest slander of all.'

This theme, together with the defence of Hitler as a man who was solely concerned with the 'conquest of communism', is another favourite with fascist journals. The Canadian, Arcand, in *L'Europe Réelle*, says: 'Hitler is the greatest conqueror in European history. He had to get through Austria, Czechoslovakia and Poland in order to land his great blow against the Soviet Union.'

'The pact with Stalin was the chloroform applied by the surgeon before the operation.'

Added *Nation Europa*: 'Germany was forced to root out the Eastern pest in its midst. The allegation of the six million murdered Jews is a libel undoubtedly engineered by Moscow and unfortunately also by short-sighted spokesmen of Jewish organizations.'

European fascist movements have in the past few years shown particular interest in the growing right-wing activity in the United States. In June 1962, *Nation Europa* devoted most of its contents to discussing the implications of this political shift in America.

'Anti-communist groups and very active right-wing societies are springing up all over the country,' says the publication. 'The American's quiet indolence and naïve optimism is definitely a thing of the past. Especially in the army and even at universities the Leftist Liberals encounter resistance. There is growing national opposition to which we German nationalists can talk.'

Nation Europa explained that the 'weakness of the right-wing is at present due to a lack of unity among the various factions ranging from the Republican conservatives under Barry Goldwater to the members of Rockwell's Nazi Party.'

The activities of international extremist movements are not always confined to scrawling slogans on walls in the dead of night or writing furious articles in each other's journals. Violence is an inherent part of the fascist creed and co-operation between ultra right-wing elements is again shown in the terrorist campaign in the Alto Adige.

This Alpine region in the South Tyrol was ceded to Italy by Austria in 1918. About 220,000 German-speaking and 120,000 Italian-speaking people live there, and the area has a certain amount of autonomy. But there have been constant demands by German extremists in this province situated just south of the Brenner Pass, for greater freedom.

Helped and financed by fascist groups from Belgium, Austria, France, and Germany, a terrorist campaign was launched in the

Alto Adige and carried out in three stages. There was first a preparatory and organizational propaganda period from 1956 to 1959, a logistical and para-military phase with supplies of arms and explosives between 1959 and 1961, and the employment of armed groups and execution of attacks from 1961.

The aim of the movement is to overthrow Italian rule in the province and scores of plastic and dynamite explosions have rocked the area during the past few years. Between 1961 and 1963 there were over 150 acts of sabotage which caused some £2,000,000 damage. Recently assassination has become an increasingly important feature of the terrorists' activities and members of the security forces have been killed.

In 1963, 162 people—including Austrian and German citizens —were charged with terrorist activities. Later sixty-eight terrorists were tried in Milan—some receiving long prison sentences.

In April 1964, the Italian Government announced that the suspected leader of the underground army in the Tyrol, an Austrian, had been arrested in Rome, together with eleven other members of the organization who were preparing a new wave of terrorist activity. Two months before this, in February, a young West German, Herbert Kuehn, was charged in East Berlin with terrorist bombings in Northern Italy, France, and East Germany. The Essen-born Kuehn had taken part with the OAS in the bombing of Paris cinemas, helped the 'South Tyrol Liberation Movement' in eight terrorist attacks in Northern Italy and detonated bombs in public buildings in East Berlin.

The twenty-two-year-old German extremist was in fact a member of a fascist group who had earlier planned an attack on the radio station Europe Number One in Saarbruecken.

The court was told that Kuehn had once approached the British Nazi Party to propose a federation of such parties in Western Europe, but had met a cool response from two of Colin Jordan's lieutenants. A member of the German 'Reich Party', Kuehn, before receiving a prison sentence, confessed to all his terrorist activities and explained that he was an anti-communist because of the Soviet blockade of Berlin in 1948, because of the crushing of the 1953 rising in East Germany and because of the Berlin Wall.

Although an extreme example, this German symbolizes the

outlook of the young men who have joined the re-emergent fascist parties in post-war Europe. His activities also give yet another indication of how the extremist groups co-ordinate their efforts.

But it is not only fanatics like Kuehn who lie behind the Alto Adige extremists. Right-wing members of the German Christian Democratic Union have supplied money and other material assistance to the terrorists. Fascist periodicals in Austria and West Germany lend constant support to their violent methods.

Despite the number of arrests, the 'South Tyrol Liberation Movement' seems only to gain in strength and daring. In September 1965, Italian troops fought an all-night machine-gun battle with heavily armed terrorists of several nationalities in the mountains of the Alto Adige after the extremists' 'commandos' launched an attack on the barracks of an Alpine regiment.

At a second trial in Milan in January 1966 a further 58 alleged terrorists, including many Germans and Austrians were accused of 160 acts of violence. The indictment showed that the autonomist direction of the movement had been superseded by a pan-German Nazi philosophy. Several of the accused were avowed fascists, one of them being Dr Norman Burger, a university lecturer and leader of a Nazi group dissolved by the Bonn authorities. Another boasted that he was a 'stainless Nazi'.

The early spring of 1961 saw one of the most important changes in plans for the fascist international's future activities. The scene was Madrid, the exact meeting place highly secret. Gathered around the table were such men as 'Scar-face' Skorzeny, Degrelle, Rudel and several other high-ranking Nazis. It was decided at this meeting to try and make Ireland the future home for their activities in the same way as the Argentine had been used in the days immediately after the war.

The methods chosen were the same as those which had been directed against Peron; the country was to be flooded with capital in such a way that the Government would become dependent on the men who control the money purses. Now Ireland was to become a kind of 'refuge' on the door-step of Europe for fascist-minded extremists.

During and after the war the followers of Hitler had transferred large sums of capital to Buenos Aires. The exact total is not known—perhaps will never be known—but many millions of pounds in looted gold, jewellery, precious gems, securities and hard cash found their way to Latin America. Peron was given a good proportion of this money in one form or another to enable him to make the Argentine less dependent on the United States and other foreign countries. In return Peron agreed to give these runaway Nazis sanctuary, new identities where necessary, and a chance to re-establish themselves.

And how well the Argentinian dictator kept his side of the bargain!

After the fall of Peron, it seemed from the Nazis' point of view as though all this effort had been wasted, for many of them were forced to flee from Buenos Aires following the temporary change of political climate.

However, they were able to go to other Latin American countries, and in particular to Uruguay, Peru, Chile and Paraguay, where they were not unwelcome. In Paraguay, for example, many of the men close to General Alfredo Stroessner, the President, were German settlers with great influence. So great, indeed, that a few years ago when the West German ambassador was invited to an elaborate celebration party by the German colony, he found himself facing a hall decorated with swastikas and Nazi banners.

Even today this Latin American republic is sympathetic to former Nazis. It is believed that Auschwitz doctor Joseph Mengele is living in the country. In January 1964, Hubert Alin, the Brussels chairman of the expert committee for the investigation of Nazi crimes of the International Union of Resistance Fighters and Deportees, said that the Nazi doctor had obtained Paraguayan nationality and was 'very probably' working there.

Investigating this report, a Brazilian journalist said that the immigration section of the Agrarian Reform Department listed Mengele's entry into Paraguay under his own name and dated it October 1958. The entry said he came from Buenos Aires, travelling on a German passport. 'The Paraguayan authorities are not interested in giving explanations about Mengele, preferring to surround him with mystery,' added the newspaper man.

Late in 1964 the West Germans revealed how they had tried to persuade the Paraguayan Government to give up Mengele.

But despite repeated requests from Bonn to surrender the war criminal so that he could face trial, Stroessner refused to hand him over. The German embassy in Asuncion was defaced with swastikas and slogans saying 'Jewish Embassy', 'Hands off Mengele', and 'Stop the persecution'. Extremists among the 30,000 German community in the country warned that reprisals would be taken if Mengele was handed over to the Bonn authorities.

But why Ireland? Why should the fascists try and make Dublin their new base?

For one thing Ireland is much nearer to Europe and the country has never been at war with Germany. Secondly there are strong German sympathies among sections of Irish society mainly because of historic bitterness towards the British.

Skorzeny and two representatives of a German and a Swiss bank had protracted talks with members of the Irish Government and they promised to transfer considerable sums of capital to aid its economic development. The Irish in turn promised to give permission for the Germans to use large tracts of Government owned land to afford them tax reliefs. The Irish insisted that the new industries should be scattered widely over the country so as to get the maximum benefit from the influx of capital.

It should be pointed out as far as the Irish Government was concerned, this deal with the former Nazis was not considered a political one. Nevertheless 'protection' for the new capital is promised within a framework of economic aid for the development of Ireland.

That there is still a massive amount of Nazi loot available for former followers of Hitler was commented on at a meeting of the International Union of Resistance Fighters and Deportees in Strasbourg in July 1965.

The resistance men had in fact met specially to ask Governments throughout the world to renew efforts to recover this stolen treasure. Switzerland, South America and Austria were described as the 'three major havens' for hidden Nazi loot, ranging from priceless art works to box-loads of gold coins.

Earlier in 1965 valuable art treasures and caches of gold coins had been dug up in the Austrian Alps and a call was made for

further searches to be carried out in Lake Toplitz in Austria—a
request refused by the authorities in Vienna.

The man who helped capture Adolf Eichmann, Simon Wiesenthal, said that much of the stolen riches were being used to
re-create underground Nazi movements. SS leaders had hidden
tons of stolen valuables in the latter months of the Second World
War. This wealth was now financing the resurgence of Nazism.

An ironic note was added to the meeting of the resistance
fighters. For their gathering took place at the very same hotel
used by leading Nazis twenty-one years previously to plan how
to hide their ill-gotten wealth. At the time an SS officer said:
'It is of the utmost importance that we hide this wealth successfully. We shall need it in the years to come to reorganize the
Nazi party in Europe.'

Who are these growing bands of new-style Nazis and fascists in
Europe?

Who are the members of the fragmented variety of extremist
parties who are forever forming various bewildering permutations
of international networks and setting up ever-increasing numbers
of co-ordinating bodies among themselves? Some are secret,
others are open in their intentions, but it does appear that there
are three main streams of recruits who join these movements.

In the first place there are the men who became imbued with
the Nazi faith long before or during the war and who neither
want nor have the mental capacity to change their convictions.
They know that they are right, that Hitler was right, that national
socialism was and still is the ultimate truth. War-time veterans
keep in touch with other veterans, and officers keep in touch with
old colleagues in their various organizations often in different
countries.

Meeting in bars and dingy cellars they swop reminiscences of
their great days when they trampled so arrogantly over Europe.
Approvingly they nod their heads in agreement as they read the
periodicals issued by the pro-fascist movements of today. Many
of these Nazis have crimes on their consciences, but they keep
their dark pasts very much to themselves.

Secondly, certain pre-war fascist leaders, for example Sir
Oswald Mosley of Great Britain and Maurice Bardèche of
France, have trimmed their sails to modern times. They do not

like to be reminded of their anti-semitic pasts and they now claim that they are not really racialists at all.

Anti-semitism is no longer the mass-appeal force that it used to be and many of these modern-day fascists believe that anti-Jewish activity is not worth the trouble it causes. The old time right-wing extremists now concentrate on the far more rewarding game of anti-communism by which they hope to make Europe a third world force opposed to both 'American capitalism' and 'Soviet bolshevism'.

What of the third type of fascist? The young with the fanatical eyes, the Colin Jordans of Great Britain, the Oredssons of Sweden, the George Lincoln Rockwells of the United States? Since setting up his 'World Union of National Socialists' (wuns) network in which he was appointed 'World Fuehrer' Colin Jordan has been sent to prison but he is now released and has not changed his convictions one degree. In Britain within the past few years he has tried all the methods used by Hitler in his struggle for power. Jordan aims at exploiting the feelings of frustration and bruised national pride due to Britain's relegation to a second-class power in the years after the 1939–45 war. In the United States, Rockwell played upon the fears of communism and exploited the sentiments of racialism and anti-Negro feeling prevalent in many sections of the community.

It is arguable that this younger fascist leader who attracts the support of certain teenagers, and in some countries university students, is potentially more dangerous than the old men linked with the past. In countries like France and Belgium for instance there are sections of the community who feel so keenly the loss of their colonial possessions that they are ready to listen to the emotional harangues of these new, younger extremists. The oas— the Secret Underground Army—in France, for instance, fitted into this fascist pattern. Its youthful leaders exploited nationalism and anti-Moslem prejudices to launch a highly successful campaign of terror against the Algerians in order to win support from and eventual control of the white settler population.

The three streams of fascist leadership have tried repeatedly to come together to form a united command and co-ordinate their activities. The setting up of new parties, and attempts at unification, followed by splits over policy with subsequent re-groupings and the formation of fresh international links under a plethora of names, has been a constant feature of political life in post-war Europe.

Such a gathering was held in Venice in March 1962, when the National Party of Europe (NPE) or as it is sometimes called, the 'European National Party' was established. Dozens of fascist and Nazi groups were represented there and delegates including Sir Oswald Mosley signed a charter known as the 'European Protocol'.

The basic aim of the resulting 'Declaration of Venice' was for Europe to become a third power, armed against and bitterly opposed to America as well as Russia. Closed, inward-looking, a white-man's club, and ruled by an authoritarian Government, the fascist Europe would oppose the United Nations. In Africa, national apartheid—on the pattern developed by Dr Verwoerd— would be imposed. States already independent would remain black, but white settler countries would stay under European domination. It was also decided that the emblem of this European National Party was to be that of Mosley's 'Union Movement'—a flash of lightning in a circle. The new party would be the central organization, under united command and directed by a 'European political bureau'.

This meeting in Italy, however, was not the first time fascists had gathered there in post-war years. As early as 1946 the creators of the MSI or 'Italian Social Movement' assembled together all the Nazi personalities it could get in touch with and who were free to travel to Rome. A 'European Study Committee' was set up and a news-sheet *Europa Unita* made its appearance as the mouthpiece of this group. Contacts were established with Nazis in Germany, Rexists in Belgium, Quislings in Norway, Mussert partisans in Holland, members of the Spanish Falanga, the National Renaissance Party in the United States and with the various fascist leaders of Europe who had fled to South America.

At the same time Per Engdahl, the energetic Swedish fascist, began to expand his activities beyond the frontiers of his own country into Norway and Denmark which had small domestic groups known as 'Reform Movements'. These were eventually merged into a 'National Scandinavian Reform Movement'.

Lord Jowitt, the Lord Chancellor, warned in the House of Lords, in December 1946: 'It is only too true that fascism and

Nazism have not been rooted out. They are there. They are dormant at this present time, but it is possible that they might once more be fanned into flame.'

With the memory of the war beginning to fade, it seemed natural enough that these Nazis and fascist-minded men should think along lines of international action. On the initiative of Engdahl and the MSI in Italy a number of meetings were convened in 1950. Representatives of various countries discussed a programme as a basis for future co-operation and it was this impetus which led to the convening of the Malmoe Conference the following year. This was the first major fascist post-war milestone.

Representatives from Italy, Spain, Germany, Austria, France, Great Britain, Belgium, Holland, Sweden, Denmark, Norway, Finland and various Hungarian exiles attended this gathering which set up the 'European Social Movement' also called the 'Malmoe International'. Among the prominent figures who elected Per Engdahl chairman was the French fascist leader, Maurice Bardèche; Karl Heinz Priester (a former Hitler Youth leader); de Marsanich (who had been an under-secretary of State for Foreign Affairs under Mussolini); Ernesto Massi of the Italian MSI; author Hans Oehler from Switzerland, and Arthur Kielsen from Denmark.

Twenty other West German Nazis were to have attended, but the Swedish authorities rejected their applications for entry permits. Nevertheless, Dr Franz Richter, alias Fritz Roessler, of the German Reich Party, got across the frontier with false papers and took part in the proceedings.

The programme drawn up by these men implied a sort of 'neutralism'—'neither Morgenthau, nor Moscow'—in fact the sort of neutralism with which Hitler had tried to unite Europe. At least sixteen movements were originally affiliated to the 'Malmoe International' and a secretariat was set up first in Rome, later moving to Trieste and back finally to Malmoe.

It was also decided to maintain contact with the Association Argentina-Europa, at that time a co-ordinating body of some twenty neo-Nazi groups under the leadership of the Nazi airforce ace Hans Ulrich Rudel, as well as with the Arab Union, and the Scandinavian-Arab Friendship League. The latter organization is run by John Alling from Denmark who worked in conjunction with von Leers from Cairo. Rudel was then in the pay of the Argentine Government advising Peron on his air force. He was thus able to travel and keep in touch with fascist groups in Lower Saxony—his favourite stamping ground.

Although the Swedish public were only vaguely interested in the marching jack-boots and the raised arm salutes of the brown-shirted members who were distributing Nazi propaganda at this May Congress in Malmoe, it provided plenty of stimulus for Nazis like Otto Skorzeny, Hitler's trigger-man and the rescuer of Mussolini, who had made his way to Scandinavia from the Argentine.

French and Swiss delegates wanted to adopt an 'active racial policy' at Malmoe, but the others hesitated to take up too uncompromising an anti-semitic line, certainly not at such an early stage. The moderates among the representatives did not wish to disturb the image they were trying to create of reasonable men who wanted the public to welcome a new 'cleansed national-socialism' purged of most of the racialist excesses of the Hitler régime.

But the more extreme elements in this movement were dissatisfied with the 'soft-pedalling' of anti-semitism—they wanted to come out quite openly with a virulently racialistic programme. A group of German, Italian, French and Swiss 'militants' banded themselves together into the 'European Liaison Office' (ELO). This movement met in Zurich in September 1951, and in Paris in May 1952, under the secretaryship of Guy Amaudruz, a Swiss Nazi leader. Contacts were established with the ex-Mufti of Palestine, Irish and Turkish nationalists, Falangists, the extreme wing of the Italian Social Movement and with the United States National Renaissance Party. Karl Heinz Priester travelled to Madrid where he held meetings with the Falangists of the 'Blue Division' who had fought on the Eastern Front in Russia.

Efforts were made to bring the two segments of the 'Fascist International' together in brotherly union and a meeting was held in Paris in January 1953, where a 'European People's Movement' (EPM) was established to 'unite all forces fighting to save Christian civilization from Judaism, Communism and Freemasonry.' Over sixty men from the USA, Germany, Italy, Great Britain, Spain, Belgium, Portugal, the Middle East, Switzerland and the Argentine sang their Nazi songs, shouted their fascist war-cries and agreed to stand together, although the two movements—the

Malmoe International and the ELO—continued their separate existences.

In Hanover, in January 1954, another attempt was made to heal the differences between the two groups and the 'United European Popular Movement' or 'European New Order' (ENO) came into existence. Following this gathering there was a great flurry of activity, with meetings being held all over Europe. Engdahl hurried from capital to capital—including numerous trips to France and Portugal, trying to put punch into the activities of fascist parties. He was loyally backed by the Malmoe International committee which at different times consisted of Bardèche (France), Massi (Italy), Wilhelm Landig (Austria), Karl Dillen (Belgium) and Hermann Schimmel from Germany. A conference was called in Luebeck for June 1954, but this was banned by the authorities; other conferences were held in Brussels (October 1954) and in the Hague in the same year.

The Swede was not the only active 'runner' for the Malmoe Movement. Dr Jan Wolthuis, a Dutch lawyer and leading light of the fascist movement in his own country, was caught illegally crossing the German border from Denmark and sentenced to ten days' imprisonment. When arrested by German frontier guards a notebook was found on him containing the names of leading members of the European Social Movement.

Several highly secret meetings were held in Madrid in the next few years attended by delegates from Egypt, Syria, Portugal, several Latin American countries, including the Argentine, Brazil, Uruguay, and Mexico, as well as fascists from Vienna, Brussels, Munich, Wiesbaden and other European centres.

Further meetings included an ENO conference at Lausanne in 1956; another gathering of the same group in Milan in 1958, and the establishment of a 'Young European Legion' as an 'International Youth Movement' in Vienna in 1959. There was a second 'Lausanne Declaration' fascist gathering in Switzerland in April 1960.

Another international group which came into existence in January 1961 is called the 'Northern European Ring'. Fascist bodies from all over Northern Europe belong to this 'NER' which held one of its conferences in Norfolk, England, in May 1961. The movement took as a symbol the sunwheel of the Nordic hero Hermann (Arminius). Nordic history plays a large part in the

'philosophy' of this group. Its policies are based largely upon
Hitler's racial theories, but there is a tendency to use the word
'Nordic' rather than 'Aryan'. The journal of the 'Northern
European Ring' was at first the 'Northern European' subtitled
'Voice of Nordic Racial Nationalism' originally printed and pub-
lished by Colin Jordan's 'British National Party'.

In the past few years the number of meetings and new group-
ings has been on the increase. Some of the gatherings are held
openly, others more secretly—some successful, while others are
complete failures. For instance, the congress called of six hundred
splinter groups from all over Europe, for May 1961, at Wiesbaden
to unite in one 'Emergency Association of Societies Loyal to the
Reich' had to be abandoned at the last moment because of lack
of support. At some meetings the visiting delegates have been
banned by the authorities.

October 1960 saw fascist banners and slogans with swastikas
on show at a meeting in Paris where thirty delegates from Nazi
and fascist movements from France, Belgium and Switzerland
met, despite protests, to study the best means of propagating
their theories. Two years previously the fascist chiefs of Europe
had met at Herblay (Seine-et-Oise) shortly before Christmas in a
hall decorated with slogans like 'to defend the white man is to
defend civilization', 'one doctrine, one fight—national socialism',
'Fascism is the only sincere movement'.

In April 1965 the 'ENO' met again in Italy with delegates
attending from all over Europe. Stirring speeches denouncing the
'racial chaos' for which the 'Pluto' and 'People's democracies'
were responsible were made. 'If mankind is to have any future,
the white race must remain unmixed,' delegates were told. And
in case the point had not been clearly understood, an international appeal to 'support South Africa' was launched.

The movement's journal *L'Europe Réelle* in an article entitled
'National Socialism will not Die', said: 'Hitler and the patriotic
parties of twenty countries yesterday tragically failed in their
European dreams.

'At a moment when all races take stock of themselves, it is sad
to see that the white race renounces its defence on the grounds of
a decadent humanitarianism, cleverly fostered by the enemy. At
the same time, the repression of the forces of sanity is practised
in most countries of so-called democracies.'

In the same edition of this out-and-out Nazi journal, Churchill is attacked as a 'war criminal who ought to have been in the dock of a second Nuremberg Trial together with Eisenhower.' The bombing of Dresden is described as a 'more murderous crime than Hiroshima' while the memoirs of Otto Skorzeny are highly praised.

What progress was the 'National Party of Europe' making after its inauguration in Venice in 1962? Reported Sir Oswald Mosley in his paper *Action* in the spring of 1965: 'A very great advance.' The British fascist leader complained, however, that lack of funds was holding up the forward march of the movement.

'We have all the ideas and none of the cash. But in this great age of decision it will be the ideas that count in the end. For in the coming crisis saving ideas alone will attract the dedicated élite of Europe,' says Mosley.

It can thus be seen that a wide, shifting conglomeration of fascist or semi-fascist movements and organizations exist in Europe and other parts of the West. In July 1963 several Members of Parliament in Britain warned their colleagues in the Commons about the international ramifications of the Nazi movement. The West German Federal Ministry of the Interior stated that there were in existence some 450 organizations and publishing houses outside Germany which were associated with International fascism. There are also about fifty periodicals of one size or another circulating in Europe, written in several languages including French, English, German, Swedish, Italian and Arabic, which are racialist in nature and support fascist and the new Nazi movements.

An indication of how these journals support and sustain each other was shown by an edition of the *Trommler* published in Austria in 1964. This Nazi publication drew the attention of its readers to the merits of a newly-formed 'Irish National Youth' group as well as the excellent reading matter to be found in fascist journals published in several European countries. Its correspondents include extremists as far afield as Australia, South Africa, Britain, Ireland, Spain and Sweden.

In November of the same year a group of anti-Nazi experts representing sixty organizations from all over Europe appealed to Governments throughout the world to ban organizations advocating the Nazi régime or racial hatred. They warned that the Nazi-fascist movement was being built up into one single coherent organization using anti-Negro and anti-communist propaganda as their main platform.

The leaders of these extremist organizations claim to have something like 4,000,000 supporters organized in 10,000 sections and cells all over the Western World. It is difficult to check the validity of these assertions but it would be hardly surprising if the figures have not been greatly exaggerated.

Although these movements are numerous and their supporters are to be found in most Western countries, clearly the economic situation today has little in common with that prevailing at the time of the Weimar Republic. It may be rash to predict, but it hardly seems likely that the social and economic conditions in Germany and Italy at that time will be repeated today.

However, there can be no certainty about this. There can be no certainty that once de Gaulle is no longer on the scene, the elements who backed the OAS in France and Algiers and who are now behind the CNR (the Comité National de la Résistance) may not create a right-wing extremist régime in Paris veering towards fascism.

The members of the fascist movements in Europe are looking hopefully for such an outcome.

All that can safely be said is that at the present time and in the present circumstances the modern fascist organizations are not important politically, nor do they pose an immediate threat to our way of life.

Should circumstances change—and it would take a bold and foolish man to say that this is impossible—then their present irrelevance could alter dramatically. Today these fascist and Nazi parties appear slightly ridiculous with their tin-pot leaders, pompous statements and mumbo-jumbo programmes. They have no mass backing. Their newspapers and magazines are ludicrous and boring. All this may be true. But then, was not Hitler with his tiny fistful of supporters slightly ridiculous, pompous and ludicrous, if not outright laughable in the twenties?

How quickly the political climate can change even in such advanced democratic countries as Great Britain and the United States has been clearly demonstrated in the past few years. The influx of coloured immigrants into England, for instance, has

provoked a certain amount of racial prejudice which in the past
has either lain dormant or not even existed.

How this racial prejudice can be whipped up and then exploited
by an ambitious politician belonging to a generally considered
responsible and respectable party was quite clearly shown by the
Conservative candidate in the Smethwick constituency during the
1964 British election.

In the United States the rising tide of right-wing extremism
under the guise of an 'anti-communist crusade' crystallized into
the figure of Senator Barry Goldwater fighting his presidential
campaign against Johnson on quite naked nationalistic lines. It
was the sort of campaign which would have won the warm
approval and in many ways duplicated the early methods of
Hitler and Mussolini.

True, one extremist Tory Member of Parliament riding to a
short-lived victory on a wave of anti-coloured hysteria does not
necessarily mean that Britain is turning to fascism, but it does
indicate that there are undercurrents of racialism ready to be
tapped by men searching for any means to climb to power.

Again, in the United States, Goldwater was heavily beaten by
President Johnson, but the atmosphere of unthinking passion and
fear stirred up by his campaign is paying handsome dividends in
the form of rapidly increased membership for extremist right-
wing organizations up and down the country.

The present-day fascist groups in the West, whether they be
Oswald Mosley's 'Union Movement', George Lincoln Rockwell's
'American Nazi Party', the 'Tacuara' in Latin America, the MSI
in Italy, the terrorists in Canada and the South Tyrol, or the
Afrikaners' Nationalist Government in South Africa, all claim
that their main concern is to prevent the spread of communism
and to protect the interests of their fellow countrymen.

But this claim is as dishonest and invalid as was Hitler's boast
that he wanted the Third Reich to be Western civilization's
shield against bolshevism. And the world knows only too well
what happened when the Nazi dictator took active steps to
'protect' the future of the Aryan race.

In this book I have tried to outline the circumstances surrounding
the re-birth of fascism in the West. The fascist-like tendencies
of former President Nkrumah of Ghana; the EOKA extremists

of Cyprus and one or two reactionary Middle Eastern countries might well be placed in the same category. The fast-growing 'Soka Gakkai' in Japan, too, bears a striking resemblance to Mussolini's fascist movement with its massive militaristic chauvinism.

But as these countries are neither involved in international fascist movements, nor do they fit the broader pattern of fascist activity as I see it in the West, I have not included them in this volume.

The Re-emergence of Fascism

CHAPTER I

Great Britain

To COMPARE conditions in Britain today with those prevailing in the Germany of the early 1930's would at first sight seem a barren exercise. There is in that country no rampant inflation; no mass unemployment, and no Hitler exploiting a long history of racialism and nationalism to sweep aside a weak and ineffectual Government.

Why then do fascist leaders like Sir Oswald Mosley and Colin Jordan feel so confident that they may yet attain positions of influence and even seize the reins of power within the foreseeable future? Why the revival of fascist activity which has been one of the features of political life in Britain during the past few years? A revival stirred by controversy over the influx of coloured immigrants and the exploitation of racial prejudice by some right-wing politicians as well as small bands of fanatical extremists.

Why the sudden atmosphere of brooding violence; the burning of wooden crosses, bomb attacks on synagogues, threats against the lives of politicians?

The basic answer to these questions is to be found in the discontent generated by the declining economic power of Britain's middle classes evident since the end of the Second World War. Among the reasons for their change of fortune has been the strength of the trade unions and the almost continual full employment since 1945. This has ensured that the earning capacity of the manual workers has caught up with and in many instances overtaken that of the bank clerks and other white collar commuters who so cherished their pre-1939 'superior' status in society.

The resultant resentment felt by the small shopkeepers and suburban wives living in their neat, semi-detached homes would hardly supply sufficient material to encourage inflammatory right-wing movements. But allied to the loss of economic and social status, certain segments of Britain's middle class have been embittered by the fact that the country is no longer a major world power.

Rebellion at loss of personal and national prestige was at first expressed by turning against the traditional party of the middle class—the Conservatives. They either stayed away altogether from the polling booths or voted for the Liberals and produced such political aberrations as Orpington.

But voting for Mr Grimond has proved to be entirely unsatisfactory. The Liberals with their hazy programme have failed to supply the channel through which the chauvinism and pent-up frustrations evident in sections of the angered middle class could find an outlet. And it is from this reservoir of discontent where right-wing extremists like Jordan and Mosley hope in the future to find growing support.

In addition both men realize full well that there is today a ground swell of antagonism towards coloured immigrants among a wide strata of working-class people in Great Britain. This prejudice of race is a highly emotional and explosive issue exploited in the past by ambitious opportunists in other lands with disastrous and bloody consequences for all mankind.

Bruised nationalism and a nascent racialism feeding on class discontent, however, are only some of the ingredients of successful fascism. Should economic conditions deteriorate and mass unemployment spread throughout Britain, then extremist right-wing movements—in one guise or another—may well find willing ears for their violent demagoguery.

Nobody believes more firmly in this analysis than Sir Oswald Mosley, who has pinned all his hopes on an economic decline in Britain. He is convinced that racialism and unemployment will present him with his greatest chance yet of achieving his aim of increasing his influence and eventually becoming Prime Minister.

In an issue of his newspaper *Action* in 1963, Mosley draws an encouraging lesson from Hitler's life:

'Hitler agitated against the Jews and the Versailles Treaty with impassioned oratory and much propaganda skill from 1918 to 1928. He polled in 1928 2·7 per cent of the votes recorded—just under half of our Union Movement's average vote in Britain today. Five years later he was in power with more than 40 per cent of the votes. What happened in the interval? The answer is the great unemployment following the great inflation.'

Again, in Mosley's *The National European* journal of September 1964, the would-be fascist leader of Great Britain warns of an impending economic crisis in the country with 'small firms and employers, pensioners, and all on fixed incomes suffering in conditions of inflation.'

'What are our chances?' asks Mosley.

And he answers: 'None until crisis.'

Following further electoral defeat in 1965, Mosley remained undaunted and in *The National European* of May 1966 said that he found in his non-success 'a strong enough base for a rapid advance when the great economic crisis comes of which we alone have warned the country for years past. Quite often in recent times movements with a lesser vote have been in power very soon afterwards, when their time came.'

To prepare the ground for his take-over, Mosley has carefully tried to eliminate the twin aspects of his pre-war policies—anti-semitism and violence—which has led the British public to reject him and stamp the contemptuous word of 'fascist' on any movement which he commands.

But the leader of the 'Union Movement' has in fact been completely unsuccessful in creating the desired image of the 'new, reasonable' fascism which men like Maurice Bardèche of France and Per Engdahl of Sweden have assiduously worked at since the end of the war.

Both these men claim that they are not 'anti-semitic'. But in fact they remain as racialistic as ever. And so does Sir Oswald Mosley. When he trains his young recruits he has the following advice to offer:

'If the British public thought that you were going to put a curly-haired child of two into the gas ovens, then they would never vote for you. But wait until a child is twenty and has his hand in their pocket. Then say to them: "There's a nice strong government called the Union Movement that can take his hand out again and they will listen to you."'

Mosley's racialist bigotry, indeed, his whole provocative approach to the coloured problem is expressed in the philosophy of 'send the black men back to their own country'. He made his stand quite clear when at a meeting in Trafalgar Square in 1960 he said: 'Two-thirds of Africa should be given to the blacks and the other third to the whites with strong frontiers to prevent them mixing.'

Echoing the extremist policies of the South African Government, Mosley explained: 'We would give territories to the blacks that we didn't want and that would be useful to them.'

At this meeting one of the 'Union Movement's' organizers, thirty-one-year-old Peter Dawson, said that plans were being made to protest against the marriage of Eartha Kitt to a white man. 'If she appears on the London stage, we protest,' he said.

Dawson was sent to prison for threatening behaviour following an incident outside the Ritz Hotel in London when Sir Edward Asafu-Adjaye, High Commissioner for Ghana, was knocked down. 'Black savages, we'll smash you back to the jungle,' said Dawson, who was under the impression that the startled Sir Edward was Patrice Lumumba, the then Congolese Prime Minister who happened to be visiting the hotel at the same time.

Another Mosley supporter at the scene, forty-six-year-old stockbroker's clerk George Doolette, demonstrated his own feelings by shouting: 'Kick the black bastard.' And just in case the point had not been fully taken by the less subtle-minded, a third Mosley man, twenty-seven-year-old Robert McIntyre, shouted: 'Murdering black bastards—we will kick your faces in.' Doolette warned grimly: 'I tell you that things will be very different in five years' time when Mosley is Prime Minister.'

A small incident perhaps. But is not this the sort of racial-induced violence and bullying intimidation associated with fascism as it strives to overthrow democratic rule?

Mosley now claims that he is dedicated to achieving power through the normal processes of parliamentary elections. But in 1949 when the memories of the Second World War and the horrors perpetuated by his former friends and allies were still fresh in the mind, his supporters, flanked by a powerful body of mounted and foot police, went marching through the East End of London—for the first time since 1936.

Mosley's object was clear. He wanted to stir up trouble by holding a fascist rally in an area where many Jews live. Back in 1947 he made no bones about his sentiments concerning democracy when in answer to the question: 'If you gained power would you permit an Opposition?' he replied: 'No. Our object is to eliminate opposition.'

Again and again since his release from prison at the war's end, Mosley has repeated his tactics of holding meetings where trouble could be expected. Again and again his rallies have been organized in sensitive areas where fighting might break out and the resulting publicity gain him recruits. His aim is to create unrest and a sense of insecurity—necessary ingredients in any possible fascist revival.

For this reason Mosley decided to stand as a candidate in North Kensington in the general election in 1958. It was in this area, around Notting Hill, where race riots took place in the previous year.

The moment his nomination was known the colour immigration issue became of paramount importance in the fight for the seat. Persistently Mosley hammered away at the vexed issue of racial discrimination, making statements like these: 'Every white man in a job knows that he has got a coloured man at his elbow, ready to take that job at a cheaper rate.'

'When the white woman is going out to work in the cold dawn the blacks are coming back from their all-night parties.'

'It will cost only eleven million pounds to send them back to the West Indies with their fares paid.'

'All the places including your beautiful squares will be inhabited by the blacks.'

With these crude, racialist views being proclaimed from his public platform Mosley was given, understandably enough, a warm welcome when he went to see that other staunch defender of 'Western civilization', Dr Verwoerd in South Africa. It is understandable, too, why shouts of 'Sieg Heil' and 'Down with Hitler' are heard whenever Mosley or his supporters make speeches.

Meetings and Mosley marches in the East End of London in 1963 were, however, hardly novelties. Even as the war was raging the first symptom of post-war fascism made its presence felt when a lean, black-haired young soldier from East Anglia, Victor Burgess, was court-martialled after being found with fascist literature in his possession.

Sentenced to forty-two days' detention, Burgess was then interned and following his release began to hold meetings in Hyde Park.

Soon he was joined by an ex-school teacher member of the pre-war 'British Union of Fascists'—Jeffrey Hamm. The men had something in common, for Hamm had also been interned—in South Africa—for a period during the war before he was freed and returned to Britain.

As a result of their joint labours, the 'British League of Ex-Servicemen' was born, but as happens so often in extremist political movements, the leaders squabbled and Burgess set up the opposition 'Union for British Freedom'.

By this time Mosley had been released from jail. 'My views have certainly not been modified by my experiences,' he declared. 'On the contrary they have been intensified.'

The fascist flame began to flicker with increasing vigour. Secret discussion groups met and fascist 'book clubs' made their appearance. 'Corporate clubs' were formed at universities and men like Alexander Raven Thomson, one of Mosley's pre-war 'storm-troopers', re-entered the political field.

A Mosley 'News Letter' began to be distributed and in October 1947 the leader of Britain's pre-war fascists published his book *The Alternative*, which laid down his new modified cult. But the semi-mystical prose of the work only served to show that he was quite unrepentant about the past. Indeed, in his *My Answer* Mosley promises quite clearly that 'Great Britain shall be born of the National Socialist and fascist creed.'

Confidence thus restored, Mosley set up a new political party, the 'Union Movement' at the beginning of 1948. Fifty-one different fascist organizations, book clubs and societies, ranging from one-man bands to larger groups, sent three hundred delegates to a school in Pimlico on a wintry Saturday afternoon in February. Outside stood the strong-arm 'bodyguard', and as Mosley marched in with his right hand raised in salute, the three hundred delegates rose to greet their leader.

Provocative meetings, marches and demonstrations followed, as usual in the traditional areas of Hackney, Dalston, Tottenham and Islington.

But it was too soon after the bombings of Coventry and London; too soon after the atrocities of the concentration camps for even a modicum of success to come Mosley's way. He moved to Eire in 1951 where during the war he had friends and influence.

Buying an isolated mansion in Ballinasloe, County Galway,

Mosley told his disappointed British followers: 'I will speak in England again when the efforts of our movement from without and from within have scrapped some of the bars. It is easier to break locks from outside than from inside. . . . My service to the Union Movement in England will therefore be unchanged.

'I believe that I can better serve the British people as well as the European idea from a position of greater strength outside England.'

An indication of what Mosley's 'European idea' meant became clear when his association with the former Nazi, Werner Naumann, was revealed by Dr Adenauer in Bonn in 1953. Sir Oswald, however, denied that he had ever given help to the fascists under Naumann who were planning to put Nazism back on the map in Germany.

Mosley's self-imposed exile to Eire did not last very long and soon he was back in Britain making repeated attempts at a come-back. By 1958 he was publishing a monthly magazine entitled *European* from his Vauxhall Bridge Road headquarters in West-minster. The 'Union Movement's' weekly mouthpiece called *Union, Incorporating Action* was shortened to *Action*.

Mosley's new venture on to the political scene was not without success and prompted the Trade Union Congress to say in September 1958: 'Sir Oswald Mosley and his followers are fan-ning the flames of racial violence.'

The 'Leader' planned yet another come-back in January 1960. This time his 'Union Movement' took steps to combat the boy-cott of South African goods launched by people in Britain who were protesting at the racial policies of Dr Verwoerd's Govern-ment. Saying that he would use 'all means to defeat the boycott', Mosley again reiterated his belief that apartheid should be estab-lished over the whole African continent.

Came this stirring message to fascists and their supporters in Britain: 'I will be back soon. Back in the East End and in all the big cities.'

A month later the inevitable happened. Mosleyites and 10,000 supporters of the boycott clashed amid wild scenes in Trafalgar Square under the shadow of the South African flag fluttering above nearby South Africa House.

This was but one of dozens of meetings of the 'Union Move-ment' which exploded into violence during the past few years.

During 1962 and 1963 there were a series of clashes, minor riots, disturbances and running fights with anti-fascists as Mosley and his men organized rallies in Kensington, Bethnal Green, Earl's Court, Dalston and Hackney, as well as in Birmingham and Manchester. In Sheffield in January 1963, Sir Oswald Mosley, now sixty-six years old, claimed that his membership was increasing. 'This section of our membership consists of businessmen and professional people, many of them influential men.'

If any doubts lingered about the feelings of Mosley's supporters, they were soon dispelled by the scenes at a social event in Islington in August 1962, when his followers greeted him with shouts of 'Sieg Heil' and sang boisterous German marching songs. Christopher Woodhouse, Junior Minister at the Home Office, said in the same month: 'A war has been fought to get rid of a gang of creatures which counted Mosley as their best—and thank God—only friend in this country.'

Even more to the point, the *Daily Mirror* commented: 'Mosley deals in hate. He trades in racial discrimination.'

Strong words, but certainly justified, for Mosley was the man who said before the war: 'Our object is no less than the winning of power for fascism, which we believe is the only salvation for our country.'

Mosley places great importance on the international links between extremist right-wing movements throughout the West and he attends and helps arrange many gatherings of European fascists. One such meeting was planned for London in December 1960, when the 'Friends of Europe' organized a 'European Rally' in Seymour Hall in Marylebone. Invited to appear on the platform with Mosley was Ulrich Rudel, one of the leaders of post-war Nazism in Germany. Another invitation went to Filippo Anfuso, former foreign secretary to Mussolini and now a member of the fascist MSI in Italy. Representatives from France, Austria and Sweden gave notice that they would attend.

But unfortunately for Mosley, who was to have acted as chairman, permission was refused for Rudel to come to Britain and the Marylebone Council hurriedly banned the rally from taking place at Seymour Hall.

Mosley has on several occasions met Rudel. There was a gettogether in Bonn in July 1960, when Otto Skorzeny joined the two men. Ranging further afield, Mosley in 1959 visited Cape

Town where he again met Dr Verwoerd and several cabinet ministers in connection with the activities of his own British 'Union Movement' and its branch in South Africa.

In May 1963, Mosley described some of his international fascist activities in *Action*: 'Just back from Bologna where I was invited to address the first annual congress of Giovane Nazione. Jean Thiriard (the Belgian fascist leader) was in the chair. He has since done splendid work in publishing the policy of the Declaration of Venice in several languages. University representatives from all over Europe were there. . . . All support ardently "Europe a Nation"—our own policy—and agreed the necessity of a united legal European party. Good work was done. It was a chance to meet the new men of value to the European future.'

Mosley's 'Union Movement' with its lightning flash insignia was also represented at a European Easter camp in 1963 organized by the extremist MAC party from Belgium and the fascist 'Jeune Nation'. And in September of the same year an on-the-run OAS gunman was picked up by the police in a London flat where he had been given shelter by one of Mosley's members.

In July 1964 Mosley gave a press conference in Milan organized by the Nazi 'Jeune Europe' movement, before making further political contacts in Germany.

Senator Goldwater was praised by Mosley's newspaper. 'The experience of America will be repeated in different ways in other countries and finally popular anger will break the political stranglehold of the liberal "Establishment" everywhere and will allow true patriots to emerge and defend our civilization against Communism.'

As a token of thanks for support, the American John Birch Society paid for an advertisement in Mosley's *The National European*, pronouncing itself as a movement against 'the Reds'.

Not content with stirring up racialism in Britain, Mosley flew to Buffalo, New York, to give a lecture. He was booed and met with shouts of 'hate-monger', 'racist', and 'remember the millions gassed at Auschwitz'. Emmanuel Celler, chairman of the Judiciary Committee in the House of Representatives, protested about Mosley's visit: 'He should be barred from entering the United States because he is still an avowed Nazi.'

Replied Mosley in New York: 'I am not an anti-semite.'

Despite this disavowal Mosley has shown again and again

where his real sympathies lie. In February 1965 he advertised his party in the New York Nazi paper, *The Free American*, which told its leaders: 'The man the Jews hate. Find out why from the Union Movement.'

The editor of Mosley's paper *The National European* contributes to the international Nazi journal *Nation Europe*. This paper together with other fascist periodicals and books are all advertised in Mosley's 'European Bookshop' list.

Mosley explains his attitude to the Jews in the following way: 'My quarrel with the Jews arose from the fact that they were trying to drag us into a war with Germany. Since the war I have never attacked the Jews except when Israel was trying to drag us into a war with Egypt.' And significantly he adds that if ever he obtained power the Jews would not be 'harmed provided they obeyed the *new* laws that would have to be devised to bring to an end certain practices.'

The 'Union Movement' leader maintains that in any case Britain should 'never have gone to war with Germany'.

'Fascism,' he explains, 'has been the subject of the most intense and mendacious propaganda in history.' And taking up the repeated theme of post-war fascists in other countries, Mosley goes on to say: 'I completely condemn the crime of some Germans in killing defenceless prisoners in their power, but what I feel about Hitler is that he did a great deal for the German people in solving the unemployment problem and raising their standard of living.'

Mosley has had a chequered career. Educated at Winchester and Sandhurst, he became Tory M.P. for Harrow at the end of the First World War. He then joined the Labour Party and became a minister at the age of thirty-two. He might well have attained the office of premier had not his impatient ambitions sent him off the political rails. Branching out on his own Mosley launched the 'British Union of Fascists' at the same time as the Nazis were establishing their rule in Germany.

The movement had its successes and reached its numerical peak of 5,000 members before two events occurred which firmly turned the public from him. Firstly, people were upset by the antics of the 'Horst-Wessel' chanting Blackshirt followers, and the brutal way they handled hecklers at their meetings. The worst example of this was his Olympia rally in 1934 where the viciousness of his 'storm-troopers' shocked even some of his own sympathizers. Secondly, there was the 'Night of the Long Knives' in Germany when Hitler killed off Roehm and Von Schleicher and at the same time gave the world an inkling of his true nature and the methods he intended adopting in the future.

These factors more than anything else turned potential support away from Mosley and from then onwards the influence of the 'British Union of Fascists' gradually grew less and less. There were continued outbursts and disturbances in the East End of London, for long the traditional home of Jewish refugees and immigrants who had settled in Britain. When war was declared Defence Regulation 18b was promulgated and Mosley was thrown into Holloway Jail.

Perhaps to use the word 'throw' is not quite accurate, for Mosley could hardly complain about his treatment. Certainly he fared far better than the enemies of his own friends in Germany who went to the concentration camps.

With his second wife, Mosley was comfortably installed in a four-room prison flat where the couple were able to cook their own meals and Sir Oswald helped by doing the washing-up. He was even allowed to invite in his sympathizers among the other people detained for their fascist inclinations. So ended the first stage of Mosley's crusade of ridding Britain of its 'putrescent' democracy.

Mosley has never ceased pursuing his fascist aims and today is still the head of the largest extremist group in Britain. But he is not the only man in the field. There are three others, Andrew Fountaine, Colin Jordan, and John Bean. All three—and in particular Jordan—scorn the modern, moderate façade of fascism which Mosley and others have tried to create with such immense effort. They brook no compromise with their basic fascist and Hitlerian ideals and make a point of co-operating with other fanatical Nazi groups in Europe, the United States and Latin America.

The political careers of these three men have been connected, but perhaps the least publicized of the trio is the thirty-eight-year-old chemist, John Bean. For the past ten years he has been working behind the scenes as ringleader and policy-maker of the racialistic, semi-revolutionary parties which have sprung up in Britain. He heads the 'British National Party' which claimed an active membership of about five hundred when formed in 1960.

Bean aims at merging all the fascist, nationalistic and extremist groups in the country into one party—a racial one—which would rid Britain of coloured people and remove Jewish influence in the business and industrial life of the land.

He admits quite openly that if he had been in Germany when Hitler came to power he would have joined the Nazis. But guardedly he adds that he would not have had anything to do with the throwing of men, women and children into gas ovens.

The political fortunes of Bean are connected with Andrew Fountaine, who owns land only a fifteen minutes' drive away from the Queen's home at Sandringham. A tall, handsome man, addicted to fast cars, forty-five-year-old Fountaine, who fought for Franco's army during the Spanish Civil War, is wealthy and openly loathes Jews as well as coloureds. Explaining his racialist attitude to any who will listen, he says: 'We all feel some sympathy for all the Jews who suffered during the last war. But they should not be allowed to make that suffering an excuse to take it out on the people who live in Britain.

'Many tens of thousands of Englishmen gave their lives to rescue the Jews from being persecuted and they ought to appreciate this. The only reward the Englishman gets and in fact got was ingratitude, for the Jews were shooting Englishmen in the back in Palestine. My solution would not be the passing of anti-Semitic laws, but to clean up Britain by preventing industrial monopolies and take-over bids practised by Jews. We would not do anything specific against the Jews, but simply erect a climate in which they would not want to live.

'Then they would go and live in other countries like Israel. We must stop the Jews getting and increasing their hold on the economy of this country.'

Fountaine emerged into the world of fascism in 1953 when he started an organization called the 'National Front'. This collapsed through lack of funds and support, as Fountaine could not continue to run the whole organization by himself.

Bean, who at one time had been a member of the ultra-right wing 'League of Empire Loyalists', then joined up with Fountaine to form the 'National Labour Party', but this group was destined to live only a short while and it was followed by the 'White Defence League'—a virulent anti-Negro organization—in

1958. The founder of this group was Colin Jordan, at the time an English and mathematics teacher in a Coventry Secondary Modern School.

Jordan was fortunate enough at this stage to get the financial backing of Mrs Mary Leese, the wealthy widow of the pre-war founder of the 'Imperial Fascist League', Arnold Spencer Leese. The various groups merged and the 'British National Party' was formed. Andrew Fountaine became the president with John Bean and Colin Jordan among the leaders.

It was not only such domestic issues as exploiting anti-coloured feeling in Notting Hill which interested these men. Jordan, for one, was a leading light in the organization behind the 'Northern European Ring' which started the international campaign to free Rudolf Hess from Spandau Prison. Pamphlets printed in Coventry in seven languages were posted up on the walls of houses in Landsberg, Bavaria, and distributed throughout Europe. They also reached South Africa where they were publicized by the fascist 'Boerenasie' organization from their headquarters in Pietermaritzburg, near Durban.

In July 1963 the 'National Socialist Movement' from its headquarters in Princedale Road, London, continued the campaign started by Jordan of spreading unadulterated Nazi philosophy. Leaflets printed by their thousands were distributed 'in every corner of West Germany' claimed John Tyndall, national secretary of the movement. He added: 'Thousands of these leaflets were printed by us and handed over to contacts we have for distribution in Germany. We have all sorts of contacts in Germany, and Germans living outside Germany.

'It is part of our policy to encourage the growth of national-socialism in Germany again.'

With a black swastika in the top right-hand corner, and printed in German, the pamphlets stated:

'National Socialists of Germany!

'We in Great Britain salute the heroic victory thirty years ago of the National Socialism Movement under the leadership of Adolf Hitler and its monumental achievements.

'We know that there is no political freedom today in Germany under Jewish democracy. Any signs of National Socialism are rigidly punished.

'We beg you to maintain your belief in National Socialism. This belief is still alive and will continue to live among the younger generation.

'A new movement is starting in the outside world. The renaissance of the National Socialist Movement has begun. We have joined forces with the Nazi movements in the United States and in other countries. We are beginning the struggle for our ideas and for the liberation of the world from Jewish domination.

'The day will come when the swastika flag will fly again.

'We shall triumph.

'Sieg Heil!

'Germany Awake.'

A number of similar pamphlets had a fortnight previously been plastered up on a Jewish synagogue in Frankfurt.

Prior to these events in 1963 there had been a clash of personalities in the 'British National Party' and Jordan was expelled. Explained John Bean: 'All Jordan ever wanted to do was to be a disciple of Hitler, and by aping the jackboots, uniforms, customs and ideology of Germany in the thirties, he was doing our movement more harm than good.'

Jordan was not, however, a man to let his ideas remain buried for long and undaunted he went ahead building up his own 'British National Socialist' movement, the most extreme and uncompromising of the fascist organizations in the country. Said Jordan: 'I decided to form, finally, an out-and-out Nazi movement.'

Although uniforms are banned in Britain, in the privacy of his headquarters Jordan and his followers dressed themselves up in grey and black uniforms. Adorned with swastikas, black ties, black trousers, black boots, and chanting their slogans, his followers demonstrated quite clearly their racialist and anti-democratic principles.

In August 1962, a rally with delegates attending from Belgium, Holland, Germany, Austria, Italy and Spain was held in the Cotswolds and Jordan claimed that an agreement was drawn up at the meeting whereby he had been appointed 'Fuehrer' of a new world-wide 'Nazi International'.

The main objects of this movement were:

(a) To form a monolithic, combat-efficient, international political apparatus to combat and utterly destroy the international Jewish-Communist and Zionist apparatus of treason and subversion.

(b) To protect and promote the Aryan race and its Western Civilization, wherever its members may be upon the globe, and whatever their nationality may be.

(c) To protect private property and free enterprise from Communist class-warfare.

(d) To work towards the unity of all white people in a National Socialist world order.

(e) To work towards suitable arrangements with non-white leaders of other races to advance racial dignity and justice for each race on the basis of total and absolute geographic separation of the races.

(f) To work towards the just allocation of suitable and reasonable portions of the earth's surface for the exclusive sovereignty of the Black race, the Yellow race, the Brown race.

(g) To work towards an eventual world order, based on race, with just representation from each racial group.

(h) To find and accomplish on a world-wide basis a just and final settlement of the Jewish problem.

'We are aiming at setting up an international network which will co-ordinate all our efforts,' Jordan said. And he added: 'The Nazi leader of the United States, George Lincoln Rockwell, supports me.'

The American 'Fuehrer' who came to Britain on the 28th of July after crossing the Irish border from Shannon, stayed in the country a few days and visited Jordan's camp at Temple Guiting in Gloucestershire. He also paid a call at a week-end rally held under canvas at Andrew Fountaine's estate in Norfolk, run by John Bean's 'British National Party'.

At this camp, members were given lectures on how to deal with anti-fascist demonstrators. They were told: 'We shall be a major political force within five years.'

A number of international supporters of fascism pitched their tents alongside their English colleagues and took part in the festivities. They included Jose Martinas of Barcelona, who is a member of the Spanish Falange Party, at least one German neo-Nazi, a Frenchman who had served with the OAS in Algeria a few months previously, and an official Italian MSI delegate.

The Spaniard, Martinas, told the campers: 'Our movement is spreading rapidly and we are here to discuss ways of forming a link with our British colleagues. We are taking reports back with us to our respective organizations.'

Over the tents fluttered a 'European Nationalist' flag—a white circle and cross on a red background.

Rockwell's presence proved a major embarrassment for the British Government and he was expelled from the country and flown back to America. Previously, in May 1961, another meeting was organized by the 'British National Party'. But this time the authorities had been more alert, for the forty 'guests' with Nazi sympathies who came to Britain to attend were told by airport officials that they could not enter the country.

As the manifestations of fascist and Nazi activity increased in Britain, more and more people began to feel anxious about this renaissance of extremist movements. Opposition soon gathered force and Jordan's August week-end camp was broken up by villagers who resented the presence of the British Nazi and the American guest. Even more trouble was in store for Jordan. With his party secretary, John Tyndall, he was summoned to appear at Bow Street Magistrates Court later in the same month.

The two men stood in the dock wearing dark suits and the sunwheel badge of their party in their lapels, while the court was told that in July 1962 they had addressed a public meeting in Trafalgar Square when they used 'words of such an insulting nature that a breach of the peace would have resulted.'

Tyndall had said at the meeting: 'In our democratic society the Jew is like a poisonous maggot, feeding on a body in an advanced state of decay.'

His leader, Jordan, had this to add: 'Hitler was right. Our real enemy was not Hitler, but world Jewry.

'In September 1939, the blackest day in British history, the long and intensive Jewish campaign was crowned with success. . . . Britain declared war on Germany.

'The coloured invasion is taking place . . . because the real rulers of Britain—the Jews—want it.

'The Jews want it because the breakdown of racial identity and racial pride, the encouragement of a mongrel population, is essential to the long-term security of their overlordity.'

After listening to the evidence, the magistrate told Jordan: 'In my view the words were so offensive to the very, very large majority of people in this country, whether Jews, Christians, Gentiles, or what, that you were positively asking for trouble by going on and using this sort of defamatory language on this occasion.'

Jordan was sentenced to two months' imprisonment and Tyndall to six weeks'.

As leader of the most bigoted of all Nazi movements in Britain, Jordan is fanatically Nazi in outlook. He stands for the expulsion of Jews and coloured immigrants from the country and also wants the abolition of democracy which he terms 'decision-taking by head-counting'. He is striving to see established in Britain a 'Racial Nationalistic Folk State' which would seek to promote the 'great ideals of racial preservation and betterment . . . embodied in the creed of National Socialism and uniquely implemented by Nationalist Socialist Germany under the leadership of Adolf Hitler'.

When he married Françoise Dior—niece of the late Christian Dior—in October 1963, there were scenes of melodramatic Nazi 'realism' at his party headquarters in Notting Hill. On the wall was a picture of Hitler, and over a table draped with a swastika flag the couple made a stern declaration that they were 'pure-blooded'. There followed a blood-letting ceremony onto a copy of *Mein Kampf*, while in the background a record player thundered out Wagner's 'Wedding March'. Jordan's supporters then rounded off the ceremony by singing the 'Horst-Wessel' Nazi marching song.

The going for the would-be dictator of Britain, however, was not easy on the political front. In October 1962 Jordan was sent to prison for nine months and with him to the cells went three other men. They were all members of 'Spearhead'—the élite corps of the 'National Socialist' movement who trained and went on military manœuvres with their swastika badges, uniforms and jackboots. The charge levelled against them was that they had run 'Spearhead' in a way 'likely to cause reasonable apprehension that it would be used for physical force.'

The investigation had been ordered after police found drawings of skulls and cross-bones, swastikas, a German eagle and slogans like 'Race War Now', 'Free Eichmann Now', 'Don't Hang Eichmann', scrawled on a wall in a Kent village. Another drawing found at the same time was of a Jewish-looking man smoking a big cigar and the words 'We will be back' written beneath.

The police watched closely and discovered that twenty-eight-year-old John Tyndall, and forty-two-year-old Kerr-Ritchie, a war hero and holder of the Croix de Guerre, but now styled the 'Goebbels' of Britain, had been drilling eighteen men in full 'Spearhead' uniform of grey shirts and jackboots. Photographs were taken and later it was discovered that Jordan had been training his men in the arts of Judo at his party offices in Notting Hill.

At the trial one corner of the court-room was piled high with photographs of swastikas, portraits of Hitler and other Nazi leaders, German steel helmets, jackboots and field telephone equipment. All these items plus two walkie-talkie radio sets, seven canisters of sodium chlorate weed-killer and tape recordings of Nazi songs had been found at the headquarters of 'Spearhead'.

Jordan explained that his 'Spearhead' movement was in the nature of a 'task force'. Defiantly he added: 'Spearhead will march on. Whatever happens National Socialism in this country and throughout the world will march on.'

The movement aimed at attracting members who had to be 'between sixteen and forty-five of a Nordic type, reasonably robust and have a basic understanding of racial nationalism'.

'The Spearhead man steps forward and marches on as the storm-troopers of the National Socialist revolution in Germany did, continuing the struggle,' said Jordan. Any new 'Nordic type' recruits who joined 'Spearhead' were earnestly entreated to obtain portraits of Julius Streicher which were a 'must for your drawing-room wall'.

The weed-killer amongst the exhibits was sufficient to fill one hundred explosive hand-grenades when mixed with sugar. On the canisters the words 'sodium chlorate' had been struck through and in their place was scrawled 'Zichlon B' which was a chemical used in the gas chambers of German concentration camps. On one tin was written: 'Place a few crystals in a sealed room full of Jews.'

During the trial Jordan said: 'We are the National Socialists and we are anti-Jewish and we are proud of it. The Spearhead member is to fight, if need be, to the last man and last breath. Emphasis is placed on physical fitness, thereby the better to work and fight.'

In actual fact the 'Spearhead' group had been launched by John Bean, but in the early part of 1962 he quit the organization because he said that he was opposed to the 'brainwashing' of members that was going on.

Before he was sentenced, Jordan boasted: 'Nothing will stop us. We are gaining ground all the time. Within ten years with the decline of democracy and general dissatisfaction I will be in power.' Then he added: 'We have done it in the service which we conceive to be for our race and nation in training young men to liberate our country from Jewish control and coloured immigration.'

Sympathetically the other Nazi 'Fuehrer' across the Atlantic, George Lincoln Rockwell, sent Jordan a consoling letter saying: 'Every day in prison will be a medal of honour.'

During the eleven-day trial Jordan laid his final plans for an emergency council to run his Nazi party while he was in prison. He chose Rockwell, who had earlier been elected as his deputy, to take over the role of 'head of the World Union of Nazis'. Jordan used this term for he says that he does not like to be called 'Fuehrer'. 'That title belongs to Adolf Hitler and I can never hope to equal him or deserve his title,' he explains.

Jordan, the Birmingham-born son of a university tutor, first became fascinated by the Nazis in 1938 when he was still a fifteen-year-old schoolboy. Dutifully he joined up when war broke out and after he had failed to become a pilot in the Fleet Air Arm, he was transferred to the RAF. He completed his army service as an instructor in the Education Corps after a spell in the Royal Army Medical Corps.

But the fanatic in him was never far from the surface; in 1946, when he was at Cambridge University studying history, he wrote to Leese, the racialist leader of the 'Imperial Fascist League' to ask for details of his policy. Leese replied: 'The Jews are our misfortune. Democracy is death. Fascism is the only solution.'

And it was on these principles that Jordan based his future life.

Although a member of the right-wing 'British People Party', he went out on his own and formed the 'University Nationalist Club'. In 1949 he graduated with a second-class honours degree, and for a while after this his only political activity consisted ot writing for magazines. Jordan then became a soap salesman in Scotland. Certainly there was no time for such frivolities in his life as girl friends. 'I had no time for women. Political activity occupied all the spare time I had,' he said.

Realizing that the short hours and long holiday periods of the teaching profession would leave him with ample time for his fascist activities, Jordan decided to take a job in a Leeds school. He became a leader of the extremist 'League of Empire Loyalists' in 1955, but this movement's policies were too mild for the hot-headed Jordan. He moved to Coventry—ironically a city which had suffered heavily during the war at the hands of the Nazi bombers—and became a teacher there.

Then followed his association with John Bean and Andrew Fountaine before Jordan finally formed his 'National Socialist' movement and took command of the militant 'Spearhead'.

Party members were instructed to infiltrate into political organizations, schools, cultural societies, sports clubs, churches, trade unions, and the Territorial Army.

Finally the activities of 'Spearhead' led Jordan to the Old Bailey and the nine-month jail sentence. Said one of his followers: 'Even though the leader has gone to jail we will go on . . .'

Jordan, at this moment, has no more than 250 active members, but several wealthy backers have made donations to his movement. The British Nazi leader certainly knows where to find his potential friends, for in a letter addressed to Colonel Shazly of the United Arab Republic, Jordan asked for £15,000 to set up a private radio station off the English coast.

The letter, which was prompted by the anti-Jewish propaganda pumped out by war-time German Nazis now working for Cairo radio, included a request for £2,500 as a personal salary for the year.

When he was released from prison at the end of May 1963, Jordan showed that he had not changed his convictions. He immediately began to formulate new plans for the take-over of Britain. As he left the front gate of Wormwood Scrubs he greeted his supporters who had turned out to welcome him with a Nazi salute. He said: 'I would say that ten years from now we will be in a position as a result of certain developments I have in mind seriously to contest for power in this country.'

'I think that in fifteen years I shall be leading the country.'

He warned: 'If normal conditions prevail we will fight in a normal way. If abnormal conditions prevail then we shall fight in an abnormal way.'

The May issue of the *National Socialist* which appeared shortly before Jordan was released carried a large picture of Hitler on the front page with the headline: 'His spirit lives on', boldly printed above. Underneath the picture the caption explained that, 'On this date—April 20th—we celebrate the 74th anniversary of the birth of Adolf Hitler, heroic leader of the Third German Reich, whose generous wish for peace and friendship with Britain was thwarted by World Jewry and its accomplices.'

'Hitler was right!' adds Jordan in one of his pamphlets which was shown to the House of Commons during a debate in July 1963. 'Democracy means Jewish Control. National Decline. Racial Ruin.'

In March 1963, the movement had celebrated the thirtieth anniversary of Hitler's seizure of power in Germany by secretly testing bombs in pine forests near Bovington Camp in Dorset. Late in 1962 Britain's top Nazi was dismissed from his teaching job in Coventry and in the following year expelled from the National Union of Teachers for 'conduct detrimental to the profession's interest and honour'.

Understandably, Jordan sprang to the defence of Ian Smith's break-away Government, and when the Rhodesian Premier visited Britain, the Nazi leader demonstrated outside No. 10 Downing Street. For his pains Jordan was sentenced to three months in jail for insulting behaviour. (The sentence was later quashed and a fine of £50 substituted.) Earlier Jordan was ejected from the Strangers' Gallery in the House of Commons after shouting slogans in support of national socialism and Rhodesia's UDI. 'Wilson is betraying the interests of our race in Britain by coloured immigration,' he bellowed.

From his Phoenix bookshop Jordan has on sale the usual motley collection of fascist 'literature' including the speeches of Hitler, Himmler and Goebbels. In addition swastika badges, records of Nazi songs and 'Hitler was right' stickers are available.

Altogether some 175 fascist and extreme right-wing organizations have sprung up in Britain since the war, but most of them have faded away—their members now belonging to the three main movements in existence today. Tiny groups such as the 'National Union of Fascists', 'The Friends of Europe', and the 'British Nazi Party' now and then make their voice heard. But they consist of only a handful of supporters.

The fact that the Jordans, Beans, Fountaines and Mosleys have failed so abysmally in the past is no guarantee that the same process of their extremist groups simply splintering, disintegrating or remaining absolutely without influence will continue during the next decade.

For the whole traditional atmosphere of tolerance and calm has changed perceptibly during the past few years. This has been due to the fact that the country has become more and more aware of the growing numbers of coloured Commonwealth immigrants who have sought employment in Britain since the end of the Second World War.

The influx of foreigners into Britain is not something new. But because of the colour of their skins, the million men, women and children from the West Indies, Pakistan, India and various African countries, who now live in the country, are plainly visible as a 'foreign' element.

In the past, racial prejudice against Africans in Britain has not been strongly pronounced as coloured visitors were students or professional men who only met middle-class Englishmen on common academic or cultural grounds. But today's immigrants are generally unskilled and unsophisticated workers whose only contact is with native-born, white-skinned British workers.

Because of the housing shortage in Britain's major cities where the coloured immigrants have flocked, the new arrivals have had to cram themselves into densely populated slum or semi-slum areas, much like the Jews who came to Britain from Russia at the turn of the century.

Different social customs and habits, the high birth-rate of the immigrants, and the resultant strain on the already utterly in-adequate welfare, housing and hospital services, has created tensions among the communities where coloured immigrants live cheek by jowl with English working-class people.

Although it is an undisputed fact that the country needs the immigrants owing to the shortage of labour in hospitals, public transport, and many sections of industry especially in the Midlands, there is a strong feeling among many British workers that their own jobs and whatever hard-earned privileges they enjoy are in danger at the hands of the new coloured arrivals.

Discrimination, whether discreet and subtle in the professional classes, banks, and other white-collar empires, or open hostility expressed by white workers if coloureds came to live next door, is widespread. So widespread that even the most liberal leaders of the Labour Party at the time of the 1964 general election were faced with the harsh reality that fully 25 per cent of their own supporters were flatly opposed to admitting any more immigrants into Britain, while fully half of the electorate demanded tighter controls of entry.

It is against this background of unease over a completely new element on the British political scene with which one must view the danger of a fascist threat.

Most politicians of the Labour, Liberal and Conservative parties have tried to adopt a responsible attitude to the vexed question of racial prejudice, but this was certainly not so in several constituencies during the 1964 election campaign.

Nowhere was this shown more clearly than in the quite open racialist tactics adopted by Peter Griffiths, the Conservative candidate for Smethwick. He quickly set the tone for the whole campaign at his adoption meeting when he promised that 'This town is not to be a dumping ground for criminals, the chronic sick and those who have no intention of working.'

Griffiths, after realizing how easy it was to play upon the racial prejudices and ignorance of the working-class electorate in his Birmingham constituency, constantly harped upon the issue of immigration for some three years before the election.

When gangs of children were heard chanting: 'If you want a nigger neighbour, vote Labour,' Griffiths said: 'We can't stop children reflecting the views of their parents. The people of Smethwick certainly don't want integration.'

And in case the point had not been clearly taken he repeated: 'I regard the slogan as a manifestation of popular feeling.'

Again and again Griffiths made statements which inflamed racial feelings and certainly cheered the hearts of British fascists. 'White girls in moral danger were seen entering Indian houses. They are abusing our hospitality.' Etc. Etc.

Little wonder that John Bean's 'British National Party'

extremists, Colin Jordan's storm-troopers, and other fanatical racialists from all over the Midlands, flocked to Smethwick to try and help the Tory campaign in the area.

The policy of hammering away at naked racialism won the day for Griffiths against the sitting Labour Member of Parliament, Patrick Gordon Walker. Against the country-wide trend to Labour, this former school-teacher recorded a swing of 7·2 per cent to the Tories. But not all Conservatives were proud of the way this dishonourable victory had been achieved and a number of Tory clergymen in the constituency complained of the blatant use of racialism during the bitter campaign. The sort of racialism which induced triumphant supporters of Griffiths to dance through the streets of the town after his victory chanting: 'Take your niggers away, Walker!'

The campaign had touched a new low in British politics and an angered Harold Wilson said in the House of Commons that the Smethwick Conservatives had sent a man to London 'who will serve his term here as a Parliamentary leper.'

There was immediate uproar in the Commons. Uproar repeated at a later date when M.P. Michael Foot said that Griffiths had been engaged in racialist propaganda.

The Tories were angry out of genuine indignation as well as a sense of unease and guilt over the way the ugly issue of racialism had been whipped up by a man sitting on the same side of the House of Commons as themselves.

They knew full well the provocative racialist views of this new colleague who says: 'There is no question of integration in Smethwick. The local people do not want it, neither do the immigrants. This applies particularly here because the majority of them are Sikhs. They have their own way of life and they don't want outside interference.

'There are certain things immigrants must not do. They must not overcrowd their houses; they must not have insanitary gardens or backyards. They must not behave in a manner which gives offence to our womenfolk. They must not spit on the footpath. They must not fill their houses with white women who, shall we say, are no better than they ought to be, who shout at coloured men in the street from upstairs windows.'

Guilty consciences certainly seem to have been pricked to judge by the astonishingly violent reaction when Michael Foot reminded Parliament that the Conservative leader at the time of the election, Sir Alec Douglas-Home, has never repudiated the type of campaign conducted by Griffiths.

Even normally responsible Tory politicians like Selwyn Lloyd have brought joy to the hearts of prejudiced electors by urging, as he did in July 1965, that immigrants who did not fit into British life should be repatriated.

The pattern of Smethwick was repeated at the Leyton by-election early in 1965 when Patrick Gordon Walker was again defeated by a Tory candidate who found himself receiving enthusiastic support from Colin Jordan, Oswald Mosley and John Bean's 'British National Party'. Said *The Economist* in January 1965: 'If there is a single new idea about Conservative policies that has got into the heads of the electorate in the past three months, it is the belief stretching far beyond Smethwick now, that the Conservatives are the party of colour prejudice. It was evident at Leyton.'

In actual fact, although the winning Conservative candidate, Ronald Buxton, disowned assistance from John Bean, the leader of the BNP claimed that he had withdrawn his candidature in the by-election in Buxton's favour after the Tory had requested him to do so.

Said Bean: 'In view of the fact that it would have led to some vote-splitting, Mr Buxton's plea was prominent in our minds when we decided to withdraw.'

Buxton admitted that he had sent the BNP a copy of his immigration brief. 'The next thing I knew was that their candidate had been withdrawn.'

In his determination to win the seat Buxton was understandably anxious that there should be no vote-splitting in the constituency. He knew full well that Bean had 'creamed off' some 3,400 of the most prejudiced votes in the Southall constituency at the general election. He did not want the same thing to happen in Leyton.

Further encouragement to the racist-minded was given by a columnist, Peregrine Worsthorne, in the *Sunday Telegraph* in January 1965.

'Large-scale coloured immigration, however well absorbed in the practical sense, would inevitably constitute a major new element of change in British society,' he warned.

'There is a limit to the amount of change that any society can digest at any period, a limit after which everything becomes so unrecognizably different that people cease to feel at home; cease to feel that they belong. Alienation of this kind is the death of patriotism, since few can love what they do not know or serve what they do not understand.

'Post-war changes in the moral climate and physical appearance of this country had brought us pretty near that limit, and to superimpose the major additional shock of large-scale coloured immigration might prove dangerously unsettling.'

Worsthorne expressed regret that the 'decent arguments for not wanting to turn Britain into a multi-racial society' are neglected by the big political parties, which by so doing 'allow Colin Jordan, on this issue, to speak for England.

'The respectable parties all pretend that in principle they are in favour of a multi-racial Britain. Most people in this country want to keep Britain white and it was hypocrisy which was causing the problem to be discussed in the worst possible manner, not so much swept under the rug as driven into the gutter.

'The correct balance of society is at stake,' added the *Telegraph* writer, who went on to say that Britain was 'still slightly off balance' owing to the entirely white immigration between the wars.

How Hitler's propaganda ministry officials would have seized on this statement had it been made prior to 1939!

After speaking about the immigrants from Hitler's Europe, Worsthorne said that they tended either to be Marxist or Social Democrat steeped in all the 'traditional prejudices of the Continental left.' Because of this boost to the country's 'Left arm' radical trends in, for example, sexual morals, in attitudes to crime and punishment, in the theatre, have swept forward at just that faster pace than would otherwise have been the case, leaving behind just that unnecessary sense of indignation and bewilderment which might have been avoided if the pacesetters had been more sensitive to the nuances of British life.'

There can be little surprise that the *Telegraph* article was enthusiastically welcomed by the extremist *South African Observer*, which reprinted it because 'it reveals a healthy awakening, at long last, to dangers threatening to engulf and destroy the British people'.

Said the editor of the South African journal: 'The British Establishment is primarily responsible for development of the evil racialism in Great Britain. It has thrown overboard the Anglo-Saxon ideal of racial and national integrity and is betraying British traditions, culture and way of life as surely as they have been betraying their own kin in Africa and elsewhere.'

The racial intolerance provoked by extremist politicians and writers playing on the fears and prejudices of the jingoistic members of the public has acted as a catalyst for the atmosphere of violence making itself felt in the country.

One of the manifestations of this was the series of attacks made on a number of synagogues in Britain during 1965. The first incident occurred in March when a house of worship in North-West London was destroyed. During the following months seven more synagogues were bombed and burned while graves were desecrated.

In addition to these attacks a Jewish home was the victim of an arson attempt and fifty-five cases of Nazi-style slogan-daubing such as 'Heil Hitler' and 'We shall free Britain from Jewish control' on synagogue walls were reported to the police.

In December 1965, a thirty-nine-year-old managing director, Aubrey Cadogan, was sent to prison for five years for setting fire to a London synagogue. Detectives unearthed a horde of vitriolic pro-Nazi literature, including books on Hitler, Eichmann and Heydrich, at his home. They also discovered pamphlets dealing with present-day fascist activities all over the world.

Two months later swastikas were daubed on the stonework and wooden gates of the Old Bailey after six young men were charged with setting two synagogues ablaze. The accused received sentences ranging from five years to six months as the judge, Mr. Justice Phillimore, hit out at Colin Jordan's National Socialist movement by saying: 'I am quite satisfied that people in charge of this movement inculcated not merely hatred of the Jews and coloured people, but encouraged active steps against them.' Once again Nazi relics such as badges of the Hitler Youth Movement, the S.S. and swastika armbands were found at the home of one of the accused.

In April 1966, four 'penitent' former supporters of Jordan's Nazi group who admitted setting fire to synagogues were freed after Judge Aarvold said: 'You are young men whose minds seem to have been snared by a philosophy that permits and even encourages the burning down of places holy to and venerated by others. You have been so ensnared and used by unscrupulous people to further their own evil designs, and one does not know whether to pity or blame you.' Explained one of the accused, 'If it were not for the propaganda of Colin Jordan and his wife I would never have done these things.'

In May 1965, Mr Reg Freeson told the House of Commons: 'Synagogues are being burnt out, shop windows smashed, and people being attacked and beaten by thugs belonging to Nazi organizations.'

A Government spokesman told him in reply: 'There is no evidence of a marked intensification of fascist and Nazi activities in our land at the present time. Last year the police proceeded against eighteen fascists and in the first quarter of this year, it is true, they have proceeded against twelve.'

Another Labour M.P., Frank Allaun, told the House of Commons about a letter which had been sent to him and other members from Colin Jordan's 'National Socialist Movement'. This said: 'The toleration and encouragement by Parliament of the coloured and Jewish domination of Britain, and the Racial Relations Bill designed to facilitate these, constitute an act of treason against the British nation.

'We give notice that it will be treated as such in the National Socialist Britain of the future, and those of you primarily responsible will then be brought to trial for this crime.'

The letter was accompanied by leaflets carrying photographs of Hitler and marked with swastikas.

Another prospective 'Fuehrer' of the country, John Tyndall, who had broken away from Jordan to form the 'Greater Britain Movement', found enough support in the new atmosphere of 1965 to open a bookshop selling the most virulent type of literature such as *Last Will and Testament of Adolf Hitler, Unconditional Hatred*, and *Bolshevism is Jewish*.

After putting up pictures of Hitler with the words 'He was right' beneath, John Tyndall's supporters announced that they intended opening up branches all over the country. Like the other extremist groups, the 'Greater Britain Movement' held provocative meetings in areas like Forest Gate, in London, where many West Indian immigrants live.

In September 1965, Scotland Yard's special branch discovered the existence of yet another violently Nazi group which had been recruiting members. Connected with extremist bodies on the Continent, this new movement has cells in various parts of the country and imports racialist literature from both Europe and the United States.

Feeling that things were at last beginning to run his way, Mosley, exuding new confidence, published on the front page of his paper, *The National European*, in May 1965, a pictorial reproduction of his old Blackshirts. The photograph, which included the 'leader' himself, bore the caption: 'The spirit and dedication of the Blackshirts of the Thirties will be needed to meet the coming Red attack on Europe.'

Three months later the journal announced proudly that contributions and subscriptions were on the upswing.

A new magazine, *The Plain-Speaker*, appeared in London to deal with what its first editorial called 'The Financial-Subversive Conspiracy'. Speaking for the 'Integralist World Association', it produced an article on 'Churchill's Achievements and Tragedy': 'A war fought only to defeat Nazism and German aggression and the sole positive results of which were the establishment of the State of Israel (not a British or any other interest and a purely Jewish affair in principle) and the spread of Communism over half the world, with the rest slipping under its sway, is a war lost, not won.'

Even the 'League of Empire Loyalists', a far-out right-wing group which had been reduced to publishing its journal *Candour* at irregular intervals, found itself caught up in the revival of extremism. Its leader, A. K. Chesterton, found sufficient backing to bring out *Candour* regularly.

Another group peddling racialist literature is the Britons Publishing Society which has been going strong since 1919. Its president, Commander F. N. Graves, claims that in 1961 it distributed over a quarter million books all over the Western world. These include, Colin Jordan's *Fraudulent Conversion*, Rudolf Hess's *Prisoner of Peace* as well as the most extreme fascist and Nazi propaganda works ever to be printed.

One of the crudest manifestations of the rise of racial extremism in 1965 was the development of a small, but virulent, British Ku Klux Klan. Copying their trans-Atlantic cousins,

English members of a new-found KKK dumped 'blazing crosses' at the homes of coloured community leaders in London, Birmingham, Leicester and other areas where Commonwealth immigrants had settled.

With the aim of spreading fear and terror among coloured people, the various branches of this movement sent threatening letters to Members of Parliament and warned immigrants that they had been 'sentenced to death'. At various times Labour M.P.s Charles Gibson, Maurice Orbach and Reginald Freeson, received KKK warnings that they would be killed.

In September 1965, police were sufficiently disturbed by a phone call threat on Mrs Joyce Butler, M.P. for Wood Green, to mount a guard outside her home. Three months before this, a London magistrate, Mrs Anne Evans, was also given police protection after the same movement told her that she had been sentenced to death. Mrs Evans had had the audacity to suggest that the 'sooner we had coloured policemen the better'.

In October 1965 security men were close at hand at Blackburn after Labour cabinet minister Mrs Barbara Castle also received an implied KKK threat. Only a week or two before this incident, three members of the Ku Klux Klan were jailed for three months for wearing uniforms at a public meeting associated with a political organization. Two of the men had previous records of racialist activities including swastika daubing, while the third had gone to prison for the unlawful possession of a fire-arm.

One of the jailed men, William Duncan, declared that the aims of his movement were to rid Britain of Jews, Roman Catholics and coloureds by every possible means including violence. All three accused, in addition to five others who faced charges, came from the Coventry area.

Perhaps it was only coincidence but before the month was out there was a mysterious manifestation of violence in the area when two explosive charges of gelignite damaged a 100-foot high pylon carrying electricity to Coventry. ·

At one of the Ku Klux Klan's meetings in Birmingham, Prime Minister Harold Wilson was described as 'nothing but a Marxist pledged to turn this country into a communist satellite'. Also using the same kind of provocative and violent language they had read about from the United States, the leaders of the Midlands group told members: 'We want the niggers sent back to their stinking countries so we can rid this country of fear and disease, lack of housing and lack of jobs.'

Coloured immigrants received letters from the KKK stating that 'Jews, Communists, Catholics and liberal English traitors are all going to get what they deserve from us.'

Indications that the Ku Klux Klan has been trying to get off the ground for some years were made by M.P. Fenner Brockway in 1957 when he said that the movement had agents in seven British towns. In the previous year a Joe Cleveland advertised the movement's activities from his room in London which was hung with swastikas and portraits of Hitler and Franco. A United States based KKK group made efforts to start up cells in Britain and a unit was uncovered at an American Air Force base in Essex.

In 1965 the recognized KKK chief in the United States, Grand Imperial Wizard Robert Shelton, felt sufficiently encouraged by the progress of English admirers that he contemplated making a flying visit to Great Britain. However, he was warned by the Labour Government that he would not be allowed to land.

Most people dismiss the curious antics of the 'British KKK' members as the work of cranks and immature publicity seekers. It is true that their numbers are minute, but as the *Sunday Mirror* warned in June 1965: 'Police reject the notion that the Klan is already at work in Britain. They see these despicable incidents as the work of juvenile delinquents or people with a childish mentality.

'Let them remember that a hundred years ago the KKK began as a prank. It was a prank that degenerated into terror, a jest that nourished blind prejudice and unleashed hatred.'

John Bean's 'British National Party' was not left behind in the more promising atmosphere of 1965. Becoming more and more active, Bean's supporters held a meeting in Trafalgar Square with banners proclaiming: 'Scrap the Coloured Commonwealth' and 'Stand by Ian Smith'. As police made arrests during the uproar which followed, Bean's followers chanted: 'Support Smith, a man with guts.'

The BNP's viciously racial *Combat* news-sheet makes regular references to its international links and recommends its readers to buy the U.S. National States Rights Party *Thunderbolt* journal.

Among its wares for sale are works by Dr Verwoerd, pre-war literature written by the English Nazi, A. S. Leese, as well as *L'Europe Réelle*, the Belgian extremist paper.

The extremism evident in fascist propaganda and the emotion evoked by implied or overt racialist statements made by some extreme right-wing politicians and writers has naturally enough created violent reaction.

In October 1965 a bomb blasted the home of Smethwick's M.P., Peter Griffiths, in his absence, shattering the entrance and causing extensive damage. Said the surprised Mr Griffiths: 'I cannot believe that I have upset people sufficiently to justify such an outrage.'

Jewish groups began to set up day and night guards outside synagogues as Rabbis urged worshippers to join vigilante squads to protect their buildings against further attack. Anti-fascist groups have sprung up whose members say: 'We are determined to see that what happened in Germany will not happen again. We will meet force with force.' As a result, groups of men and women have systematically tried to break up extremist meetings. An example was given in October 1965, when thirty militant young men succeeded in ambushing and attacking John Tyndall and his supporters on their way back from a provocative meeting in Dalston which had disintegrated in chaos.

Coloured immigrants warned, too, that they had decided to form vigilante patrols to protect themselves against further attacks from Ku Klux Klan groups.

All these are small incidents, perhaps, hardly sufficient to raise a general alarm. But it is important to remember the lesson which both Hitler and Mussolini taught any future would-be fascist dictator. It is vital for any extremist movement to create a general mood of violence. Would-be dictators must provoke physical opposition, rioting, disturbances, the setting up of opposition 'defence' groups. This leads to a disintegration of normal democratic political processes giving small extremist groups an opportunity to make progress and attract recruits.

Then as the German and Italian dictators demonstrated, the trick is to pose as the sole protector of order and thus seize power providing 'firm' government.

Even if potential extremist elements in Britain find Mosley's 'Union Movement', Jordan's Nazis or the Ku Klux Klan too distasteful for their liking there are in existence other more 'respectable' right-wing bodies. One such movement is the 'Freedom Group' which was formed for the purpose of keeping the Labour Party out of power.

The chairman of this organization, Edward Martell, has made his 'anti-Socialist' position quite clear on several occasions. In August 1963 he opposed Anthony Wedgwood Benn in Bristol, declaring that it was a bad thing to give a Socialist a walk-over at any time. Benn, the former Labour M.P. who had won his fight to renounce his title and return to the House of Commons, had expected no opposition in the by-election which resulted.

The Conservative M.P., Malcolm St Clair, who was returned when Benn was disqualified, decided to leave the field clear.

Martell fought hard calling for the abolition of family allowances, the lowering of school-leaving age, the introduction of intelligence tests for voters and imprisonment for those who advocate strikes. Nearly 19 per cent of the voters who turned out at the booths found his extremist right-wing views sufficiently attractive to support him.

The leader of the 'Freedom Group' regards such Tories as R. A. Butler and Iain Macleod as 'dangerous pink Socialists'. Commenting on Conservative Party policy in 1962 Martell called it bitterly, 'disastrous leftism that has landed the country where it is'.

His movement is composed of five independent organizations all of which are firmly under his direction. There is the 'National Fellowship', 'The People's League for the Defence of Freedom', the 'Anti-Socialist Front', the 'Free Press Society', and in addition a newspaper, the *New Daily*, which Martell edits himself.

Claiming the support of 160,000 men and women whose names he keeps on a 'master index', Martell's 'Freedom Group' in its holy war against Trade Unions ran 'freedom buses' during the London bus strike and an emergency parcel service in 1962 during the postal 'go-slow'. His members are also willing to be called upon to drive railway engines and unload cargo ships in the future if necessary to break strikes.

Trade Union practices still stand between this country and its return to 'sane Government and a national morality based on Christian principles', says the 'Freedom Group'.

In February 1964 the movement launched a campaign to infiltrate Conservative constituency associations throughout the country. The aim of the specially created small groups or 'cells' was to combat any 'softening' of Tory policy – and spread the influence of men who believe in Martell's extreme right-wing views.

It is only too easy to shrug off Martell as being unimportant; to dismiss Mosley's fascist movement and the lunatic fringe who follow Colin Jordan as worth nothing more than nuisance value in Britain today. Their organizations are small and have little real support, but the conditions for their growth could change dramatically in a country where the middle classes are suffering from economic discontent and hurt national pride and where segments of the working class are vulnerable to racialism. Conditions which provide fertile ground on which a mass fascist movement thrives.

Normally the Conservative Party would be considered completely immune to the corrosion of its high principles by any extremist pressure group. The vast majority of its candidates at the 1964 general election scrupulously avoided the immigration issue often in the knowledge that they could have won votes by 'doing a Griffiths' and stirring up racial prejudice.

But the vexed question of racialism has found its leadership floundering before the onslaught of the former M.P. for Smethwick, Peter Griffiths. Comments like 'This is a white man's country and I want it to remain so,' by veteran Tories like Sir Cyril Osborne have indicated that Griffiths is not alone in his extreme views.

The explanation for this bending by the party leadership—it is not a capitulation as yet—beneath the onslaught of irrational racialist hysteria was put bluntly by Griffiths in a speech he made in November 1964 when he said: 'At least twenty seats in London, the West Midlands and elsewhere can be won if the Conservatives take a firm line on immigration.'

His 'firm line' on immigration is, of course, the exposed portion of the anti-coloured racialism iceberg he has so championed during the past three years.

Many Tories realize the tremendous electoral asset stirring up racialism could and does provide. To many Conservatives Peter Griffiths is the new 'Messiah' showing the way to the promised land—i.e. electoral victory over Harold Wilson's Labour Party.

Griffiths is a popular draw with Conservative party groups up and down the country and is in constant demand as a speaker.

The Conservative leadership is well aware of the extremist right-wing pressure being brought to bear on its M.P.s and prospective candidates, especially in the Midlands. Bodies like the 'Birmingham Immigration Control Association', the 'British Immigration Control Association' and the 'Vigilant Immigration Control Association' have launched a campaign which in many ways resembles the tactics of the extreme right in the United States when it attacked the leadership of the Republican Party, panicking it into accepting its champion Goldwater as presidential candidate.

Both before and after the 1964 election local Birmingham-area newspapers were bombarded with indignant letters from 'public citizens'. Meetings of protest about the 'immigration menace' were held throughout the Midlands. Provocative leaflets designed to frighten workers into believing that their jobs and wage packets as well as their womenfolk were being threatened by the West Indians, Pakistanis and Indians 'flooding' into the country, were distributed. Specially printed postcards and letters were directed to Tory Members of Parliament and Conservative Party offices.

Although racialism was a muted theme in the 1966 election, and Peter Griffiths was swept out of his Smethwick seat, extreme right-wing prejudice is far from dead. For example the Racial Preservation Society started up in June 1965 by a Brighton antique dealer, James Doyle, claims to be 'deeply concerned about the effects of massive coloured immigration on the future pattern of our society and race'. With members joining from all over England, the society's journal *The British Independent* says that branches are being opened almost weekly.

The group aims to 'repatriate coloured immigrants from this country' and that one cannot 'unmongrelize a mongrelized race'. Adds Mr Doyle, 'It is biologically harmful to dilute Caucasoid blood'.

The *British Independent* is filled with provocative statements, like 'Harold Wilson is a Communist'. It applauds the South African government, and carries such headlines as 'Immigration and Health-Anxiety Growing', 'Coffee-Coloured Britain' and 'Crime and Coloured Immigration'. The Journal also Advertises 'Support

Rhodesia' car stickers (50 for 3/6). Action against the movement was demanded in the House of Commons, and when this was refused a Conservative M.P., John Hunt, said: 'Have we not reached an absurd situation when legislation passed by the House to deal with incitement to racial hatred is found to be inadequate to stop the dissemination of this kind of racial filth?'

In May 1966 Mr Hunt told the House that he had been threatened with hanging if he continued to oppose extremist racialist organizations. He said: 'One extremist organization informed me that those responsible for what they call the contamination of our land will hang on Tower Hill for their treason against the British people and the writer warned: 'Make sure that you are not among them!'' '

These 'immigration control' organizations, local 'residents' protection bodies and preservation societies find that they attract large numbers of sympathizers and active members wherever they open their doors for business. Although a comparatively new development on the British political scene their potential is enormous. For the moment their influence is felt in the pressure they put on the Conservative Party. But should these movements coalesce into a national organization skilfully stirring up racial hatred and prejudice and then exploiting the resulting chauvinism, the results could be highly damaging to democracy in Britain.

The Labour Government has played its part, too, in helping the growth of racialism. 'Socialist' leaders have strengthened the restrictive clauses of the Conservative-introduced Commonwealth Immigration Act, and have shown a strange reluctance to make use of the watered down Race Relations Bill to put an end to the racialist activities of men like Jordan, Bean and Tyndall.

What makes the situation even more disturbing is the fact that traditional democracy as we know it in this country is being eroded by the growing power of bureaucracy and the centralization of real power in fewer and fewer hands. This thought was ably expressed in an editorial in *The Times* in March 1963.

'People are being placed more and more at the mercy of authority and of the executive,' said *The Times*.

'The techniques of power, of political manipulation, of the predatoriness of officialdom, become ever more insidiously efficient. . . . Against these, the community and the individual have all too few safeguards. Parliament is not a sure one. The law is even less so.'

The point about the 'law' being 'even less so' was made painfully clear when the Lord Chief Justice, Lord Parker, had this to say when speaking in connection with a journalist who had refused to reveal the sources of his information during the proceedings of the Vassall Tribunal: 'Your duty in the ordinary way as a citizen . . . [is] to put the interest of the State above everything.'

The 'totalitarian implications' in the statement by Lord Parker were condemned in a motion tabled by two Conservative Members of Parliament in March 1963.

The Times editorial had in fact taken up the argument that the freedom of the press and consequently the whole foundation of democracy was in question following the jailing of the two journalists.

With democratic ideals being squeezed from above, with racialist pressure groups strengthening the hands of the chauvinistic right-wing of the Conservative Party, it is little wonder that men like Mosley see prospects of their creed of fascism gaining ground in Britain.

Should economic conditions deteriorate then one or another of the various movements or trends mentioned in this chapter may well attract mass support. The resulting challenge to democracy would be a strong one.

CHAPTER II

Australia and Canada

AUSTRALIA

THE influence of Sir Oswald Mosley has extended as far as Australia where one of his former admirers, Brian Henry Raven has established the fascist 'Australian Workers Nationalist Party' with its headquarters in Melbourne.

Like many another of its kind, the AWNP maintains close links with a number of international extremist organizations, but in particular with Rockwell's 'Nazi Party', with the 'Christian Knights of the Ku Klux Klan' and with Swedish groups at Malmoe.

The programme of these Australian fascists follows a pattern set by similar movements in Europe: 'Smash communism; keep Australia white; form a strong United Government and a Greater Australian Workers State.'

Raven, when inviting Rockwell to tour Australia, echoed the thoughts of Jordan and many others of the same view by saying: 'Our aims are to further the cause of white people throughout the world.'

This young admirer of Hitler is not the only right-wing extremist in Australia. Perhaps the best known is forty-eight-year-old Eric Butler of Melbourne who publishes *The New Times* and *Intelligence Survey*. He is also the secretary of the 'Social Credit Organization', and director of 'The League of Rights'. Butler also finds time to run a 'Heritage' bookshop which sells racialist literature.

Over the years Butler's magazine and his bookshop have circulated statements like these: 'Hitler worked for the Jews who wanted the countries of the world opened to their infiltration.'

'The communists work for the Jews who want world conquest,' and even:

'Churchill worked for the Jews in his destruction of the British

Empire for the achievement of which he was made an honorary member of the Council of the Elders of Zion.'

There is also reference in Mr Butler's literature to the 'vile sexual habits of Jews'.

Butler denies being an anti-semite and declares that he is 'only a Christian who opposed Judaism because he is Christian.' He sees the solution to the 'Jewish problem as the conversion of the Jews to Christianity'.

Butler is closely associated with A. K. Chesterton, the anti-semitic leader of the British 'League of Empire Loyalists' who frequently reprints articles from the fortnightly *The New Times* in his own publication *Candour*. The Australian extremist also maintains the closest contact with Ron Gostick, chief of the 'Christian Action Movement' in Canada and S. E. D. Brown, the editor of *The South African Observer*.

Acting as the Far East correspondent of the American John Birch Society , Butler is warmly praised by this far-right group as Australia's 'most significant anti-communist'. His books, *The Red Pattern of World Conquest* and *The Fabian Contribution to the Communist Advance*, are recommended to American readers.

Another man in the same line of activity is a certain D. W. de Louth of Queensland. He has his own printing press and repro-duces hundreds of different items of fascist material published in Europe—in particular from Britain and from Sweden. He also maintains contact with extremist sources in Latin America.

'The Australian National Socialist Movement' created by a New Zealand immigrant, Donald A. Lindsey, overlaps to a certain extent with the AWNP. Its major support is concentrated in South Australia and New South Wales, and counts among its leaders Arthur Smith, a Sydney dry cleaner, and E. R. Cawthorn of Adelaide University. This group has been active in importing fascist literature from the United States, Sweden and South Africa. In April 1964 the Australian Senate was asked to prohibit this tide of Nazi propaganda.

Two months later police raided the headquarters of the Australia Nazi Party and arrested five men after seizing gelignite and arms. Extremist activity seemed to be growing, for in September 1965 a new fascist movement, the 'National Australia Party' made its first public appearance in Melbourne—complete with jackboots and brown shirts. The party's national organizing secretary, Juris von Rand, a German settler, held a public meeting from swastika-painted rocks beside Melbourne's Yarra River. Explained the new Aussie would-be 'fuehrer': 'The party is violently anti-communist, strongly nationalistic and determined to clean up Australia's filthy moral climate.

'We are willing to use force to achieve our aims, if necessary. We are militantly right-wing. I suppose in fact we could be called fascists.

'One of the party's main aims is to justify many of Hitler's policies.

'Our party is not violently anti-semitic, but we don't believe that anything like six million Jews were killed in Germany. Anyway, most of them were probably criminal types or diseased.

'We are going to grow, and we are going to win. It will take time, but we cannot be stopped.'

In a minor key, another fascist—this time an immigrant from Britain—who made himself unpopular in Australia was a John Crouch who caused a stir when he told fellow aircraftsmen serving with him in the Air Force that he was a Nazi. Eventually the Air Minister, Mr David Fairbairn, announced that Crouch was to be discharged from the forces.

There is also a strong fascist element among the East European immigrants who have settled in Australia since the war. In particular, former Nazis from Hungary have been active in setting up political groups which publish racialist and extremist propaganda.

The activities of Yugoslav immigrants who belong to the fanatical Ustashas Croat movement have come under close survey by Australian security police during the past three years. This followed the trial in Belgrade in 1963 of nine Croats newly returned from Australia who had been arrested for plotting to assassinate President Tito. Investigations revealed that Ustashas had been undergoing guerrilla training in remote parts of Queensland.

A wave of terrorism between the openly Nazi Ustashas bands and other Croats in Australia caused the authorities some alarm and in May 1965 new uniformed Ustashas recruits were reported to be in training. Police raids uncovered a host of modern arms as well as training manuals and books on sabotage sent by Ustashas headquarters in Madrid.

A Labour Member of the Australian Parliament, Dr J. Cairns, claimed that Ustashas extremists had threatened his life after he disclosed that among the 44,000 Yugoslavs living in Australia at least 2,000 were Nazi inclined.

In NEW ZEALAND there is very little fascist activity, although a 'National Socialist Party' is in existence run by A. G. McKechie. It is modelled on Jordan's group in Britain.

CANADA

A NATO meeting scheduled to take place in Ottawa in May 1963 presented just the opportunity wanted by the terrorist 'Quebec Liberation Front' to publicize its activities throughout the West.

The crimson letters FLQ two feet high and crudely painted, made their appearance overnight on buildings in the centre of the city. Threats were made to bomb hotels where the Nato foreign ministers had booked rooms. And the authorities took the warnings seriously enough to divert large numbers of the mounted police to the job of hunting down the fanatical right-wing French Canadian terrorists.

Parcels were carefully examined, guards posted in and around hotel entrances, and a close twenty-four-hour watch kept in the city streets. Check points were set up and buildings where the conference was to take place were floodlit. Every possible precaution was taken for the FLQ had a list of achievements to its credit reminiscent of the OAS in its own early terrorist days in Algeria.

The comparison with the secret underground army in France's former North African colony is apt, for the 'Quebec Liberation Front' is inspired by the OAS terror campaign in Algeria, and a number of its former gunmen who had fled when the Moslems gained control of their country came to settle in Canada with other European 'pieds-noirs' settlers.

Scores of terrorist acts and bombings rocked Montreal. One such attack in April 1963 resulted in the death of a sixty-five-year-old night watchman at an army recruiting centre, and another explosion critically injured a bomb disposal man who was trying to remove dynamite from a letter-box.

During one morning in March 1963, three Molotov cocktails were exploded in the armouries of Canadian Army camps in Montreal after the letters FLQ were scrawled on to their walls.

Another incident occurred when the movement dynamited a section of railway line near Quebec City about six hours before the then Prime Minister, Mr John Diefenbaker, was to have gone by during his election campaign. An engineer spotted the damaged line in time and it was repaired before Diefenbaker's arrival. The terrorists also planted a bomb in the federal revenue department building in Montreal and hurled another explosive at the Royal Canadian Mounted Police headquarters.

Bombs made their appearance in letter-boxes, 'mountie' recruiting centres and in radio stations that closed their programmes with the British National Anthem. The 'mounties' were singled out in particular as they are considered to be 'an occupying bourgeoisie colonial force'.

Then, in July 1963, a stick of dynamite blew up the statue of Queen Victoria built at the turn of the century in Quebec. General James Wolfe, the architect of the French defeat in Canada, was also blasted off his pedestal. These last acts of vandalism were perhaps the most symbolic of all the terrorists' attacks, for the FLQ was born in the simmering discontent generated in the French-speaking province of Quebec.

The avowed object of the movement—and others like it—is to obtain independence for Quebec from English Canada by a violent struggle of its 'farmers, labourers, students and intellectuals against Anglo-Saxon colonialism and its flunkies of the Quebec bourgeoisie.'

This is what the FLQ described as its aims in its manifesto:

'Suicide squads of the Quebec Liberation Front have as their mission to completely destroy by systematic sabotage:

'(a) All the symbols and colonial institutions (federal), in particular the "mounties" and the armed forces.

'(b) All the information media of the colonial language (English) which holds us in contempt.

'(c) All enterprises and commercial establishments that practise discrimination against Quebec people, and who do not use French as their first language, but who use instead the colonial language (English).

'(d) All the factories which discriminate against French-speaking workers.

'Independence or Death.'

The movement added that its 'suicide commandos' carried special identity cards and said that if any were captured they would expect to be treated as prisoners.

The FLQ also set up a 'Tribunal Revolutionaire des Patriotes Québeçois' which was to judge 'foreign and Quebec criminals who are traitors to their country. This tribunal will deal only with the most important cases. In case of guilt, two sentences only will be passed: exile or death.'

The frustrated national pride in Quebec Province is nothing new and has its roots in the mid-eighteenth century when Britain's General Wolfe defeated France's Marquis de Montcalm on the Plains of Abraham outside Quebec City. The British gained control over most of the territory and ever since then the French settlers and their descendants have looked on themselves as conquered people. They have made repeated requests for Quebec to be granted its independence from the rest of Canada.

The French Canadians have some justice on their side. They contend that the ideal from the very beginning was for the French to be equal partners in a bilingual country. But it has not worked out that way, for the English-speaking communities have ignored the French language and culture. The inhabitants of Quebec province have discovered that when there is competition for jobs they always lose out to English-speaking Canadians. It is always the French-speaking Canadians who have to learn English—and never the other way about.

In addition large segments of industry, mineral wealth, and commerce in Quebec are in the hands of much-detested English-speaking Canadians or Americans, while the natives of the province—an area twice as large as Great Britain—have hardly invested to any extent in their own enterprises.

As a result many of the six million French-speaking population of the province feel that they are ruled by 'foreigners'. In particular, this sentiment applies to the poorer and more backward inhabitants of the predominantly Roman Catholic countryside which until 1960 lay dormant under the corrupt régime of Premier Maurice Duplessis. Then Liberal leader Jean Lesage swept him aside and whipped up the simmering nationalism of the Québeçois with the slogan of 'Masters in our own Home'. Lesage looks to France for new investment and cultural contacts to help break the economic stranglehold of the 'Anglo-Saxons'.

The strength of the desire for autonomy by the citizens of Quebec was amply demonstrated in the 1966 provincial elections when Lesage was defeated by the more conservative Union Nationale. The leader of this party, Daniel Johnson, had pulled in the extra votes by outdoing Lesage on the separatism issue.

A number of separatist movements nourished by narrow historic nationalism and racial sentiments have sprung up. Although claiming to be liberal they are in fact fascist in outlook.

Groups of tough young men hurled defiance at the authorities by holding rallies, chanting war-cries and rioting in the city streets. Slogans have been painted on buildings in the dead of night and the cry: 'Québec oui, Canada non' is frequently heard.

One of the separatist organizations is the 'Alliance Laurentienne' run by Montreal University professor, Dr Raymond Barbeau. This movement claims 2,000 members and publishes a journal with a circulation of 3,000. It aims at setting up a 'Conservative Catholic State' called 'Laurentia'.

Then there is the RIN—'National Independence Rally' (Le Rassemblement pour l'Indépendance Nationale) which wants the fleur-de-lis flag to flutter above the Union Jack in Quebec. With an estimated 3,000 membership—including large numbers of students—this movement demands the abolition of federal income tax and the setting up of a school to train diplomats for the proposed new French state. In the provincial elections of June 1966 this separatist group polled 5·6% of the votes cast.

One of its leading figures, thirty-four-year-old university graduate André d'Allemagne says: 'We are not anti-English. We admire their tradition of fair play, their justice. But we do resent the fact that they run the army, the diplomatic corps, and they determine our foreign policy and dominate parliament. We want a unilingual French-speaking nation outside of Confederation.'

D'Allemagne claims that the 'new' nationalism in Quebec is 'liberal'—standing for greater control over Quebec's resources—'not Socialism, but perhaps a mixed economy.'

In August 1963, the movement staged a peaceful demonstration while a salute was being fired from Mount Royal, Montreal, in honour of the birthday of Queen Elizabeth the Queen Mother. Two plaques in Quebec City, one commemorating the visit of King George VI and Queen Elizabeth in 1939 and the other marking the spot where General Wolfe's troops landed, were torn from their stone bases and carried away.

One of the founders of the RIN, Dr Marcel Chaput, a scientist, refuses to speak English and broke away to form the 'Quebec Republican Party' (Parti Républicain du Québec). This staunch champion of separatism insists: 'Separatism is not a dream fantasy but the legitimate desire of a people defeated on the battlefield.'

In February 1964, Dr Chaput attacked the proposed visit of the Queen to Quebec by saying: 'Some of my own people are ready to let her know—and brutally—that she is no longer welcome in French Canada.' The Royal visit had been planned as part of the celebration of the 1864 conferences that led to Confederation.

Dr Chaput told two hundred members of the 'Young Men's Canadian Club' that 'violence is a probability' if the visit took place. 'The Queen's visit is a provocation,' he added. 'French Canada is a conquered nation which wants its freedom.' He added that there was nothing that English-speaking Canadians could do to prevent the creation of a separate French nation in North America.

'Independence is already half achieved. The other half is to be achieved and it will be achieved,' he concluded.

Professor Barbeau added his voice of resentment at the visit: 'I am afraid of what might happen if the Queen visits Quebec.'

In fact the Queen came to no physical harm during her visit in 1964, but on her tour of Quebec City she was met by a cold, utterly hostile population. There were no cheers, no warm words of greeting normally associated with Royal visits. If nothing else, this demonstration of calculated rejection by the French Canadians showed to the world at large that they were in deadly earnest over their campaign for full recognition by their English-speaking countrymen.

Eventually a number of FLQ leaders were caught by the police and at their trial in Montreal the young terrorists were utterly unrepentant: 'As members of the FLQ we do not recognize the foreign law under which we are accused.

'It is true that we committed these acts, but we committed them certainly because we believed and still believe this is the only attitude that can free the people of Quebec from colonial domination and the yoke which weighed upon it.'

Despite the court sentencing nine of the men to terms of

imprisonment ranging from six months to twelve years, terrorist groups were soon active again.

During the November 1965 general election a time-bomb was found in a Montreal hall soon after Lester Pearson, the Canadian Prime Minister, had addressed a rowdy political meeting. The device was found only thirty feet from the rostrum where Pearson had stood his ground while fists flew and chairs were overturned in the rear of the hall in a fight between his Liberal supporters and French-Canadian separatists.

It was the fourth such time-bomb found within a few days. All failed to go off.

In February 1964, the Canadian Minister of Defence, Paul Hellyer, was questioned about the continuing thefts of arms and ammunition from Quebec armouries.

Even as he was making a stern announcement about the tightening-up of security measures, five young men broke into the armoury of a Canadian Artillery regiment and escaped with semi-automatic rifles and ammunition.

Shortly before this incident—in January—fifteen masked men made another spectacular grab at a Montreal military base and drove off with a lorry load of machine-guns, more semi-automatic rifles, field mortars, bazookas, bombs, radio equipment, small arms, and ammunition. Extremists then broke into an armoury at Shawinigan and stole a further fifty rifles after scrawling 'ALQ' on the walls.

A police officer in Montreal said: 'There isn't much room for doubt that these guys have a plot on their minds. The terrorists who have accumulated a stock of weapons in the raids are young, fanatical and capable of a suicide mission that would win maximum publicity for their cause.'

This series of thefts was the work of a new group, the 'L'Armée de Libération du Québec' and its political wing, the 'Comité Révolutionnaire du Québec'.

Despite their obvious dangers and fanaticism, these extremist movements have only a limited membership—mostly students or young men in their twenties. It has been left to the right-wing authoritarian Social Credit Party which deals in bigotry and extreme nationalism to whip up the major support in the province of Quebec.

Led by forty-five-year-old Réal Caouette and Robert Thompson, the Social Credit Party won a major triumph in the mid-1962 elections when it attracted sufficient votes to muster thirty seats—twenty-six alone in Quebec Province. This made it the third most important party in the country.

Founded during the depression as the 'Douglas Credit Party', the movement evolved a quaint financial system which aimed at balancing every issue of goods with an equivalent issue of purchasing power. This was to be done by monthly payments of cash from the Government to private citizens.

Although it won substantial support from French Canadians and has even formed two provincial Governments, Alberta and British Colombia, it has never been in a position to put its economic theories to the acid test of practicability.

Thompson is the official leader of the Social Credit Party, but the real driving force behind the movement was Réal Caouette with his impassioned oratory and extravagant promises. He has managed to channel much of the chauvinism of Quebec province in his direction and has succeeded in doing this by buying time on commercial television to expound his views.

Both he and the fifty-one-year-old Thompson demonstrated the extremist right wing's classical virulent anti-communist stand by dismissing the multi-million-dollar long-term contract signed by Canada and China in 1961, covering wheat, barley and flour, as one of the 'greatest hoaxes ever perpetuated on the Canadian people'.

The two men proclaimed in unison: 'Even today Australian and American troops in Indo-China are facing an enemy fed on bread made from Canadian wheat.'

Caouette, the fourth child in a settler's family of fifteen, admits that he was an admirer of Hitler and says: 'When I was a boy in the great depression I longed for prosperity. In Germany Hitler had achieved prosperity and order for his people.

'In that respect I admired him. But I never had any use for his racial theories, and of course when he went to war my admiration vanished.'

But with a careful eye on the conservative Catholic vote, Caouette adds: 'One must remember that Mussolini gave the Pope his freedom back and brought religious education back into Italian schools.' Caouette also boasts that he refused to fight for Canada during the war.

Despite the smooth excuses explaining away his leanings towards fascist ideology, Caouette ran into difficulties with his own party following 'unwarranted statements' endorsing Hitler and Mussolini as 'great organizers'.

After a two-day crisis meeting in Ottawa in July 1963 the party's National Council sacked him, but he still has great support among the rank-and-file members. He won twenty seats in Quebec province in the 1963 elections while the party in the West could only muster four successes. Fighting the November 1965 election as the head of his own breakaway 'Créditistes', Réal Caouette could chalk up but nine successes, while Thompson's 'Social Credit' party won five seats. The Quebec wing of the Social Credit Rally and a splinter group from the RIN formed Le Ralliement National in 1964, but has met with only limited success.

So impressed was Rockwell, the leader of the American Nazis, with Caouette, that he flew to Montreal to meet him, saying: 'He is my kind of man. I only know that his heroes are Hitler and Mussolini and I agree with him.'

Right-wing extremism, however, is not confined to Quebec province. Besides the Hitlerian ideals brought by some East European refugees and war-time Nazis who sought a haven in Canada under disguised identities, there are, too, a number of native-born fascists in the country. One such man is the veteran Adrien Arcand, who before the war led 10,000 blue-shirted followers of the 'National Unity Party'.

In the early days following the defeat of Hitler, Arcand remained politically dormant. But he resumed his activities by writing for international fascist journals.

Besides Arcand there have been a number of other men who have engaged in fascist activity since the war. One such extremist is Derek Sones, from Britain, who is one of the leading lights of the 'Canadian League', in Toronto. There is also André Belle-feuille, a self-styled Nazi leader from Sorel, Quebec, who said: 'I am an anti-semite and I am proud of it.' Bellefeuille held meetings where oaths paying 'reverence' and 'respect' to Adolf Hitler were given. The gatherings were marked by members raising their hands in the straight-arm Hitler salute while shouting 'Heil' in unison.

Ron Gostick, another extremist who edits *The Canadian*

Intelligence Service, claims that it is the 'Reds who promote racial revolution in the United States.'

Gostick's journal, which acts as the mouthpiece for the 'Christian Action Movement', reproduces material from other fascist periodicals. For instance, in February 1965 an article about Jews financing world-wide communism first printed by Eric Butler in Melbourne was reprinted for the benefit of Canadian extremists.

In 1963 racialist pamphlets were distributed in the country by American Nazis through the hobbies columns of Canadian newspapers. Such advertisements read: 'Nazi propaganda leaflets. An interesting hobby. Free sample.'

To those answering the advertisement a batch of five pamphlets were dispatched through the post. One outlines the party's programme promising to 'investigate, try and execute all Jews proved to have taken part in Marxist or Zionist plots.' Another pamphlet describes the Jews as a 'people of robbers' and a third, which claims to have been smuggled out of Eichmann's death cell, says that the former Nazi leader was tortured into confessing that he murdered Jews.

A strip cartoon showing Uncle Sam being kicked over a cliff by a bearded man carrying flags bearing the Hammer and Sickle and the Star of David makes up the contents of the fourth pamphlet. The last one promises to 'weed out all non-Aryans from North America.'

A few months after these racialist pamphlets had been advertised in Canada, one of the men behind their distribution was arrested in Birmingham, Alabama, on charges of incitement to riot and interference with the police. Toronto was then showered with anti-Negro and anti-Jewish leaflets, and the slogan made familiar by Colin Jordan, the British Nazi, that 'Hitler was right —communism is Jewish', was scrawled up on buildings in the city.

On the 12th November—following a day of Remembrance for the victims of two world wars—hundreds of leaflets were scattered from the top of a skyscraper. The campaign spread to the province of Quebec, especially among the students of McGill University and Loyola College in Montreal.

Further Nazi literature was widely distributed expressing sentiments like these: 'We demand the arrest of all Jews involved in communist or Zionist plots, public trials and executions. All other Jews would be immediately sterilized so that they could not breed more Jews.

'This is vital because the Jews are CRIMINALS as a race, who have been active in anti-Christian plots for nearly two thousand years.'

Protests about the growing racialist activities of Nazi groups were made by religious organizations including the United Church of Canada, trade unions, student bodies, etc. But an increasing number of extremist bodies from the United States, including the National States Rights Party, have in the past two years sent speakers and literature to Canada.

In April 1966 a committee set up by the Federal Government advocated new laws to stop the dissemination of this hate propaganda. Alarmed by the distribution of racialist literature and meetings of fascist groups which had provoked violence in Toronto, the committee commented: 'The triumphs of fascism in Italy and National Socialism in Germany through audaciously false propaganda have shown us how fragile tolerant liberal societies can be in certain circumstances. They have also shown us the large element of irrationality in human nature which makes people vulnerable to propaganda in times of stress and strain.'

The interest of the American fascists in Canada is understandable for they see north of the border a wide field for their fanatical propaganda among a powerful group who feel that for language and cultural reasons they are looked on as inferior.

The nine English provinces of Canada may regard the emergent nationalism in Quebec as a nuisance and even slightly ridiculous. But to right-wing extremists it represents an open door to the prospects of political influence and power.

CHAPTER III

The United States

As the Negro riots in Los Angeles, Chicago and other cities have demonstrated so vividly, the black man in the United States of America is kicking aside his janitor's uniform and demanding rudely and aggressively, urgently and without equivocation, his fair chunk of the American way of life. Right *now* he wants equal voting rights, equal opportunity of employment, equal schooling. And he wants the full weight of the law and the Constitution flung into the battle against racialism.

Compromise, timid step-by-step de-segregation and the token introduction of a Negro here and there into the higher echelons of Government or the administration are no longer gratefully accepted crumbs. The demand for genuine equality is without a doubt the greatest internal challenge which democracy has had to face in the United States since the Civil War.

As men of goodwill and liberal inclination brace themselves for the social and political convulsions which have yet to be faced, the opposing forces of reaction and prejudice see in the struggle their best opportunity yet of fighting their way to power.

Even if the de-segregation issue had not reached its present explosive state, there is sufficient evidence that American democracy is in any event today facing an immense challenge from the far right. This has happened before—the post-war extremist hysteria of McCarthyism, for instance, did great harm to the country before dying a natural death.

But there is something far more dangerous in the present right-wing revival which has been gathering momentum in America in the past few years. It has many forms, many shapes, a vast sweep of movements, societies, and groups of men ranging from the respectably conservative Arizonan Barry Goldwater, to the late fanatic George Lincoln Rockwell and his American Nazi Party. Throughout the wide spectrum of the reactionary right runs a consistent theme and philosophy—the obsession with anti-communism.

Sometimes hysterical, sometimes coldly intellectual, motivated either by fear, outraged nationalism, ignorance, racial prejudice, pure self-interest or genuine idealism, the men behind the 'red menace' scare are finding it more and more a magnet to attract support, publicity, money and power.

The causes behind the growing fear of communism in the United States are not difficult to pinpoint. There was the first Sputnik 'bleeping' its triumphal path through the heavens, followed by Russian rockets and Russian cosmonauts hammering home their superiority in space research achievements. Many Americans previously complacent about the all-round superiority of the United States have had their illusions swept aside with a frightening jolt. Berlin, Laos, Vietnam, the growing strength of China, diplomatic defeats or cold-war stalemate, the traumatic experience of watching Fidel Castro ride cock-a-hoop in Cuba— and nothing, or apparently nothing being done about it—all add to the feeling of panic and fright.

Sensing this widespread wave of fear, right-wing leaders and organizations up and down the country have intensified their rabble-rousing, emotional appeal to the less sophisticated American. 'The red menace is everywhere' reiterate the preachers, politicians, gospellers and lecturers of the fascist right wing.

Robert Welch of the John Birch Society has warned that even Eisenhower is part of the communist plot; the fiery crosses of the Ku Klux Klan again light up the night sky of the Southern States, while the swastikas of George Lincoln Rockwell make their appearance more and more often.

Despite the defeat of Goldwater in the Presidential election, the extreme right wing goes from strength to strength. Money from big business floods into the coffers of these reactionary movements as increasing numbers of people become worried about the international situation and look for reassurance in the strident voice of extremism.

On bought time on the radio, on television, in a flood of books, leaflets, letters and newspapers—from the slick and glossy 60-pager to the hastily printed, badly edited broadsheet, on long-playing records, tape-recordings and car stickers, Americans are warned in the name of 'God and Christianity' about the 'internal red threat'. Well-paid lecturers and trained orators stomp the country; schools and seminars are opened by the score, meetings and highly organized postal campaigns thunder against the 'commie danger'.

'Strike a blow against the Reds by sending five dollars today! Not tomorrow! Send it today!' is typical of the high-pressure salesmanship employed. The message of the 'red menace' is even put over intertwined with an 'anti-fluoridization of drinking water' campaign. One proclaims: 'The fluoridization of drink supplies is an attempt by Jewish Bolshevists to wipe out Christians by poisoning their water.'

Why only Christians would have their taps contaminated is not explained.

Many of these men and organizations deny that they are fascists, but their methods of grasping for power through violence —open or implied—are fascist in origin. And although the roots of democracy are deeply embedded in the American way of life, and freedom is a cherished tradition, there is considerable latent danger of this fascist tide gaining increasing power and influence.

Both Kennedy and Eisenhower felt sufficiently alarmed by the growing volume of right-wing pressure to warn the country against these 'so-called patriotic groups'.

'We need no such super-patriots,' said Eisenhower, and Kennedy stated: 'If their view had prevailed we would be at war today and in more than one place . . .

'In the most critical periods of our nation's history, there have always been those on the fringes of our society who have sought to escape their own responsibility by finding a simple solution, an appealing slogan or a convenient scapegoat. At times these fanatics have achieved a temporary success among those who lack the will or the wisdom to face unpleasant facts or unsolved problems.

'Under the strains and frustrations imposed by constant tension and harassment, the discordant voices of extremism are once again heard in the land. Men who are unwilling to face up to the danger from without are convinced that the danger is from within. They look suspiciously at their neighbours and their leaders. They call for a man on a horse because they do not trust the people. They find treason in our churches, in our highest court, and in our treatment of water. They equate the Democratic Party with the welfare state, the welfare state with Socialism and Socialism with Communism.

'So let us not heed these counsels of fear and suspicion.'

The Attorney-General, Robert F. Kennedy, added his voice: 'These movements are a source of tremendous danger.'

Little did he realize just how immediate the danger was, for shortly afterwards, in November 1963, an assassin's bullet struck down his brother, the President, in that fateful Texan city of Dallas.

Now the communist leanings of Lee Harvey Oswald, the killer, are well known. But despite the findings of the Warren Commission there are still many questions which remain unanswered about this political assassination of President Kennedy. In the wider sense, however, the name of the man who actually pulled the trigger hardly matters; what does matter is that the real culprit of the shooting is the deliberately engendered climate of hate, fear and violence stirred up by the right-wing extremists in the United States.

Chief Justice Earl Warren had this to say: 'Surely there is a lesson to be learned from this tragic event.

'If we really love this country and love justice and mercy and fervently want to make the tomorrows better for those who are to follow, we can at least abjure the hatred that consumes people, the false accusations that divide us and the bitterness that begets violence.'

And Senator J. W. Fulbright, chairman of the Senate foreign relations committee, added: 'Redemption for the death of President Kennedy could come from a national revulsion against extremism and violence.'

There was wide evidence that American life had been marked by 'a baleful and incongruous stand of intolerance and violence,' said the Senator.

'In an atmosphere in which dissent can be regarded as treason, in which violence is glorified and romanticized, in which direct action is widely preferred to judicial action as a means of redressing grievances, assassination is not really a radical departure from acceptable behaviour.

'It is to be hoped, profoundly to be hoped, that there will be some redemption for the death of our President. That redemption would issue from a national revulsion against extremism and violence, from a calling forth of the basic decency and humanity of America to heal the wounds of divisiveness and hate.'

Continued veteran columnist Walter Lippmann: 'The divisive forces of hatred and ungovernability are strong among us, and the habit of intemperate speech and thought has become deeply ingrained.

'It is deepened by the strains of war and the frustrations of this revolutionary age, by the exploitation of violence and cruelty in the mass media, by the profusion of weapons and by the presence of so many who know how to use them.'

President Johnson added his own voice when he called for an end to 'the teaching and preaching of hate and evil and violence in the land.'

The assassination, perhaps, could have taken place almost anywhere in the United States, but there is a certain ironic symbolism in the fact that the deed was performed in Dallas. For this second largest city in Texas has for long been a home of right-wing extremism. As Lippmann again put it: 'Dallas has long been conspicuous for its tolerance of extremists and for the inability of its decent citizens, undoubtedly the great majority, to restrain the extremists and restore a condition of honest and temperate and reasonable discussion.

'In this atmosphere of political violence lived the President's murderer, himself addicted to the fascination of violence in his futile and lonely and brooding existence.'

Two of the country's leading reactionary champions, General Edwin Walker and oil millionaire, Haroldson Hunt, live in Dallas, and Texas itself has a senator—John G. Tower—who ranks with Barry Goldwater in extreme conservatism. Chief of the 'National Indignation Convention', Frank McGhee, has in the past demanded that President Kennedy be tried for treason. His movement favours the impeachment of Chief Justice Warren and the abolition of income tax, and is one of the groups recommended by 'Nation Europa', the fascist international mouthpiece.

McGhee is backed by Captain Eddie Rickenbacker, who is regarded as the 'wise old man' of the extreme right. A First World War flying ace, Rickenbacker retired from his post as chairman of the Eastern Airlines in December 1963 to crusade for the 'American Way of Life'.

The 'National Indignation Convention' has held rallies and mass meetings to express the anger of its members at the training of Yugoslav pilots at an Air Force base in Texas. It had sufficient support to attract 2,400 delegates to a national convention it organized in 1961.

Another staunch supporter of the Convention is the wealthy super-patriot, Texan rancher J. Evetts Haley, who also says that he would like to hang Justice Warren. Haley runs 'Texans for America', an organization which spends a lot of time keeping 'subversive textbooks' out of the hands of schoolchildren. This campaign had some success, for fifty books have been removed from the shelves of Texas schools. In 1962 it succeeded in getting the State's Education Agency to alter every textbook adopted for use in Texas schools to meet the organization's standards of 'Americanism'.

Robert Welch added his voice to the climate of extremist hysteria by saying in June 1962, 'I categorically predict that the United States will be occupied by Chinese communist troops by summer 1972. This is the Kennedy plan.'

Only weeks before the President was shot, members of the John Birch Society, the Young Americans for Freedom and a Cuban counter-revolutionary organization—Alpha 66—man-handled and insulted the late Adlai Stevenson, the country's United Nations representative when he visited Dallas to make a speech. He was hit on the head with a picket sign while books and pamphlets were hurled at him. When the city officially apologized to Stevenson for the treatment he had received there, General Walker flew upside down the five American flags he normally keeps fluttering outside his house in protest. Three years previously Lyndon Johnson and his wife—both Texans—were roughed up in the streets of the city when campaigning for Kennedy. Johnson was spat in the face and called a 'dirty renegade'.

Stores owned by Jews in the main streets of Dallas were plastered with black swastika emblems, and in 1961 the city's Junior League succeeded in preventing an exhibition of the works of Pablo Picasso on the grounds that his politics were suspect.

On the very morning of the day the President was killed, a certain Bernard Weissmann, who is a leading light in an extremist group called 'The American Fact-Finding Committee', placed an advertisement in a Dallas newspaper which asked Kennedy: 'Why have you ordered or permitted your brother Bobby, the Attorney General, to go soft on Communists?'

'I am a patriot and a conservative,' said Weissmann afterwards in explanation. He added that his advertisement—which cost him 1,464 dollars (£520)—was justified as a retort to the 'attacks made by local liberal groups in Dallas against Conservatives.'

A fortnight after the assassination, police arrested an eighteen-year-old member of the American Nazi Party who was demonstrating on the site of the shooting. Wearing a swastika on his arm the youth carried a life-size effigy with a Castro-like mask. On it was a sign reading 'Don't blame Dallas—Castro killed JFK. Invade Cuba Now.'

The 'Communist conspiracy' which right-wing extremists claim lay behind the Kennedy slaying was reiterated by Martin Dies, former Texas Congressman, who wrote in the March 1964 issue of *American Opinion*, the glossy John Birch Society magazine: 'Lee Harvey Oswald was acting on instructions from Moscow when he assassinated President Kennedy.'

The John Birch Society was born in the early tide of growing right-wing sentiment in the United States shortly before Christmas 1958, when Robert Henry Wiborne Welch, Jr, from Boston, Massachusetts gave up his highly successful career as a sweet and candy manufacturer to launch the movement.

From the outset Welch, who springs from North Carolina farming stock, made it quite clear that he was aiming for political power and would seek it by plugging an uncompromising anti-communist fascist-style policy. As Hitler laid down his intentions in his *Mein Kampf*, so Welch in his *Blue Book* made it evident that he denounced democracy as 'merely a deceptive phrase, a weapon of demagoguery and a perennial fraud.'

'The men who join the John Birch Society during the next few months or few years,' he added, 'are going to be doing so primarily because they believe in me and in what I am doing and are willing to accept my leadership.'

Named after Captain John Birch, a deeply religious Georgian who had gone to China as a missionary, the Society now claims well over a 100,000 membership and is dedicated to 'fighting and destroying Communism within the United States'. John Birch, who was a chaplain with the American Army, was killed shortly after the end of the Second World War when he fell into Chinese communist guerrilla hands leading a counter-Red mission. A Chinese linguist, he seemed to have upset his captors for they shot him out of hand, although they later released the rest of the prisoners they had taken along with Birch.

The twenty-seven-year-old Southerner who had become 'The first victim and martyr in World War Three' served as an admirable vehicle for Welch's ambitions. Here was a name behind which all truly patriotic, nationalistic Americans could join under the banner of militant anti-communism.

It mattered little to Welch, the businessman turned politician who in 1947 was honoured by his colleagues as 'Candy man of the Year', that he had never even met John Birch.

Welch's technique in building up the movement is to use communist methods by setting up cells or chapters with twenty or thirty members each, all over America. He explains that he is fully justified in fighting 'reds' in the country by 'smearing them'. 'Our methods,' he admits, 'are mean and dirty, but the communists we are after are meaner and dirtier, and are too slippery for you to put your finger on them in the ordinary way.'

Using the same principles he advocated in his book *The Road to Salesmanship*, written when he was still making boiled sweets, Welch, a brilliant organizer and administrator, employs every device to further his cause including the tactic pioneered by Goebbels of the 'big lie'. Quite open and frank about his methods, Welch, who regards the late Senator Joe McCarthy as one of his heroes, makes sweeping statements and accusations without even pretending to produce evidence to back them up.

Blandly he announced that 'one half of one per cent of Catholic priests are communist sympathizers', but failed to produce names when challenged. And of John Foster Dulles—whom few would describe as being a woolly-headed liberal—Welch says: 'The man was a communist dupe.'

Believing firmly in the principle of the bigger the lie and the more important the name, the more publicity and political capital there will be available to exploit, Welch dismissed President Kennedy as an 'immoral man who can do a tremendous amount of ball-carrying on behalf of Communism here in the United States.' And President Eisenhower was described by Welch as a 'dedicated conscious agent of the communist conspiracy' and 'a card-carrying member of the Communist Party.'

Operating with high-powered business efficiency from his secluded suburban-Boston headquarters at Belmont, Massachusetts, Welch sends out a constant stream of instructions and advice to his faithful followers. More than anyone he has realized the potential support to be culled from the discontented religious fundamentalists and racially prejudiced conservative communities in the South, as well as the upper middle classes of the North who feel that their security is threatened by social change.

At secret meetings Birchers are told: 'Unless we can reverse forces which now seem inexorable in their movement, there will be only a few more years before the United States will become four separate provinces in a world-wide Communist dominion ruled by police state methods from the Kremlin.'

How to combat the hidden enemy lurking everywhere within the borders of the United States? The super-patriots—housewives, small shopkeepers, bank clerks, garage attendants and other members of the lower middle class who form the bulk of Welch's movement—are given these warnings: 'One of the hardest things for the ordinary decent American to realize is that a secret Communist looks and acts just like anybody else.'

'There are half a million of them in the United States,' warns Welch. Even worse is to follow. Grimly he declares: 'In addition there are a million Communist dupes and sympathizers up and down the land.'

Where must the enemy be sought? Everywhere. In the pulpit, on newspapers, in colleges, trade unions, libraries, in the Government—especially the Government—and even in parent-teacher associations and girl-scout groups.

In each community Birchers are ordered to start 'hate' campaigns against anyone who might fall into the category of a communist agent. Congressmen and government officials must be bombarded with telegrams and calls to action, and on a local level letters are written by the thousand, whispering campaigns are started and local government offices and library committees are constantly harassed. An alleged favourite weapon is the often repeated threatening post-midnight telephone call, though the Birchers have denied using this tactic, as well as other extreme methods.

The aim is to create suspicion and distrust, for in the United States it is difficult to stand up and defend a man who is called, no matter how unjustly, a 'communist stooge', for fear of becoming oneself a target as a 'red sympathizer'.

Schools are particularly fruitful ground for the leaders of the John Birch Society who urge children to report to their parents what they are told in the classrooms. Professors at universities and teachers at primary and secondary level who have attacked these extremists are smeared as fellow travellers and many have even been forced to resign following the noisy outcry and resultant atmosphere of suspicion aroused by Birchers who have worked their way on to parent-teacher associations. Sometimes there is resistance to Welch's tactics even in smaller communities. In March 1964 sixteen of the thirty-three teachers in the Iowa town of Pleasantville resigned because of the harmful influence of the John Birch Society there.

So strong is the pressure exerted by right-wing groups that laws have been passed on a state level making it compulsory for courses on 'anti-communism' to be taught in the classroom. Mr Max Rafferty, a superintendent of schools in California, has declared: 'We had better not be caught withholding from the nation's children the wonderful sharp-edged glittering sword of Patriotism. In a word, this means indoctrination.'

The 'Christian Anti-Communist Crusade' has placed its literature in a number of American high schools and in the State of Louisiana teachers attend a six-day summer preparation course on 'Americanism versus Communism' which includes lecturers like the highly emotional preacher Frederick Schwarz. The men and women to whom the care of American children is being entrusted are taught: 'Well-meaning but impractical do-gooders and disgruntled intellectuals are often duped into spreading the party line.'

Just in case there are parents or teachers who feel that they cannot decide for themselves whether their children are being 'indoctrinated' by communists in schools, there exists the 'America's Future Inc.' of New York which has a textbook evaluation committee carefully examining books used in schools. Parents are advised to be 'on the alert at all times to prevent attempts by the Federal Government to get their hands on the schools.'

'Look into the background and philosophy of the school board members and prospective members. Keep an eye on school libraries for leftist books.'

Parents are constantly reminded to make sure that their children are being taught the 'right of a free society to protect itself against subversion.'

Birch-inspired groups also issue cards which are placed inside stores where goods from communist countries are on sale, threatening boycotts and smearing the owners as 'red-sympathizers'. So successful have some of these campaigns been that merchants have faced ruin. In some cases stores selling goods from iron-curtain countries have had to take out licences and pay special fees.

Welch controls his movement with dictatorial firmness. So much so that it was denounced as a 'fascist group' by the Ohio Democrat, Stephen Young, who said: 'Unfortunately these radicals of the right in the so-called "Birch Society" in many communities have been practising character assassination without regard for the truth, threatening merchants with boycott and college professors and school principals with dismissal. They spread fear, hatred and suspicion.'

Welch makes no secret about his philosophy. Anti-communist and anti-democratic, he wants a dictatorial-style republic to prevail in the United States. 'Democracy, which is Government of the masses, results in mobocracy—demagogism, licence, agitation, discontent and anarchy. A republic is ideal, for its rule is subject to "laws" rather than "men", whereas democracy which breeds chaos is the worst of all forms of Government.'

The leader of the John Birch Society goes on to explain that 'democracy leads to the dangerous path of socialism and communism.'

A highly organized propaganda campaign making use of a wide variety of books, leaflets, stickers, long-play records, and tape-recordings is carried out by the John Birch Society, while its lecturers travel the country backing up appeals on radio and television warning of the 'communist menace within'.

'The Communists have moulded every major policy decision by the American Government since 1941 by their infiltration into high positions of power,' says the persistent voice of the Birchers. The clergy are singled out as among the worst of communist influences and the National Council of Churches which preaches de-segregation is made a particular target for attack.

With some predictability the Civil Rights campaign is dismissed by the John Birch Society as a 'communist plot'. In the May 1965 issue of *American Opinion* the demonstrations and riots in Selma, Alabama, were blamed on 'communists intentionally setting the stage for race war'.

This refrain is taken up by one of the contributors, ex-Congressman Martin Dies, who states that: 'Communist control of the Negro "Civil Rights" movement is now a matter of fact, or merely a matter of time.'

As chairman at one time of the Committee on Un-American Activities, Dies continues: 'We uncovered considerable evidence which left no doubt that Moscow considered the Negroes of the United States to be excellent potential recruits for the Communist Revolution. The Communists early decided to create their revolution here by promoting racial hatred between white and Negro citizens.'

By the middle of 1965 a new trend among extreme right-wing groups of including 'Social Democrats' and 'Liberals' as being under communist control made itself felt. In the same issue of *American Opinion* one of the associate editors, E. Merrill Root, author of *Brainwashing in the High Schools* and other such works, said: 'The Liberal supposes that freedom means the liberty to deny your own destiny, being and essence; liberty to become anything except what by nature you mean and are.'

To ensure the widest possible market for its message, the John Birch Society and other right-wing extremist groups have opened up scores of bookshops and libraries in American cities. These 'freedom bookstores' and 'opinion libraries' sell the work of extremist authors, and have on sale framed pictures of Welch, General Walker, and Joe McCarthy. They also serve as meeting places for the John Birch Society and other similarly-minded groups.

Books like Rosalie M. Gordon's *Nine Men Against America*—a vitriolic attack on the Supreme Court—are a good selling line in these shops. A large selection of right-wing fascist-tinged literature is pumped out by mail-order firms like the 'Bookmailer' of New York, run by a former CIA man, Lyle Munson, who claimed that in 1961 he sold over 2,000,000 items of printed material.

Another official of the Birch movement is Tom Anderson who says in his magazine *Farm and Ranch* that 'co-existence is immoral'. 'It is a gutless, impossible delusion and fraud. State Department employees and overseas staffs are international Socialists, dupes, and do-gooders who are serving the Communist cause unwittingly by following the Communist line. Some are undoubtedly Communist. Some are merely gutless traitors . . . many of these people, deliberately or not, are delivering us to the enemy.'

'Eisenhower,' said Anderson, 'is the most overrated man since Santa Claus.'

In his fight against both the Republican and Democratic parties, Anderson, who comes from Nashville, calls them: 'Socialist Party "A" and Socialist Party "B". Our leaders are not fighting Communism—they're promoting it—treason is the reason,' says Anderson.

Other targets for the Welch venom are the United Nations, which is a 'hot-bed' of communist conspiracy, and the American defence programmes which are expensive and 'all part of a Communist plot to sap American strength.' The inconsistency of labelling the Soviet Union as the violent enemy plotting on every side to overthrow the capitalist system of the United States, and then attacking the Government for spending money on arming itself against this enemy is never challenged by the audiences who flock to hear Welch. In fact the attacks on State spending are a main plank of the Society's platform which aims at 'cutting Federal Taxes'. All social welfare programmes which stem from the money raised by these taxes are lumped together as costly steps on the road to 'Socialism' and hence inevitable 'Communism'.

Another subject which arouses the fury of the John Birch Society is the American Supreme Court, which is described as 'being engaged in destroying the Constitution of the United States'.

'The Supreme Court is one of the most important agencies in the Communist world for global conquest,' says Welch's movement.

The main attack is directed against Chief Justice Earl Warren, and Birch members send tens of thousands of letters to their Congressmen calling for his 'impeachment'. The cause of all this anger is that the liberal faction of the Supreme Court, symbolized by Warren, has supported numerous reforms in civil liberties. It ordered the racial integration of the public schools in 1954 which has subsequently hastened the growing impetus for complete equality for the Negroes not only in the South but throughout the country. Warren is the quintessence of liberalism to the fascist-minded in America, for he has done much to counteract the hysteria stemming from post-war McCarthyism.

Another method of spreading anti-communist propaganda was thought up by William Douglass, a member of the John Birch Society, when he established the 'Let Freedom Ring' movement. 'We disseminate anti-Socialist pro-American broadcasts via a telephone tape-recording. Your customer dials a number (just like time and weather) and gets two minutes of anti-Communist dynamite.'

As a result a ninety-second sermon of fear called a 'patriotic message' can be dialled any hour of the day or night in more than thirty American cities. 'Let Freedom Ring' scripts paint a picture of 'communist conspiracy' behind the United Nations, the Supreme Court, the White House and the National Council of Churches. One message proclaimed that Eisenhower had once attended a meeting to discuss 'the best way to surrender you and your family to the Reds'.

Were it only the unbalanced and unthinking segments of the lower middle class who followed Welch, the power, influence and latent threat of the John Birch Society would not be considered too seriously. But it is not only the shopkeeper and small businessman who pay their annual subscription of twenty-five dollars for the privilege of taking part in the Welch crusade against the 'Bolshevist menace'. Backing him with the prestige of their names and wealth are generals, admirals, professors, former FBI men, clergymen, judges, diplomats, and, above all, rich industrialists.

For them 'better dead than red' is a bitter truth and they hope to hold on to their positions and their wealth by supporting the man in whom they see their last and only hope against socialism, creeping welfarism and the ultimate evil—communism. They are also angry and worried by the growing bureaucratic power of Washington and resent paying for expensive welfare schemes.

One such man was Spruille Braden who was among the first to

join the John Birch Society. A former U.S. ambassador to Cuba, Colombia and the Argentine, Braden called the American foreign aid programme 'counter to religion because it benefits atheistic Communists and their henchmen.'

Also on the National Council which advises Welch on the running of his movement, have been at one time or another three former presidents of the National Association of Manufacturers—William J. Crede, Ernest G. Swigert and the late Cola C. Parker. Other backers include Clarence Manion, former dean of the University of Notre Dame Law School, and Professor Revilo P. Oliver of the University of Illinois, where he teaches classics.

Professor Oliver claims that the American Central Intelligence Agency is overrun with crypto-communists. On the subject of education Oliver says that 'college courses on contemporary problems are usually sheer, pure, unadulterated Communism with a little polish on the surface.' The professor aroused nation-wide indignation when he claimed that a communist conspiracy lay behind President Kennedy's assassination because 'he was becoming a political liability to them.'

'Kennedy's memory will be cherished with distaste,' said this Birchite.

Manion, who describes himself as an 'unreconstructed McCarthyite', edits a weekly newsletter, the *Manion Forum*. Another Council member is the Roman Catholic priest, Richard Ginder, who writes at length about the red conspiracy in *Our Sunday Visitor*, a national Roman Catholic publication pushed through the letter-boxes of nearly a million American homes each week.

Adding his weight to the Council, too, is T. Coleman Andrews, who was Commissioner of Internal Revenue during part of President Eisenhower's term of office. Andrews, naturally enough, concentrates on the issue of the 'Abolition of federal income tax'.

Welch claims that membership forms are 'rolling in all the time', but is rather coy about just how many firm Birchers he has on his books. It is known, however, that his major support lies in the states of Texas, California, the rural eastern area of Washington and right across the deep South.

Henchman Tom Anderson says dryly: 'We grow like a fungus.'

The Society's membership includes a large proportion of

Roman Catholics, and combined with the endorsement of the movement by some Church of Rome clerics, this has set limitations to recruiting members from the strong rightist Protestant element in the community and the bible-thumping fundamentalists.

But the religiously inclined who do not care for Welch and the John Birch Society need have no fear about not finding a suitable outlet for their super-patriotism. They can choose from literally dozens of big-business high-pressure religious groups run by demagogues, self-ordained priests and charlatans of every description who are cashing in—and cashing in handsomely—on anti-communism and racial bigotry by selling their own particular brand of Christian tolerance and brotherhood.

One of the most successful men in the hot-gospelling field is the highly energetic Billy James Hargis, who pulls in the crowds under his banner of 'For Christ! Against Communism!' And crowds there certainly are in their tens of thousands to hear his message of the dangers of 'internal Communist treachery'. They contribute their dollars, too; one has only to look at Hargis's 'Christian Crusade' headquarters, his superbly equipped travelling 'evangelist' bus complete with two baths, and his 700-acre farm in Oklahoma.

The son of a Texas truck driver, the Reverend Billy Hargis in 1955 hired a public relations firm which specializes in boosting 'down-and-out' preachers. He soon found that anti-communism, added to his hell-fire fear-of-God message, brought in the crowds as well as hard cash. Now his 'religion' with its own *Weekly Crusader* newsletter, and monthly *Christian Crusade* magazine, has grown into a million-dollar-a-year business.

And little wonder, for Hargis sells his line hard, with such messages as: 'Announcing brand-new patriotic pamphlets by Billy James Hargis. New material, new design, new approach to getting inexpensive but truthful anti-Communist information to the masses. Ideal for mass circulation to churches, schools, civic clubs, fraternal groups, etc.'

His book *Communist America—Must It Be?* is advertised as 'one of the most illuminating volumes on the communist menace yet published, clearly written and easy to understand.' Its warnings are melodramatic: 'If the average American citizen doubts that his beloved country is in mortal danger, that his wife and children are on the verge of the embrace of Communist rape and enslavement, let him look anywhere about him.'

Day in and day out the great message is sold to the gullible with every publicity gimmick known to advertising. Hargis's simple and easily digested theme of 'God and country' is broadcast over radio and television to millions, and is propagated in his weekly column appearing in some two hundred American newspapers. His book *Communism and You* is described as an 'excellent first lesson in the methods and aims of Communism' (25 cents each, or five for one dollar), his records and tape-recordings and even special Christmas cards and photographs of himself in gold frames are aimed at the very large fundamentalist section in the United States.

Hargis, who dismisses the concept of the 'brotherhood of man' as 'hogwash', has his major following in the South. He is working hard to increase his flock in the North of the United States and claims that 10,000 new paying 'crusaders' become his disciples every month.

Initially the Rev. Hargis makes his appeal on religious grounds —the first ten minutes of each lecture are about God; the rest, and that can mean anything up to an hour, is an undiluted no-holds-barred anti-communist harangue.

The Kremlin, he says, has set the year 1974 as the deadline for the conquest of the United States. The Russians will succeed for the Government is heavily pro-communist. Marxist teachers are being introduced everywhere; how can the United Nations be trusted when they do not even open their meetings with a prayer?

Strongly racialistic, Hargis boasts a complete collection of the works of Allen Zoll, a professional anti-semite.

At his special 'Leadership in Anti-Communism' school held in Tulsa, Oklahoma, where pupils pay up to $100 a week to learn how to 'stem the forces of liberalism and thus stop the growth of socialism and communism', the message that Negroes 'are inferior to whites in mental capacity' is taken very seriously. His teachers preach that efforts to integrate schools are all part of the communist plot. It is pointed out that Negroes are not patriotic and are prone to 'stampede in battle'.

Even more of this heady stuff follows. 'The chief difference between Congolese and U.S. Negro soldiers is that the Congolese eat more white people than Americans do.' The National Council of Churches also comes in for attack as a 'hotbed of Communism'.

In between racialist lectures the scholars at Tulsa are told that the communists have turned Government departments into a Kremlin-directed base to overthrow the three vital American pillars of health, education and welfare. The object of this carefully thought out programme is quite clear, for many fundamentalists are terrified of the 'red-menace' which embraces the horrors of 'liberalism, socialism and atheism'. They are worried about the growing trend towards racial de-segregation, the increase of federal power, and the social changes now taking place in America as the struggle for Negroes to reach equality takes a new, urgent path.

Basically Hargis appeals to the racially bigoted, ill-educated and poorer classes in the United States, but he gets the backing of more well-to-do followers because they are concerned about the heavy taxes they have to pay to the Federal Government which they believe to be tainted with communist ideas and inclining towards socialism and state welfarism through its schemes for medical and social aid.

The wealthy businessmen, the oil barons, and other industrialists who pour a stream of dollars into Billy Hargis's pockets may not buy his five-cent pamphlets or fancy-looking fifteen-dollar books. Nor do they much enthuse over his 'folksy album' of long-playing records which offer 'pure beautiful gospel music plus the enchanted voice of the preacher with some of his choice sermons, combining as they do the spiritual and the patriotic'.

They are not over-impressed by his claims that 'God has built this movement through me', nor do they feel in need of his food supplement called 'Nutri-Bio' to create 'glowing good health' which he peddles as a side-line. But they do see in him a protector —as German industrialists once saw a champion in Hitler— against the menace of bolshevism.

Helping Hargis with his crusade are men like Benjamin Gitlow, former head of the Communists in America, an FBI informer and one of a number of former party members now making a lucrative living by lecturing and writing 'exposures'; and the retired Major-General Charles A. Willoughby, former intelligence chief for General Douglas MacArthur, and who now writes a 'foreign intelligence digest' for Hargis's newspapers.

Hargis maintains close contact with East European exile groups in the United States and in one of the issues of his *Christian Crusade*, Prince Michel Sturdza of Rumania, writing on 'Co-existence and the Russian Captives', attacked Churchill's 'Machiavellian elasticity which condoned the burning of hundreds of thousands of civilians in the non-military city of Dresden and a few post-war years later enabled him to accept an academic award from Chancellor Adenauer on the advice of other cynical German politicians.'

Modesty is not one of Hargis's virtues and he is constantly advocating his own works with titles such as: *The United Nations—Destroying America by Degrees*; *The Facts about Communism and the Churches*; *The Communist Programme for the American Farmer*; *Walter Lippmann—Poisoning Public Opinion*; and *Uncle Sam—MD*, a timely article on federal aid to the aged, 'which is merely a foot in the door for the complete socialization of medicine'.

In his constant appeal for funds, Hargis reminds the faithful that gifts and legacies of shares, cash and property are always welcome. A strong supporter of the John Birch Society, Hargis dreams of bringing together all the fragmented sections of the extreme right on the American continent in one cohesive movement. He convened a not very successful meeting in Washington in 1962 for this purpose.

All criticism of his movement, his methods and his aims, or doubts about his sincerity are dismissed as 'red smears' and only serve as a spur to this man of religion.

Hargis is a great admirer of Major-General Edwin A. Walker, who more than any other man represents the ultra-conservative military wing in the United States. Walker, who dislikes democracy and all its trimmings, feels that the only way to beat communism is to start a preventive war. Men like the General who hold these views never go into details about the nuclear horrors of such a war, but their philosophy is made quite clear should they ever be in a position to seize power.

'Why not now?' they ask. 'Why don't we stamp out the pestilence?' 'Why not die for a good cause?'

The aim of these military men—many of whom are retired generals and admirals—is to exert as much pressure as possible on the Government and thoughts of seizing power have certainly crossed their minds. A right-wing fascist-style military junta of 'super patriots' would firmly lead the United States back on to the path of rugged independence and traditional virtues even if this meant having it out once and for all with the 'commies'.

General Walker became actively engaged in politics after he was relieved of his command for trying to indoctrinate his troops in Germany with his extremist views. The John Birch Society and others of the fascist fringe in the United States made much political capital from his 'martyrdom'. 'The purge of General Walker,' said Billy James Hargis, 'is but an example of the extent to which the Fabian Socialists now in control of our nation will go to extend their programme.'

'We know now that it is their intent that all pro-American anti-Communist material shall be erased from troop information programmes, and that all right-wing personnel in the Armed Forces of the United States shall be eliminated to make way for the Fabian Socialist take-over—aided and abetted by international Communism, its agents and its sympathizers.'

A veteran of the Second World War and of Korea, General Walker has spent thirty years in the armed forces and pleads passionately for an end to 'subversion in high places'. He ran into trouble when he invited right-wing extremists to lecture to his GI's, and then resigned from the army so as to be completely free to put over his message in the United States without official restraint.

'For twenty years,' he says, 'the United States Government has acted as if it were the agent of the Soviet Union.' Walker attacked Eisenhower for 'co-existence', and Kennedy for 'carrying out similar appeasement policies'. He has also turned his attention to the United Nations which he describes as 'a tower of Babel'.

'We should pull out of this unholy alliance with the enemies of God,' says the General.

It is not only foreign affairs which interest Walker. He fulminates against the growing role of the Federal Government in state and local affairs and went so far in action as well as word that he was arrested on federal charges—later dropped—of seditious conspiracy and inciting insurrection at the University of Mississippi at the time of the enrolment of the first Negro student there.

Calling himself the 'scapegoat' of the Government's 'unwritten policy of collaboration and collusion with the international Communist conspiracy', General Walker is but one of many military leaders who have shown their troops right-wing propaganda films, given them lectures on the evils of communism, and allowed seminars run by extremists to be held on their bases and at their training camps. Troops are told that the major threat to America is internal rather than external communism and even mildly liberal social legislation is held out as socialism, 'that is, a fancy name for naked communism'. Foreign aid, cultural exchanges, disarmament negotiations and international programmes of aid to under-developed countries are nothing more than 'sops to the communist enemy'.

The spreading of this type of 'education' among American military forces was becoming so widely pronounced that Senator Fulbright warned: 'If the military is infected with this virus of right-wing radicalism, the danger is worthy of attention. If it believes the public is, then the danger is enhanced. If, by the process of the military "educating" the public the fevers of both groups are raised, the danger is great indeed.'

So worried was the Administration that the Secretary of Defence, Robert McNamara, forbade military officials to express views which were politically partisan or contrary to established national policy.

Naturally enough, this aroused the anger of Welch, Hargis, Walker and other extremist leaders. 'The Government is dictating a no-win policy towards the Communist conspiracy,' retorted Walker. Despite his wild statements, his cold personality and his lack of political training and education, General Walker is still a powerful figure on the right in the United States. He gathers much sympathy for his crusade against communism and his attacks on the Administration for its 'muzzling of the military'.

It must not be thought that Walker's admirer, Billy Hargis, is the only man who has cottoned on to the idea of mixing God with anti-communism. There are dozens of others in the field all doing very nicely with tens of thousands of supporters all eager to hand over their dollar bills for the cause.

One of the most successful is an Australian preacher, Dr Frederick Charles Schwarz, who settled in California in 1953 and now commands powerful backing from multi-millionaire corporations. Schwarz spreads his Baptist evangelism with the message of the 'internal danger of Communism'. In addition he campaigns against liberals, racial integration, the United Nations, large sections of the Protestant clergy, federal income tax, the World Council of Churches, mental health legislation, professors, the Supreme Court, the Administration in general, and the fluoridization of water supplies.

A lay preacher in the Australian Baptist Church before he realized the potentialities of the American market, Schwarz is a highly successful showman and his 'Christian Anti-Communism Crusade' raked in half a million pounds in 1961. His father, a Jew in Austria before becoming a convert to Christianity and emigrating to Australia, inspired his son to become a doctor in medicine and theology. This has stood the exuberant Aussie in very good stead in the United States where his oratory seems to hypnotize his audiences. His wife still lives in Australia where Schwarz says she is secretary of the 'Crusade' down-under.

Schwarz sells his ideas through the usual publicity channels of bought time on commercial radio and television, books, pamphlets and records. He has also thought up the idea of spreading the message in the form of strip cartoons. His comic book for 'children' shows communists throwing the aged and infirm into 'concentration camps' as part of some scheme to breed a super-race by eliminating the weak and sick.

In particular, Schwarz concentrates on 'Schools of Anti-Communism' which have held seminars in Arizona, California, Florida, Hawaii, Indiana and dozens of other spots up and down the land, but all directed from his headquarters at Long Beach, California. Helping him in his task of showing the Americans the true path to salvation, are men like Herbert Philbrick, former FBI undercover man in the American Communist party; Robert Morris, former chief counsel of the Senate Internal Security sub-committee and one-time president of the University of Dallas; W. Cleon Skousen, ex-Salt Lake City police chief and member of the FBI whose book *The Naked Communist* achieved a big success among right-wingers in the United States.

Also backing Schwarz are business firms like the Allen-Bradley Company of Milwaukee, and Patrick J. Frawley, the Californian industrialist who heads the 'Technicolor Corporation'. One of Schwarz's greatest triumphs was a meeting in Hollywood in 1960 when over four million on television saw Senator Thomas Dodd and C. D. Jackson, the publisher of *Life* magazine, speak on behalf of his movement. Actors John Wayne and James Stewart were there to add their support to his mainly middle-class audience.

Schwarz was originally brought to the United States by a Carl McIntire who branched out on his own after he was dropped by the Presbyterian ministry for breaking church law. He set up the 'Bible Presbyterian Church' and the 'American Council of Christian Churches' with branches in Europe, and claims to have a following of over three million in affiliated denominations. A close friend of McIntire's is the Air Force Chief, Edgar Bundy of Illinois, who operates the 'Church League of America' and the Abraham Lincoln Republican Club. Bundy supported Joe McCarthy, and he was the man who triumphantly revealed that the communist 'menace' was at work even in the ranks of the United States girl-scouts movement.

Behind Schwarz and Hargis, and dozens of other 'preachers of religion' who have smaller and more localized followings, is the immensely powerful 'Harding College' and its controlling body, the fundamentalist 'Church of Christ' run by Dr George Stuart Benson. This 'power-house of the extreme right' situated in the shadows of the Ozarks at Searcy, has been built up by the sixty-five-year-old Benson, a former missionary in China, to a bustling arts college with up-to-date facilities set in magnificent surroundings. Its thousand scholars are supported by such generous donors as the former chairman of General Motors, Alfred P. Sloan, who gave a donation of three million dollars. Other industrialists have contributed many millions more to ensure that a constant stream of highly skilled, persuasive, ultra-conservative propaganda is pumped out from 'Harding College'.

There is the usual barrage of books, television and radio programmes, travelling schools, seminars and leaflets, and Benson has also produced films such as 'Communism on the Map' which makes dramatic use of colour to show how the world is gradually turning pink as a prelude to its ultimate fate of 'deep red'.

Even though this motion picture has been dismissed as an 'irresponsible mingling of facts and falsehood and a gross distortion of historical events', it has been seen by millions.

'Freedom Forums' complete with speakers, free literature, films like 'Communism in Action' and 'Communist Encirclement', are hired out in bulk for presentation to big industrialists who often compel their employees to attend during business

hours. These 'Freedom Forums', which last several days, proclaim the basic message that the United States 'is the last
important bastion of resistance to Godless enslaving Communism'. They have made their appearance in schools and on
military bases complete with such lecturers as Schwarz, Skousen,
Benson himself, and the retired General Albert Wedemeyer. This
German-trained military man is held in high esteem by Barry
Goldwater. He believes that the United States was wrong to
destroy Germany and Japan in the Second World War. 'Thus the
principal bulwarks against Communism in the areas of the United
States and Allied interests were removed,' he says.

Listeners at 'Freedom Forums' are told that the 'Communists
are at our throat. Socialism, the last step before Communism,
arrives in deceptive forms—medical aid to the aged, federal aid to
education, rent controls, social security, foreign aid, liberalism
in religion, and above all, the sinister growing power of organized
labour.'

Benson, the son of an Oklahoma farmer, says that his mission
is to create leaders of resistance to the spread of socialism and
communism and he warmly recommends the John Birch Society
to those who seek his guidance. Like the chief Bircher, Robert
Welch, Benson advocates the Republican form of government as
opposed to democracy. He is vehemently opposed to 'planning'—
which he says, begins as 'isolated interference with the free
economy and ends as the controlling mechanism of the authoritarian state.'

'The cost of Government is growing at an alarming rate and
excessive taxes of industry reduce the incentive to produce,' he
proclaims, keeping a careful eye on the grateful cheques rolling in
from big business. Should there be any hesitation about the size
of the contributions, the doctor throws in such comments as:
'Work laws must be passed to keep employees out of the clutches
of "big labour".'

Nervous businessmen do not, however, rely solely on the efforts
of professional 'defenders of the faith'. There are a number of
powerful industrialists and manufacturers who personally play a
direct role in the emotional 'anti-Commie' movement. The Texan
oil-baron, H. L. Hunt, for instance, not only advocates his
products to millions of listeners who tune in daily to his radio and
television programmes called 'Life Lines', but at the same time

he uses the Rev. Wayne Poucher to warn his captive audience of the 'threat of atheistic Communism from abroad'.

Poucher, a 'Southern Church of Christ' priest, is the 'Life Lines' spiritual guide and talks at great length about the 'subversion from within'. He says that income tax is 'now graduated to the point of confiscation in the higher brackets'.

'An ever-growing clamour for welfare and security has played into the hands of the planners who offer many programmes in the name of humanity and security. These planners are socialists who today chart much of the course of our lives and are continually grasping for new areas of control.'

In case the television and radio message is missed, oil-man Hunt, who supported the late Senator McCarthy, and is now an admirer of the John Birch Society, runs his *Life Lines* newsletter three times a week from editorial offices in Washington.

One of the country's major savings and loan companies, the 'Coast Federal of Los Angeles' under the presidency of Joe Crail, supports its own 'free-enterprise' department distributing millions of free leaflets, news-sheets and brochures every year which ram home the message of anti-communism. Hundreds of other American businessmen do the same thing and many firms distribute Schwarz's anti-red comic book with the company's name printed on the back. As one businessman expressed it: 'Anti-communism builds sales and raises employee performance.'

Before his death in 1966, D. B. Lewis, of Los Angeles, combined selling dog food with intense interest in politics. As president of the 'Organization to Repeal Federal Income Taxes Inc.' Lewis declared: 'The income tax is one of the most vicious laws ever passed,' and added with good measure: 'I'd blast the Communists off the map in twenty-four hours.' Lewis also supported and acted as sponsor for the 'Dan Smoot Report' on thirty-two television and over fifty radio stations in Western states.

Dan Smoot, a well-spoken former FBI agent from Texas, readily admits to being an extremist and says: 'I equate the growth of the welfare state with socialism, and socialism with communism.' Besides broadcasting on radio and television, he edits a widely-read newsletter, the *Dan Smoot Report*, which has been going strong since 1955. This publication is recommended by Robert Welch as 'thorough, scholarly, interesting and devastating.'

Then there is the 'America Security Council' run by former FBI man John M. Fisher, who provides reports and information to more than 4,000 companies about individuals or organizations they are considering employing in one capacity or another. Fisher's 'Council' was formed in 1953 to 'keep a continuing check on the Communist threat' and claims to have the largest private file on communism in the country. On the 'Council's strategy committee' are right-wing extremists like General Wedemeyer and the retired Admiral Ben Moreell.

With the massive financial backing 'Harding College' obtains from American industrialists, Benson sends teams of men to Europe to make films which depict the evils and failings of 'welfarism'. His weekly column 'Looking Ahead' is sent free to thousands of newspapers, and the leaders of scores of extremist and fascist-inclined groups obtain their basic material from the College.

But not only are fundamentalists caught up in the hysterical fear of communism preached by the 'anti-red' religious evangelists. There are other extremist movements scattered all over the United States varying in size and importance.

One such body is the 'Advocates of Our Lady' of Chicago—a Catholic group who want to establish a world-wide Catholic social, political and economic order. The Governments of Spain and Portugal, with their form of fascist dictatorship, come nearest to their ideal. The group violently attacks Protestants and 'USSR-Communist-Judaism-Freemasonry-Kremlin' treason. With remarkable self-confidence and candour the 'Advocates of Our Lady' warn that all liberal Catholics who have collaborated with the enemy will be hung or burnt at the stake 'when we take over the reins of Government'.

Another extremist man of religion is the Rev. Gordon Winrod who lost his job as assistant pastor of a Lutheran Church at Little Rock, Arkansas, because as he put it: 'I dared speak against the Dictatorship, the Jews.'

Speaking on the platform of the Nazi 'National States Rights Party', the Rev. Winrod declared: 'All Jews are immoral, revolutionary and anarchistic. Beware of them for they are like a plague of vermin crawling upon our body politic.'

This ranting priest publishes a monthly *Winrod Letter* for 'Christ and Country' as well as a number of books, including

Arnold Leese's *Jewish Ritual Murder* and the German Nazi-produced edition of Martin Luther's pamphlet *The Jews and their Lies*.

The same refrain is taken up by the 'American Gentile Youth Movement' which produces labels and stickers saying: 'Hitler Failed. . . . He let them live.

'To have peace and prosperity forever EACH NATION MUST KILL ITS OWN JEWS.

'When the last hour for the Jew in America strikes—there will be No Passover! Jews, America is your last mile!'

'We, the People!', another organization, also of Chicago, run by Harry T. Everingham, is strong enough to publish its own journal called *Free Enterprise*. 'We, the People!' which started out as an evangelist body, has for its chief aim the abolition of income tax.

One of its officials is Ezra Taft Benson, Secretary of Agriculture under Eisenhower for eight years. His son, Reed, is an important figure in the John Birch Society. Benson gives loyal support to his son's activities and says: 'The John Birch Society is the most effective non-church organization in our fight against creeping Socialism and godless Communism.' In September 1963, Benson called Welch: 'One of the greatest patriots in American history.'

Very vocal on the anti-tax front are a colourful couple, Kent and Phoebe Courtney, from New Orleans, Louisiana. Besides editing their *Independent American* monthly magazine, the red-haired Courtney with the help of his energetic wife publishes a *Tax Pax* bulletin from their deceptively ramshackle-looking headquarters. A former pilot, Courtney thunders against the iniquities of income tax and in his publications reprints articles from the most bigoted and reactionary sections of the American right-wing press. Disseminating his ideas, too, on his own radio programme, this extremist under the wing of the 'Courtney Conservative Society of America' believes firmly that the only way to oppose communism is by 'direct political action'. His major immediate aim is to set up a third political party and he claims that he has growing support from militant anti-communists and racial segregationalists throughout the country.

Tax Pax bulletin number 43 made its own contribution to the 1964 presidential campaign when it launched an attack on Nelson

Rockefeller, calling him 'The International Socialist'. So extreme is the stand taken by the Courtney couple that they have even dismissed Barry Goldwater as a 'Judas goat who is tainted by Socialism'.

Another group which finds Goldwater far too liberal for their liking is the 'Patriotic Research Bureau' of Chicago run by Elizabeth Dilling who believes that even the John Birch Society is dominated by Jews. But then Elizabeth Dilling finds Jews behind most movements and she has even described Hitler as a 'Jewish tool'.

In the same vein is another anti-semitic movement run by a Mr C. Leon de Aryan who edits the old-established monthly *The Broom*, which mixes racialism with his personal creed of vegetarianism.

The 'Ruth Company' of Denver, Colorado, is greatly concerned with the London 'smog dilemma' which it claims is caused by the 'money-mad Rothschilds who will have the historical brick and stone buildings in London falling down by the anhydrous nitric acid engendered by their diesel buses.'

If only, adds Joseph P. Ruth, who sends his literature to Britain, if only the Rothschilds would 'make a deal' with us and install our diesel exhaust gas conditioners converting diesel exhaust to a non-toxic salt.

'But the Rothschilds, who have controlled England since 1877, find it cheaper to let the public suffer to their own great profit. To garner gold into their coffers, the Rothschilds and General Motors Corporation put the unwary public into coffins.'

If the various purveyors of religion and the numerous fragmented movements of extremism from the eccentric to the fascist do not openly propose or advocate violence as a political method, it still remains a latent threat. America is a violent country—four presidents, Abraham Lincoln, James Garfield, William McKinley and John Kennedy have died at the hands of assassins, and attempts have been made on the lives of Andrew Jackson and Theodore Roosevelt. In more recent times gunmen have tried to shoot down Franklin Roosevelt and Harry Truman.

American history is streaked with violently coloured episodes which have risen to the surface during times of social crises or national upheaval. The 'Know-Nothings', for example, in the middle of the nineteenth century gained immense support from native-born Americans who were fearful of the new immigrants swarming into the country from Europe. With their political allies, the 'Know-Nothings' even gained control of New York and swept the board in the Southern States.

The labour and union troubles at the turn of the century made Americans fearful of the creed of communism which triumphed in Russia at the end of the First World War. There were riots and bombings against democratic socialists, and leaders of workers' movements were beaten up, thrown into prison, deported and even killed in a wave of hysterial violence.

The unemployment of the 'thirties and Franklin D. Roosevelt's 'New Deal' aroused a general fear and big businessmen poured funds into the organizations of the men who would defend them against the 'creeping communist menace'. Congress was even told about a plot organized by some Wall Street brokers to bring about a right-wing military *coup d'état*. Fascism imported from Germany found its followers among Americans in the 'Christian Front' and the brown-shirted 'Bundists', who swore eternal loyalty to Hitler.

After the Second World War, Senator Joe McCarthy set the pattern for the present wave of extremism with his witch-hunt tactics, seeing communists lurking behind every American bush. He did not openly advocate the use of force, but today violence is accepted by many in the United States as part of the country's way of life. And one of the chief symbols of this violence is the hooded and white-robed figure of the Ku Klux Klan fanatic.

Today this movement has nothing like the alarming vigour and arrogance, and only a fraction of the mass membership of the period between the two World Wars. But nonetheless the Ku Klux Klan is a force to be reckoned with, especially in the Southern States of Alabama, Georgia and Florida where even the police are sometimes found to be members of the movement.

The strength and influence of the KKK is such that out of fear or sympathy with its aims, local southern juries ordinarily set Klansmen free no matter what the accusation and evidence levelled against them. From 1955 to November 1965 there were twenty-nine civil rights killings in the Deep South. Only two white men have been convicted. One got ten years for manslaughter, the other was placed on probation.

Ever since the historical declaration of the American Supreme

Court in 1954 ordering the de-segregation of schools throughout the country, the Ku Klux Klan has attracted the racially bigoted white American who is fearful of the growing economic strength of the Negro and his demands for equality in all walks of life. The acrid smell of burning wood drifts across the countryside as Klansmen once again light the warm Southern sky with their flaming crosses.

Violence is their reply to the advance in human rights. And so violence explodes in the form of bomb attacks on the homes of Negro leaders, beatings up with iron chains, the carving of the 'KKK' initials on 'uppity nigras' and in the summer of 1963 a bullet in the back for nationally known Negro leader Medgar Evers.

In the same year further violence erupted in Birmingham, Alabama, where four little Negro girls were killed and twenty-three people—mostly children—were seriously injured when a bomb exploded in a church.

This was the fortieth bombing which had taken place in Birmingham since white supremacy groups had poured into the city following racial disturbances there. A member of one such group, the pro-segregation 'Citizens Council' in Greenwood, Mississippi, was later charged with the murder of Evers. But after two trials juries were unable to agree and he is now free on bail.

In March 1964, white mechanic William Sterling Rosencrans, who the police said was a close associate of North Florida Ku Klux Klan leaders, was charged with bombing the home of a Negro boy who had cracked segregation barriers at a Jacksonville elementary school.

White businessmen and even the mildest of liberals are continually warned by Klansmen that they will be boycotted and 'face even worse' if they surrender to the demands of the Negroes and lower the barriers of segregation. In February 1964 a bomb exploded and a cross was burned in the town of Princess Anne in Maryland in a bid to stop negotiations between a bi-racial commission and restaurant owners who had refused to serve Negroes on their premises. A few days later the Congress of Racial Equality asked the FBI to investigate the burning of 150 crosses near Negro homes, churches and schools at Baton Rouge, Louisiana.

Operating through its squads of perverts and hoodlums, the KKK was held responsible for the mutilation and murder of three civil rights workers who were found in a Mississippi dam in June 1964.

In the following year, in October, Richmond Flowers the Alabama Attorney-General stated that members of the Ku Klux Klan have been implicated in at least twelve of the seventeen racial murders in the previous two years.

'Members of the Klan are believed to be responsible for many of the unsolved beatings, bombings, arson and other forms of violence that have occurred in the South.

'People laugh at them in their sheets and robes. The average Klansman is of low intelligence and with no economic or social standing in the community. Many are portraits in despair.

'Because of apathy an effective education programme is absolutely necessary to inform the responsible citizens of our communities just what kind of a vicious, perverted organization the Klan really is.'

Just how vicious was shown earlier in 1965 when Mrs Viola Liuzzo, a white mother, was shot dead after a civil rights march between Selma and Montgomery.

Although the killing aroused anger throughout America and President Johnson denounced the Ku Klux Klan as a hooded society of bigots, the strength of the movement in the South was shown when the suspected killer, Collie Leroy Wilkins, was acquitted by white jurors despite two attempts to bring him to justice. Later he was jailed for ten years on a conspiracy charge.

At a Congressional investigation of the Ku Klux Klan in October 1965, it was stated that some potential witnesses were frightened off by 'fear of Klan harassment, economic reprisals, cross burnings, bombing and even death.

'The witnesses are unwilling to give information even if arrangements are made for them to leave Southern States. They fear reprisals against their wives, children, brothers, sisters and parents.'

The inquiry was told that the Ku Klux Klan network was spread wide operating in seventeen of America's fifty states. Congressmen heard how the United Klans of America had instructed members in the use of explosives, incendiary devices, firearms, booby traps and guerrilla warfare. Plots to slay President Johnson and blow up the White House had been hatched.

Claiming that they are a fraternal Christian organization with their roots in the Civil War, the members of the KKK follow their forebears who got together to protect themselves against the dangers presented by the newly privileged Negroes after the South was defeated.

The 'Great Invisible Empire' of the Ku Klux Klan grew rapidly from its early days as a rural organization of degenerate whites. It attracted members by their hundreds of thousands after the First World War and wielded such power with a claimed four million membership that it eventually influenced the election of Governors and even marched triumphantly through the streets of Washington.

In the 1930's the KKK found common cause with the American Nazis as its members continued to torture, castrate and murder its victims.

The Ku Klux Klan is anti-Jewish, anti-Negro, anti-Roman Catholic and has in the past instigated numerous lynchings as well as blowing up Negro schools and Jewish synagogues. Now it makes common front with the equally racist White Citizens' Councils in Mississippi, and the members of the 'American Nazi Party' who have joined them in rioting in Georgia and other Southern states.

The Imperial Grand Wizard of the KKK, Robert Shelton, declares in his Alabama drawl: 'Jews and Niggers are part of the communist conspiracy.' Shelton, a thirty-six-year-old car salesman, describes Negroes as 'poisonous as rattlesnakes' and says he intends 'keeping them in their place . . .'

His followers are told: 'We know from evidence that Negroes are making preparations for setting up a black supremacy state with you and I to be their slaves.'

'The Bible proves the Nigger is inferior to us white Anglo-Saxons. The Jew is inferior too. God is a segregationist.'

Explains Shelton: 'We hold it is obligatory upon the Negro race, and upon all other coloured races in America, to recognize that they are living in the land of the white race by courtesy of the white races; and the white race cannot be expected to surrender to any other race, either in whole or in part, the control of its vital and fundamental governmental affairs.'

The Ku Klux Klan is not a united movement; it is rent by internal dissension and there are dozens of off-shoots such as 'The KKK of Alabama', 'Dixie-Klans', 'The Christian Knights of the KKK', besides the group run by Shelton which is one of the most successful since the post-1954 renaissance. The 'National Knights of the Ku Klux Klan', which claims to control forty-three separate Klan groups throughout the United States, is another organization which has come into prominence. It is controlled by an Atlanta segregationist lawyer, James Venable.

Members of the movement claim that they originated in the Scottish clans and go back to the days of Rob Roy. Now they are organized into a complex hierarchical system with the colour of their hoods—white, blue, scarlet and so on—denoting the various ranks which bear the exotic names of the Exalted Cyclops, Kladd, Klavalier, etc.

But if Dixieland was once able to rule the roost with its extremist movements breathing racial superiority and practising violence, the Negro today is showing that he is no longer satisfied with the role of passive victim. In open opposition to the segregationists, non-violent Negro movements led by men like Martin Luther King have come into being. But there is a powerful element among the Negroes of the United States who see extremist activity as their only salvation. This extremism has engendered its crack corps of black spartans who are close in spirit and behaviour to the storm-troopers of Hitler. They are active in learning the arts of Judo and polishing up refinements in the effective use of knives, broken bottles and knuckledusters.

These strong men, calling themselves the 'Fruits of Islam' are the disciplinary bully-boys of the Black Muslims , the fastest-growing movement among the twenty million Negroes in the United States.

As racialist in approach as Vorster in South Africa with his policies of 'apartheid' and white supremacy, the 'Black Muslims', who have a membership of between 100,000 and 200,000, reject out of hand the white man as well as his religion of Christianity. Their ultimate aim is for all Negroes to move back to Africa or Asia before the predicted holocaust which will destroy white rule in the United States and set the country on fire. This was the frightening prediction made in 1934 by the founder of the movement, W. F. Fard, a strange figure who claimed that he was an Arab from Mecca. Fard disappeared as mysteriously as he had come on to the scene, but while he was around during the bitter climate of the depression his outright condemnation of the white races made a deep impression on Negro communities in the United States.

One of his most enthusiastic converts was Elijah Poole, the son of a Baptist minister in Georgia. The seventh of thirteen children, Poole, when he was eleven, saw white hoodlums of the Ku Klux Klan string up a Negro youth from the branches of a willow tree and shoot his body full of bullets. The Negro boy swore revenge for the lynched man who had been accused of raping a white girl.

He moved north to Detroit and came under the sway of Fard whose racial theories were only distinguishable from those of the Ku Klux Klan because they substituted the words 'white man' for 'nigger'.

When Fard apparently went back to Mecca, Poole took over the Black Muslim movement and, shifting its headquarters to Chicago, set up a university and took upon himself the new name of 'Elijah Muhammad'. He then claimed that in fact Fard had been Allah in disguise, and the prophet had made the former Poole his official messenger from on high.

Although 'Elijah Muhammad' preaches that all his faithful will eventually go back to Africa, he demands as an interim measure that a part of the United States—one-seventh—should be set aside as an all-Negro State. Little wonder that George Lincoln Rockwell, leader of the American Nazis, approved and came along in support of the Black Muslim meetings. Was this not the same racialist spirit which Hitler himself had taught? It seemed to Rockwell a good idea to identify the country's Nazi movement with another group whose philosophy is so similar to his own.

Believing in 'separation or death' the Black Muslim organization is run on strict disciplinary and puritanical lines, and its members predict bloody wars between whites and blacks before the end of the twentieth century. Their voice is pitched in the same key as the extremist white groups like the John Birch Society, and the all-white anti-communist 'Christian' preachers with their anti-Negro rantings. They are being joined in ever-increasing numbers by frustrated Negroes bitter over what seem to them the insurmountable racial barriers in the United States.

During the last war, Muhammad and many of his disciples were thrown into jail—an action which they immediately turned to advantage. For in the prisons of America the Black Muslims find some of their most enthusiastic converts—and today there are at least three of their groups or 'temples' at work behind prison walls. Following the death of President Kennedy, Black Muslim prisoners in a jail at Lorton, Virginia, set off a 'near-riot' applauding the news of the assassination. White prisoners and other Negroes pounded on their cells with cups, plates and other objects in anger at the Black Muslim reaction.

When released from jail the newly-recruited members of the organization are given shelter, a friendly welcome, and are taught the rules of their acquired religion.

The philosophy of the Black Muslims bears little relation to the Koran which preaches against discrimination and racialism. Backed by the disciplinary toughs of the 'Fruits of Islam' the leaders keep a tight rein on the movement and allow no deviations from their stern rules. The womenfolk wear white robes and head-dresses and are kept under close watch. 'We must protect our most valuable property—our women,' proclaim the banners at meetings. Consorting with whites is considered the ultimate crime, to be punished by expulsion or a violent beating.

Sexual behaviour in the movement is strictly disciplined, the moral code high, and any woman who dares to go with her hair uncovered or shoulders bare is considered immodest. Make-up of any kind is forbidden.

Told that they are the descendants of a mystical tribe who lived on the Nile known as the Shabazz, the Black Muslims have built up a modern school in Chicago where their children, who are unusually well-behaved and disciplined, are taught Arabic. Conservative in dress, the men are encouraged to go in for crew-cut hairstyles and wear star and crescent buttonhole badges with white ties. Spurning pork, corn bread and tobacco, the followers of Muhammad gain a certain self-respect by joining the movement, and are grateful at the identity and sense of belonging which their membership bestows on them.

Taking a leaf from the book of their opponents in the white camp, the Black Muslims collect funds with the same high-pressure techniques normally associated with the promotion of soap or motor-cars. Magazines are produced in great abundance and, again copying their white opponents, the Black Muslims buy time on at least forty radio and television stations. Jumping on to the 'no-tax' bandwagon—always a good way of winning popularity—the Black Muslims want the American Government to exempt all black people from paying taxes 'as long as they are deprived of equal justice'.

They hold rallies, collect money and build their own temples, and as a step towards having their own separate Negro state in the United States they have set up clothing factories, stores, supermarkets and even farms where food is produced to their dietary rules. Restaurants have been opened for the true children of Allah, and to finance all these activities the leaders call on members to donate one-third of their income to the cause.

When Muhammad began to take a back seat in the movement because of his age, the Black Muslims turned to their prospective new prophet and leader, Malcolm X, a good-looking man with immense charm whose powerful and emotional oratory won over vast numbers of new recruits to the movement.

An ex-thief, bootleg whisky and dope runner who served prison sentences for larceny, Malcolm X told his enraptured audiences: 'There's a great day coming.' This extremist leader's real name was Malcolm Little. But like all followers of the Black Muslims, including their most famous recruit, world boxing champion, Cassius Clay, he dropped his given 'slave' name and adopted the letter 'X' in its stead.

'Islam must replace the "betrayal" of Christianity,' said Malcolm X. 'The white man is the devil, the black man is divine. The day is long past when the races can, or should, live together, for an integrated society will always be a white society and the Negro will live and work as a gelded white, a free slave on sufferance.'

'The future of the American Negro lies in one or two separate and sovereign Negro States. The enemies of the future are the moderates of either colour, the National Association for the Advancement of the Coloured People, the Jews and the Federation Constitution as now interpreted. The means to this end is through the seizure of all national Negro organizations and resources.'

Malcolm X ran into trouble with his leader Elijah Muhammad in December 1963, and was suspended for expressing joy at

President Kennedy's assassination by talking about 'chickens coming home to roost'.

Undeterred, Malcolm X broke away from the Black Muslims in March 1964 to start up his own movement called 'Muslim Mosque Incorporated' which is dedicated to revolution and violence. 'There can be no revolution without bloodshed,' he announced, and warned that his party planned to 'plunge into the civil rights movement'.

'Negroes,' said Malcolm X, 'will be turned from non-violence into active self-defence against white-race supremacists all over the country.

'Here in the United States it is perfectly legal to own a rifle or shotgun. Therefore, we Negroes should form our own rifle clubs with which to defend our people when they are clubbed by police and bitten by the police dogs. We must defend ourselves in time of emergency.

'You will find that the meek little Negro lamb has become a roaring, raging lion who is no longer content to stay out in the streets, but who will invade the home of the white, his kitchen, his parlour, his bedroom.'

Malcolm X then predicted that in the future there 'will be more racial violence than Americans have ever witnessed.

'We aim to sweep out of office all those Negroes who act as puppet politicians and who take orders from the whites. In my new Muslim Mosque movement, the accent will, above all, be on youth. If any whites want to help us, they can, of course. But they can't join us. You can't mix bananas with dried leaves,' added Malcolm X.

The extremist Negro leader did not live long enough to see his prediction of increased racial violence come true, for he was assassinated in February 1965 at one of his meetings. But the movement he started marches on and still recruits members.

It is not only the urban Negro who is turning away from moderation in his quest for full equality, but even in the Deep South a hundred years of Negro passivity is being transformed into violence and a reaching for the gun.

In June 1965, for instance, Louisiana Governor John McKeithen said that he was 'concerned' about a heavily armed Negro group in the South calling itself the 'Deacons of Defence and Justice'.

The 'Deacons' came into being to watch over Negro homes at night. They have opened fire on harassing whites at least twice in Louisiana, and have branches in Mississippi and Alabama.

Their vice-president, thirty-two-year-old Ernest Thomas, said in Bogalusa that Deacons carry pistols and rifles and are out to dispel the Southern notion that Negroes will not fight back.

The main area of racial discontent, however, is not to be found in the South where, before 1940, 80 per cent of the Negro population lived. Rather is it to be found in the giant industrial cities of the North and West which attracted hundreds of thousands of Negroes in the great economic boom of war years.

Today millions of Negroes live in slum areas in cities like Los Angeles where they are surrounded by working-class whites and belts of the plusher middle- and upper-class suburbia.

Theoretically equal to his white neighbours, the Negro, however, has found that in practice he is very much an under-privileged citizen and was the first to lose out when the economic boom lost some of its great post-war impetus. Chronic workless-ness and poverty has hit the Negro communities of the industrial cities hard. And it is the large unemployment problem prevailing in the United States which so strongly exacerbates the racial question.

As long ago as 1963 Willard Wirtz, the Secretary of Labour, warned that unemployment statistics reflected a critical situation which could develop into one of the most explosive social prob-lems in the nation's history. He was referring particularly to a heavy increase in the number of youngsters out of work.

Total unemployment in America, he said, was 4,100,000 and the number of out-of-work teenagers had reached a record 21 per cent by March 1964. It is therefore hardly surprising that teen-agers make up a large proportion of the crowds who flock to hear anti-communist preachers like Billy Hargis and Frederick Schwarz, and that numerous supporters of the Nazi leader, Rockwell, are in their early twenties.

When we consider that the Negro unemployment figure is three times higher than the national average—there are about 900,000 Negroes, including a quarter of a million teenagers out of work—and that three times as many Negro children as white pupils drop out of school before their studies are completed, then it is not surprising that there is a large pool of discontented coloured Americans who are becoming more and more restless about racial discrimination.

The Negro crime and delinquency figures are also higher than the national average, and the Black Muslims and similar movements make good use of the opportunities this offers them. Their policy inevitably leads to violence. Riots have been provoked in prisons by Black Muslims and tension is slowly being built up in Negro quarters all over the country. In Harlem knives, bottles and fire-arms are being used more and more frequently in clashes with the police, as well as in inter-gang battles. In one such instance in Harlem in June 1963, Negroes were stabbed and police injured following a battle between rival 'African Nationalists' and 'Black Nationalists'.

But the grave discontent among Negroes in slum areas cannot always be counted upon to be channelled into joining groups like the Black Muslims. This was demonstrated with the utmost clarity in the Los Angeles riots which caused thirty-five deaths and $40 million worth of damage, and which so startled white Americans.

Countless reasons were offered by 'experts' to explain away the savagery and wanton destruction wrought by the Negro bands bent on arson and plunder. But the real answer lay in a report published by the Department of Labour which showed quite clearly that the blame for the rioting lay in three centuries of slavery, prejudice and economic exploitation of the Negro.

The up-to-date statistics in the report drove home the earlier figures given by Wirtz. More than one Negro family in four is fatherless, while half of all Negro children spend part of their lives in broken homes. Unemployment, illegitimacy and marriage break-ups have led to dependence on the Government for national assistance. Fifty-six per cent of Negro children exist for part of their lives on welfare hand-outs while the corresponding rate for white children is 8 per cent.

Illegitimacy is high—over 43 per cent among Negro families in New York, for instance.

The reasons for the despair, anger, frustration and simmering discontent caused by poverty and lack of opportunity, the restlessness caused by the break-up of family life, are vividly illustrated by these cold statistics. As Billy Graham grimly prophesied after the Los Angeles explosion: 'We are caught in a great racial revolution. What we have seen in Los Angeles is only the beginning.'

Calling for new laws to deal with men who exploit the explosive racial situation, the evangelist added: 'I am convinced that there are sinister forces at work taking advantage of the race problem, whose ultimate objective is the overthrow of the American Government.'

Perhaps it is mere coincidence, but the cramped, squalid ghetto of Watts which produced the Los Angeles racial riots is set in the same city where extremist right-wing groups preaching hatred and violence are particularly active and successful.

The discontent at their poverty and lack of opportunity in achieving real equality with white Americans was eloquently shown when the Negro population of Watts rioted again in March 1966.

The cry 'Get Whitey' is heard more and more frequently in the black slums of American cities. An arsenal of bombs and weapons and a secret rifle range was unearthed in New York. During 'long hot summers' of racial rioting, violence has erupted in such cities as Chicago, Cleveland, Omaha, New York, Newark and Detroit. The cry of 'Black Power' went up in each city.

Explained Negro leader Roy Wilkins, 'Black power means anti-white power. It is a reverse Mississippi, a reverse Hitler, a reverse Ku Klux Klan. It is the wicked fanaticism which has swelled our tears, broken our bodies, squeezed our hearts and taken the blood of our black and white loved ones.' Added a Government official: 'Black power really means that the Negro no longer agrees with the principle of non-violence. It means he's going to fight back with bullets and maybe even bombs.'

Analysing the Negro problem in June 1965, President Johnson warned that the isolation of Negroes from white communities was increasing.

'Negro poverty is not white poverty. Many of its causes and many of its cures are the same, but there are differences— deep, corrosive, obstinate differences—radiating painful roots into the community and into the family and the nature of the individual. These differences are not racial differences. They are solely and simply the consequence of ancient brutality, past injustice, and present prejudice.

'Of course, Negro Americans as well as white Americans

have shared in our rising national abundance, but the harsh fact of the matter is that in the battle for national equality, too many, far too many, are losing ground every day.

'We are not completely sure why this is. Negroes are trapped, as many whites are trapped, in inherited gateless poverty. They lack training and skills. They are shut in slums without decent medical care. Private and public poverty combine to cripple their capacities.

'Perhaps most important is the breakdown of the Negro family structure. For this, most of all, white America must accept responsibility. It flows from centuries of oppression and persecution of the Negro man . . .

'Only a minority—less than half of all Negro children—reach the age of eighteen having lived all their lives with both of their parents. When the family collapses, on a massive scale, the entire community itself is crippled.

'We have failed to find American justice for the American Negro. It is the glorious opportunity of this generation to end the one huge wrong of the American nation.'

This constructive and progressive attitude by President Johnson on the Negro problem evoked the wrath of the fascist-minded in the United States. The extremist J. Evetts Haley accused the President of being 'pro-Socialist'. In a book *None Dare Call It Treason*, published a few months previously, the author attacked Johnson and his family, together with all other presidents since Roosevelt for 'conditioning the American people to retreat in the face of the Communist enemy.'

Another group—this time for whites only—who openly propagate violence and the use of knives and bullets are the 'Minutemen' who are preparing for the day when the 'reds' will take over. All over the United States small secret groups of these 'Minutemen', each cell independently organized, carry out manœuvres in camouflage suits and bury caches of small arms, mortars, grenades, machine-guns and supplies of food in preparation for going into hiding.

The members practise markmanship and learn Judo as well as hold furtive weekly meetings where they study such works as Mao Tse-tung's *Modern Guerrilla Warfare* for the inevitable day when the Red Flag flutters over the Capital.

Started in 1959 by a drug manufacturer, Robert Bolivar

DePugh, the 'Minutemen' hold guerrilla warfare seminars in various parts of America and have even set up their own factories for the manufacture of ammunition, small arms and survival equipment such as compasses and masks against nerve gas and bacteriological warfare. The movement advertises for new recruits with this sort of appeal: 'Pledge yourself and rifle for a "Free America".' In July 1966 the forty-three-year-old DePugh set up a new political party, the 'Patriotic Party'.

The 'Minutemen' claim to have something like 25,000 members and say that they are fighting the communists in advance by sending out vitriolic pamphlets and news-sheets and keeping dossiers on suspect 'liberals' and 'Red sympathizers'.

DePugh, who lives in Missouri, and who was an artillery officer in the Second World War, aims to beat the communists when they have taken over the country by guerrilla warfare tactics and then recapture the United States and restore the 'Constitutional Republic' based on 'freedom and liberty'.

Unlike other extremist movements in the country, the 'Minutemen' are not concerned with making profits. Each cell has to look after its own finances and is utterly dedicated to its role as a fascist-style para-military organization. In June 1965 Senator Thomas Dodd warned that the 'Minutemen' aimed at developing a 'vast underground army'.

Two months before this, the movement ran into trouble when the Californian Attorney-General Thomas C. Lynch condemned the 'Minutemen' and four other extremist groups as 'a threat to the peace and security' of the state. 'They have lost faith in our system of Government. They embrace violent racial and political doctrines,' said Lynch.

'They continually plot armed activity while skirting outright sedition.' In April 1966 a plan to kill Senator William Fulbright was uncovered.

One member of the group who was arrested was found to be guarding 33,000 rounds of ammunition, rifles, pistols, gunpowder and dynamite caps. Another 'Minuteman' had in his possession seven machine-guns, six rifles, four hand guns, thousands of rounds of ammunition, dynamite caps, fuses, hand grenades and seven booby traps. In July 1966 a private arsenal including rocket propellant was uncovered in Los Angeles.

But even under the 'commies' life will have to go on. Besides the 'Minutemen' there are groups of 'Minutewomen' whose more immediate job is to search for communists in schools. These prospective mates of the future guerrillas operate from their Los Angeles headquarters. They have chapters in several cities where they spend their time searching out 'reds' in schools and carefully screen textbooks to ensure that no communist-tainted or leftist thoughts are allowed to sully the minds of their children.

Most of these groups on the extreme right-wing in the United States concentrate on the issue of the 'internal communist menace', for it supplies a facile psychological outlet for the worried and less sophisticated Americans who feel that by attending meetings, buying books and playing their role as fee-paying contributors, they are being patriotic and doing their duty to flag and country—as well as protecting their own future.

By seeking out local 'reds' and writing letters to their Congressmen, these citizens consider that they have done their 'bit' and need not concern themselves with having to think about the international challenge of communism.

But a policy of isolationism does not have the power it once did and many of these right-wing groups are looking beyond the borders of the United States to form links and join in the activities of fascist organizations in Latin America, Europe and Africa.

The 'Minutemen' claim to have started groups in Canada and have made contact with the OAS and other right-wing activists in Europe. The Ku Klux Klan also has members in Europe and the Argentine. From its headquarters in Waco, Texas, the 'Aryan Knights of the KKK', run by Horace Sherman Miller, are in close touch with the Tacuara terrorist organization in Buenos Aires.

The Klansmen also have connections with groups in Brazilian cities where they go under such titles as 'Vigilantes of the Night' and 'The High Order of the Black Cloaks'. In the days following the capture of Adolf Eichmann, an article written by the anti-Jewish agitator in Arab Jerusalem, Antoine F. Albina, stating that 'Eichmann could not be guilty' appeared in a publication of the Ku Klux Klan in Atlanta, Georgia.

Branches of the KKK have been active in South Africa and its influence spread to Great Britain in 1965.

The John Birch Society launched a campaign in 1962 on behalf of General Salan, the former head of the OAS terrorist movement in France. It was hoped that such a campaign described as a 'few

strong breezes of justly enraged opinion from American people'
would sway de Gaulle in his policies towards the chief of the
underground army. For the more simple-minded of its followers
who knew little about events in Algeria, de Gaulle was painted by
the John Birch Society as the 'man who was selling out France
to the Reds'.

In the Society's *bulletin* members were urged to write letters to
five French newspapers and to *The Times* of London to stress
that trying General Salan for his life a second time (the first
trial was held *in absentia*) 'is so contrary to every principle and
custom in the law of modern civilized peoples as to constitute a
disgrace to the French nation.' The *Bulletin* claimed that the vast
majority of the French people would certainly agree with this
sentiment.

The slickly edited monthly magazine of the John Birch Society,
American Opinion, published a letter from Jacques Soustelle,
formerly Governor-General of Algeria, addressing an appeal to
the American people on behalf of the tens of thousands of settlers
who had fled from Algeria. Readers were told that the betrayal of
these people into communist hands by General de Gaulle could
have been prevented by a sufficiently responsible American press.

The reasoning behind the pro-Salan campaign was that de
Gaulle, who is dismissed as a 'comsymp' (communist sympathizer
in John Birch Society terminology) is said to keep a careful watch
on public opinion. It therefore suggested a 'veritable' flood of
letters to the French newspapers. The journal then gave a detailed
account of the circumstances of General Salan's trial and quoted
as the core of the OAS leader's defence, the statement: 'I do not
have to vindicate myself for refusing to let communism be established (in Algeria) one hour from Marseilles.'

Welch also keeps his eye on Africa and when President
Tshombe of Katanga was still holding out against the United
Nations in the Congo, the John Birch leader weighed in heavily
on his side, pouring scorn on the efforts of the United Nations to
restore order. About Britain, Welch says that the country is 50 to
70 per cent under communist control.

The most internationally-minded extremist in the United
States was the leader of the American Nazi Party, George Lincoln
Rockwell. Early in 1963, after he was 'elected' as the international
commander of the world-wide Nazi movement, Rockwell started

making plans to hold an 'International Nazi Congress' in the Argentine and wrote to the leaders of the Argentine 'National Socialist Party' to start organizing for this project. The self-styled 'Fuehrer' of America, forty-four year old Rockwell was the son of a radio comedian. He was a former Navy Commander who was dismissed from the Naval Reserve in 1960 for his Nazi Party activities. Rockwell owned an extensive library of anti-Semitic literature and plaques of Hitler, and he not only came to Britain in August 1962 to meet Jordan but he also travelled to Europe and Canada where he made contact with other fascist leaders.

In the United States, the American Nazi and his uniformed 'storm-troopers' have frequently demonstrated outside the White House against racial integration in the South. Besides publishing his *Storm-trooper* news-sheet, Rockwell also spent a great deal of time making speeches wherever he could find an audience. In February 1963 he spoke to students at Chicago University despite protests and demonstrations against his presence there.

The 'Fuehrer', whose brown-shirted followers have their headquarters in a farmhouse in Arlington, Virginia—ten minutes' drive across the Potomac River from the White House—described Hitler as 'our spiritual leader' and he offered studio-sized portraits of the German chief to his supporters for framing.

As violent in aim and deed as their 'heroes' of the Third Reich, Rockwell's followers are often in trouble with the authorities. In 1961, two of his party members, twenty-six-year-old Richard Braun, and thirty-one-year-old Robert Garber, were jailed for a year for attacking a thirteen-year-old Jewish schoolboy on his way home from a dance. They dragged the youngster into their swastika-bedecked premises and threatened to beat him with a lead pipe.

The two heroes were later described by Rockwell as 'brave and honourable men who are proud to go down fighting for their country'. In May 1963, four teenagers with swastika armbands and with anti-semitic literature in their possession, machine-gunned a classroom and the home of a woman teacher who had given them bad marks.

Five months later police arrested a fifteen-year-old boy who had overturned tombstones in a New York Jewish cemetery. The youth's garage was equipped as a 'Gestapo headquarters' and decorated with swastika flags, several German army helmets, swastika armbands, pictures of Hitler and Eichmann, and news-paper cuttings about Nazi death camps.

In February 1964—just three months after the assassination of Kennedy—police in Los Angeles arrested two students who were found in possession of a rifle, 500 rounds of ammunition and American Nazi party literature. The secret service men who were called in were understandably alarmed as President Johnson was due in the city the very next day. Together with the rifle and ammunition found in the car was a portrait of Hitler and a Nazi publication which had a photograph of President Johnson on the cover with a gunsight pattern across the head and the word 'Next?' above it.

Rockwell proclaimed that when he came to power he would build a modern state in Africa and offer ten thousand dollars to every 'nigger family' to migrate there. He also added that 80 per cent of the Jews are traitors and that he would kill them. He claimed that Jews control Russia through terror and force, and in addition they rule the U.S. through manipulation of Jewish financial power.

The American 'Fuehrer' has also taken a hand in the de-segregation disturbances in the Deep South and travelled with a bus-load of Negro-baiting followers behind racially mixed groups of 'Freedom Riders' who were demonstrating for equality. Travelling in convoy, Rockwell's storm-troopers wearing red and black swastikas tried to stir up trouble in different Southern states during race riots.

The Nazi 'leader' also toured the South on the same day as the giant civil rights march was taking place in Washington in order to organize counter-demonstrations. Rockwell wrote: 'The nigger revolution will openly threaten to plunge its final dagger into the beating heart of our Republic.'

After the Negro rioting in Chicago in the summer of 1966, Rockwell stirred up further trouble in the city by holding a rally there. Telling a massive crowd of supporters and sympathizers that they must prepare for the 'white revolution', Nazi party leaders called on their followers to carry out counter-marches into Negro areas. The result was predictable. In the ensuing riots 16 people were injured and a number of Negroes beaten up.

Originally a follower of Senator Joe McCarthy, Rockwell soon found that witch-hunt policies were too lukewarm for him. Like his English counterpart, Colin Jordan, the American Nazi had been imprisoned for his activities, but this did not discourage his ambitions of becoming President of the U.S. 'by 1972'.

In his official *Stormtroopers Manual* Rockwell explained why he became a fully-fledged 'Nazi'. 'Everywhere I draw the largest crowds because I am controversial. Millions of people who would pay no attention to more "conservative" right-wingers are fascinated by a Nazi. Like birds before a snake.'

Rockwell praised the activities of Billy James Hargis as 'sincere' and 'doing good', but a 'little unenlightened as he only preaches to the converted'. He should aim at the 'brain-washed liberal nigger-loving youth of our nation and the pinko and communist labouring masses who are now listening to and following the Jews.'

With this type of provocative racial propaganda being pumped out, incidents of violence are only to be expected.

As an example in November 1965 vandals broke into a synagogue in Holyoake, Massachusetts, and after daubing the walls with huge black swastikas set fire to the building.

Another extremist group, the 'National States Rights Party', counts thirty-one-year-old Maynard Orlando Nelson among its leaders. Nelson, who also runs his own 'Real Political Institute' in Chicago, is a close ally of twenty-seven-year-old Matt Koehl, who in turn was a member of James Madole's 'National Renaissance Party'. An associate of Nelson's is Dr Edward R. Fields, a Louisville chiropodist and a veteran of extremist activity who co-ordinates contacts with other groups such as the Ku Klux Klan and the American Nazi Party. Connected with the 'National States Rights Party' is John W. Hamilton, formerly with the 'National Citizens Protective Association', of St Louis, which publishes the *White Sentinel*, and John Kasper, who has served a term of imprisonment for subversive activity in Tennessee.

Proudly proclaiming its slogan of 'White Men Unite', the 'National States Rights Party' is one of the fastest-growing right-wing groups and boasts in its publication *Thunderbolt* that it is 'America's Largest Third Party'. For sheer virulent racialism, *Thunderbolt* stands supreme. In an editorial it had this to say about Nazi war-criminal Julius Streicher: 'The greatest anti-Jewish patriot of this century was Julius Streicher. Here was a man who was clearly murdered to appease the Jew.'

'For years *Der Stürmer* was the world's leading journal against international Jewry. There can be no doubt that the Jews would like to have us murdered also for telling the people about their devilry. There was never the slightest bit of evidence that Streicher (a newspaper publisher) could have been in any way connected with any war crime. He simply had offended the International criminal Jews and thus had to pay with his life. For this reason we have decided that Julius Streicher must not be forgotten. And above all that these murdering Jews killed this man for using the freedom of the press to expose the crimes of the Jews. In honour of Julius Streicher, we have published the most famous edition he ever printed.'

Thunderbolt then reproduced a special 'ritual murder' edition of *Der Stürmer* which appeared in 1934 and which provoked the Archbishop of Canterbury to say: 'It seems almost incredible that such a publication recalling the worst excesses of medieval fanaticism should have been permitted in any civilized country.'

Consignments of this U.S. printed *Thunderbolt* soon afterwards arrived in Western Germany and were seized by the police.

The publication is edited by Dr Fields and James K. Warner, and it advertises five other papers produced by the party: *The Attack*, *The Storm* (both of New York), *Arkansas NSRP Newsletter* (Little Rock) whose editor is Ann Bishop, *The Florida Patriot* which is edited by Dewey Taft, and the *Ohio Newsletter* (editor Irving Thacker). Two other journals appear in Louisiana and Missouri.

The party has branches in thirty-five states, often with each group taking its own name. In Pennsylvania it goes under the title of 'The National Association to Preserve Free Speech', and in Nebraska it is called the 'Ultra American Service Association'. The 'Blue Shirts' of Louisiana under their leader Leonard Butler acknowledge their association with the party but say rather gloomily that their chanting of 'Viva Fascismo' slogans seems to discourage many new members from joining.

Like other publications in Europe, James Madole's the *National Renaissance Bulletin* came out with a 'Hitler Birthday' editorial calling the Nazi dictator the 'George Washington' of Europe. It declared that 'German National Socialism taught its youth to have courage, respect for labour and ardent fidelity to their parents, race and nation.'

Although he has lost some of his members to the American Nazi Party Madole is still active. He has numerous Arab connections and is particularly strong on his pro-Nasser anti-Israel campaigns. Internationally-minded, Madole often publishes European extremist writings and recommends *Mosley—Right or Wrong*, one of the works of the British fascist chief; *The World Conquerors* by Louis Marschalko, the Hungarian Nazi; *The Jewish Ritual Murder* by the late Arnold Leese, as well as other 'vital books on racial nationalist topics'.

Madole's new journal *The Free American*, which replaces the *International Nazi Fascist*, was edited by a Dan Burros in New York. Interspersed between such slogans as 'Hitler was right' and 'Perish Judah' are advertisements for Rockwell and Jordan's new movement, 'The World Union of National Socialists' (WUNS) and such offshoots as the Canadian 'Anti-Jewish Combat League'. *The Free American* has agents in Germany, France and England. Burros, a former member of the American Nazi Party, committed suicide after his Jewish origins were made public.

The editor of yet another publication, the *American Nationalist*, Frank L. Britton made a point of linking anti-Jewish and anti-Negro propaganda. Britton denied all past Nazi crimes and, taking up the refrain from present-day European fascist publications, he denounced the *Diary of Anne Frank* as a 'hate fabrication intended to keep alive the vicious myth that the Germans deliberately exterminated the Jews.' The German–Israel reparation agreement was abused as 'the greatest blackmail operation in all recorded history'.

Britton also deplored 'race-mixing' among Hollywood personalities and made provocative announcements of the kind that 56 per cent of Negroes at the American military base at Camp Lee 'were dull and feeble-minded'.

Although the *American Nationalist* is now no longer published, its past articles and editorials are so cherished by the fascist-minded and extreme-right in the United States that they are continually reprinted.

Associated with the fascist movements is the Young Americans for Freedom group, composed mostly of college students and organized into University chapters. One of this group's particular heroes is General Edwin Walker, and at its mass meetings are displayed banners which proclaim: 'Stamp Out Communism',

'Tear Down the Berlin Wall', and 'Invade Cuba'. The Young Americans for Freedom claim a 20,000 membership.

One of the widest-read publications preaching racial hatred in America is *Common Sense*, a fortnightly which describes itself as 'America's newspaper against Communism'. Connected with the 'Christian Educational Association', its contents are so filled with racialist material that the House Committee on Un-American Activities has described it as the source of 'some of the most vitriolic hate propaganda ever to come to the attention of the Committee.'

Common Sense has the doubtful distinction of having been condemned by the United Nations and all Presidents of the United States since Herbert Hoover.

An interesting theory put forward by the slightly more squeamish supporters of the right-wing racialist groups who cannot swallow undiluted anti-semitism, is known as 'Khazarism', evolved by an apostate Jew called Benjamin Freedman, a former salesman.

The Khazars, according to this theory, were an Asiatic tribe in Southern Russia who were converted to the religion of Judaism in the sixth century and then scattered among various European races. Because they were rather a cunning lot, the 'Khazars' took over control and today the people who call themselves 'Jews' really came from Russia 1,400 years ago.

With this theory in pocket, members of the various groups who read Freedman's articles in *Common Sense* and other journals of the same hue are able to reply to allegations of being anti-semitic by saying with clear consciences that 'it is not true—there's simply no such thing as Jews.'

Other writers in *Common Sense* are not convinced and complain rather bitterly that 'everyone seems to be Jewish'.

The editor of this journal, Conde McGinley, died in July 1963 but his work is continued by his son, Conde Junior.

Another journal, called *Human Events*, has seen its circulation leap upwards from a struggling 13,000 in 1960 to 100,000 two years later as it caught the full tide of rising right-wing sentiment.

William Buckley's *National Review*, a bi-weekly, boasts a 72,000 circulation, although it aims at a slightly higher intellectual level than most of the other publications in the field by directing its appeal to 'right-wing' thinkers. Buckley is a strong supporter of the 'Young Americans for Freedom' Movement.

A wealthy, romantic figure, Buckley, whose razor-sharp wit and intelligence once won him the accolade of being a 'kind of sick Kennedy', is staunchly anti-communist. His extremism led him to support Senator Joe McCarthy in his witch-hunt hey-day, and, although a staunch Catholic, Buckley criticized Pope John's famous '*Pacem in Terris*' Encyclical as a 'venture in triviality'.

Like others on the extreme right-wing, he demands the abolition of collective bargaining in industry, unemployment compensation and all welfare legislation.

Hundreds of right-wing groups, made up of zealots and crooks, the idealistic and the cynical, the simple-minded and sometimes the highly intelligent, have come into existence during the past few years. There are so many of them that an organization known as the 'Alert Americans Association' of Los Angeles lists over 2,000 in its 'Directory of Rights Groups'.

Starting up, splitting, disintegrating and then re-forming again under a variety of names and leaders with bewildering speed, this fragmented right-wing tide obtains its support from all corners of the country. It is particularly strong in Texas, Arizona, California and in the Deep South. For instance, Gerald L. K. Smith, who runs his *Nationalist News Service* on undisguised racialist lines, has his greatest support in Missouri. Smith also runs a monthly magazine, *The Cross and the Flag*, which advises followers to infiltrate their way into the John Birch Society. The object of this exercise is to try and get Welch's supporters to add the names of Jews to the Society's list of red conspirators and traitors in the United States.

Some of these movements are militantly religious, some are 'respectable' and primly conservative, concerned only with saving the nation from the 'commie menace', while others are quite openly fascist. The National Catholic Welfare Conference said it was convinced that three-quarters of these extremist groups are making 'a financial racket of the fight against Communism'. But all such criticisms are shrugged off by ultra right-wing movements as 'communist-inspired smears'.

Although they may be dismissed as 'worthless fanatics' and 'screwballs' and bundled together with the Black Muslims as necessary growing pains in the development of American democracy, the organizations making up this lunatic fringe are a powerful influence in the land and many of their activities are kept under the closest surveillance by the FBI.

Of more immediate importance, these right-wing movements exert constant pressure on the American legislature. Well organized campaigns designed to block progressive and enlightened social and foreign programmes have met with considerable success. Representatives like John Rousselot of California and Edgar Hiestand joined the ranks of the John Birch Society. It was Rousselot, a thirty-six-year-old former Republican Congressman, who said: 'Democracy is one of the worst of all forms of Government.' Various Congressmen and Senators have sponsored resolutions calling for the abolition of federal income tax and taken up the cause of the 'martyred' General Walker.

Another man greatly admired by the extremists is Senator Strom Thurmond, the South Carolina Republican, who is a militant anti-liberal in the forefront of the battle to prevent the spread of de-segregation.

The darling of the reactionary right, however, is Barry Goldwater, the Republican Senator from Arizona who often echoes the words of the John Birch Society. 'The members of this movement,' he says, 'are good, sincere citizens.' And taking a leaf out of Welch's book, Goldwater warns: 'The real danger to our nation, to our way of life and to the cause of freedom throughout the world comes from the leftists in our midst who even today counsel a soft attitude towards Communism, both at home and abroad.'

The 'get tough with the communists' line was repeated in February 1964, when the Senator commented on the action of Castro, who had cut off water supplies to the U.S. naval base at Guantanamo in retaliation for the arrest of Cuban fishermen off the coast of Florida. 'Our flag can be spat upon and torn to the ground, and as an American I'm sick and tired of it. I think I can promise President Johnson the backing of the American people if we don't take this one lying down.

'This points up once again that we've reached such a low in our foreign relations that any bum can kick us around. This is another result of an indecisive foreign policy. Whenever a weaker country thinks it can thumb its nose at a stronger country and get away with it, it is going to do this.'

And in similar vein he turned his attention to Indo-China:

'I would drop a low yield atomic bomb on the Chinese supply lines in North Vietnam or maybe shell them with the 7th Fleet.'

Goldwater, when campaigning for the Republican presidential nomination, won the applause of the right-wing extremists when he urged that American warships be used to prevent British buses from being shipped to Cuba. 'United States Marines should have restored Guantanamo's water supply stopped by the Cubans,' he added.

'It might lead to some shooting in Cuba, but that's all,' said the Senator blithely, forgetting how the whole world nearly met its nuclear Armageddon on the last occasion when there was the threat of 'some shooting in Cuba'.

In March 1964, Goldwater told factory workers in New Hampshire that the United States should recognize a Cuban Government in exile and train and equip refugees and mercenaries to overthrow Dr Fidel Castro's Government.

'People say this might cause war. It might. But we're going to have to go to war some time if we keep backing up. The sooner the United States moves against Cuba, the cheaper it's going to be and the less the chances that American troops will have to be used.'

Little wonder the extreme right in America saw the man from Arizona as their sturdy knight riding out to challenge the red menace. 'If elected President,' they agreed, 'he will stop our drift into communism.'

Says Welch: 'Goldwater is the man who comes nearest to measuring up to all the needs and qualifications for the Presidency.'

Not only in the United States, but extremists all over the Western World pinned their hopes on a Goldwater victory. Said the Nazi *Nation Europa* published in Germany: 'A win for Goldwater would be so world-shaking an event that nothing more would be needed to bring down in ruins the walls which communist tyranny in central Europe can maintain only with help from the West. And Roosevelt's gang in the State Department will lose their jobs.'

Throughout the election campaign Goldwater appealed to the narrow nationalism, frustrations and petty racialist prejudices of millions of lower middle class Americans such as shopkeepers, clerks, garage-owners and small-time employers.

His speech-making echoed the jingoistic speeches and approach used by Hitler in the early 1930's in Germany. Only instead of Jews, Goldwater played upon the white American fear of growing Negro demands for a place in the sun. And just like Hitler, Goldwater attacked socialism and communism as the dogmas of the very devil.

Warned Trade Union leader, George Meany: 'Goldwater is not a crackpot. In the 1930's the people of Germany said Hitler was a crackpot. But he captured control of a political party and seven years later we had a most catastrophic war.'

With the landslide defeat of Goldwater in the November election, it might have been thought that the far right would retire mortally wounded following the rejection of its extremist champion.

But far from it. A virtue was made out of necessity and proudly the right-wing faction of the Republican party proclaimed: 'Twenty-seven million Americans can't be wrong.'

This, of course, was the number of votes which Goldwater did pull in against Johnson, and William Buckley, quick to seize on this crystallization of right-wing opinion, launched the *American Conservative Union*. Amply supplied with funds from reactionary big business supporters, the *Union* began issuing a broadside of propaganda in the form of magazine articles, syndicated newspaper columns, radio and television broadcasts, etc. By the middle of 1965 the number of broadcasts costing £3,500,000 a year totalled well over 7,000 a week and reached the four corners of the United States.

The 'fungus' of right-wing extremism seemed to have received such a shot in the arm by the Goldwater election campaign and the publicity which it evoked, that right-wing groups all over the country reported booming business. For instance, the John Birch Society announced somewhat incredulously that its own membership had doubled and now stood at something like 160,000.

To handle the sudden deluge of application forms flooding into its offices, the John Birch Society now employs over two hundred staff, including sixty full-time field co-ordinators. Salaries alone amount to £10,000 per week and gross annual income has doubled in two years to well over a million pounds.

With five regional offices being kept busy, Welch estimates that shortly he will need—and expects to get—£350,000 a month from members and sympathizers.

With growing arrogance and soaring ambitions, Welch says that the 'United States is an insane asylum run by its worst patients'. Hoping to 'control the thinking of the American people by 1968' the leader of the John Birch Society expects to double his membership by the end of 1967 and then redouble it in the following year. His avowed aim is to have at least 1,000 members in each of the 435 Congressional districts by the end of 1967. If he can achieve this he feels that he will be able to exercise important national political power.

In recent months Welch has been concentrating his activities on penetrating the ranks of the police, and active Birch cells have been set up in local police departments. Establishing a new body called 'TACT' (Truth About Civil Turmoil) the Society plans to have committees in every American community. These 'TACT' groups will promote the theme that the entire struggle for Negro rights is a communist plot.

This latest development is to take full advantage of and exploit racial feeling in the country. Leaders of the violently anti-Negro 'White Citizens Councils' in the South who are on a par with the Ku Klux Klan are cordially invited to write for *American Opinion*. One such article blasted the civil rights movement as a threat to 'our country, our race and our civilization'.

Welch's printing presses are now pouring out books, brochures and news-sheets by the million. Sales are handled in over three hundred of his 'American Opinion Libraries'. One of these items of literature which appealed to the twenty-seven million who voted for Goldwater in 1964 said that the forty-two million 'camp followers' of President Johnson had 'voted for repeal of our Declaration of Independence: Voted for scrapping the United States Constitution entirely: Voted for encouragement and support by the Federal Government of racial agitators to instigate more riots.' And finally: 'Voted to condone and accept the gradual destruction of all moral principles.'

American Opinion, Welch's show-piece glossy journal now has the largest circulation of any political review in the whole of the United States.

Billy James Hargis is another who is now going from strength to strength in the post-election climate. His 'Christian Crusade' broadcasts its message over four hundred radio stations every week. One of his rivals, the Rev. Carl McIntire, who is not only anti-communist but also anti-United Nations and anti-civil rights, does even better with broadcasts on some 618 radio stations weekly. In the south the Ku Klux Klan claims a swelling membership.

William Buckley, a good-looking and compelling television performer, caused a stir when he became the third candidate in the campaign for New York mayoralty late in 1965. His quite deliberate aim was to take votes from the liberal Republican Congressman, John Lindsay, and so prevent him from capturing one of the most powerful political offices in the United States.

Buckley's reasoning was that if Lindsay won the election it would be a powerful victory for the Republican Party's left wing and thus crush the ambitions of the party's Goldwater adherents. Hence the reason for his candidature—even if it meant that the Democrats might sweep the board. Buckley failed to stop Lindsay winning, but by securing over 300,000 votes—13 per cent of the poll—he proved that 'Goldwaterism' is by no means a dead issue in American politics.

In November 1966 former film star Ronald Reagan, who is a staunch Goldwater man, won a smashing victory over incumbent Democrat Pat Brown in the election for Governor of California. A passionate anti-Communist, Reagan is firmly opposed to civil rights legislation and was associated with the John Birch Society.

With one American voter in ten living in California, the significance of this victory cannot be under-estimated. Goldwaterism is far from dead, and undaunted by his presidential defeat, the man who ran against Johnson is now talking about a come-back and plans to run in the 1968 senatorial election.

The significant point about the ground-swell of right-wing activity in the United States today is that it is a far greater danger to democracy than any previous extremist convulsion. Its backers and leaders have for the first time in American history made a powerful dent in one of the great established parties—the Republicans.

Nelson Rockefeller warned of this danger: 'The far right-wing, including the John Birch Society, is making a determined and ruthless effort to take over the Republican party, its platform and its candidates on its own terms.'

These ultra-conservatives have immense financial backing and thanks to the highly developed mass communications media now in existence are able to reach the ears and eyes of tens of millions of Americans with their persuasive propaganda.

Adlai Stevenson asserted in February 1964 that the advocacy of excited, ill-considered and foolish acts by American right-wingers can do 'untold harm'.

'For it begets a frame of mind among the ignorant and thoughtless in which extreme courses seem natural . . .'

In 1966 historian Arthur Schlesinger warned that irrationality on the right and left wings of politics could be preparing the way for a 'new McCarthyism' in the United States. 'The late Senator McCarthy's anti-communist crusade was possible because of hostilities and frustrations caused by America's part in the Korean war.

'If history repeats itself, and it sometimes does, the war in Vietnam ought to produce something roughly comparable to the McCarthy phenomenon,' he said.

The matter was put in a nutshell by the sober, warning voice of Bishop Everett W. Palmer of Seattle who said: 'There is a frightening likeness between certain anti-communist movements now in vogue across America and events which transpired in Germany and Italy prior to the rise of the Nazi and fascist régimes.'

CHAPTER IV

Italy

IT WOULD have been most surprising if the political force of fascism had come to a complete stop when Mussolini and other fascist leaders perished in Northern Italy in 1945.

The shock defeat, the invasion by the victorious Allied armies and the flight by many of the top Italian fascists to Spain and Latin America dealt a crippling blow to the twenty years—the Ventennio—of fascist rule in the country.

If nostalgia was still strong among some Italians for the days of glory, the pomp and circumstance, the mass meetings, the chants and ceremonial trappings of Mussolinism in its hey-day, then certainly these feelings were kept discretely quiet in the years immediately after the war. Despite rumours of some neo-Nazi activity, of the rebirth of neo-fascism in the Movimento Sociale Italiano (Italian Social Movement) or MSI, the outside world was not aware of any great revival until 1962 when the sound of marching jackboots was again heard reverberating in the streets of Rome.

The occasion was the Rome Municipal elections in June of that year when the MSI made a full-blooded attempt to increase their share of the vote. It is estimated that a million pounds—part of which is believed to have come from abroad—was spent by the MSI on the election.

The streets were showered with fascist leaflets, and the air was thick with electioneering programmes and promises calling upon the electorate to vote for this extreme right-wing party. Speeches blared out over powerful loudspeakers in vans thundering up and down the city night after night, and the party even arranged for leaflets to be dropped from an aeroplane on to the heads of guests at the President's annual garden party.

Just in case there should be any doubt about the political ideas behind the MSI, squads of fascist youth marched into the narrow streets of the traditional Jewish quarter on the banks of the Tiber with its crowded tenement buildings to provoke incidents and riots. The lower middle-class residents of this one-time compulsory dwelling-place for the Jews of the Holy City responded with angry violence and several clashes broke out before jeeploads of police arrived to restore order.

This was not the first time that fascist hoodlums had shown their faces in Rome. In October 1960, goose-stepping squads raided the same area. After upsetting street-stalls, smashing windows, beating up old men, singing Nazi songs and chanting fascist slogans, they fought pitched battles with groups of young Jews. One of the fascist leaders, Franco Cecchetti, collapsed with a smashed skull and was taken to hospital in a critical condition.

Two years before this—in May 1958—there were other demonstrations provoked by members of the MSI in this one-time ghetto. Chanting 'Long live Mussolini' and 'Death to the Jews', they smeared swastikas on the walls of the Great Synagogue, defaced the tablet on the front wall which commemorated the six million Jewish martyrs who died at the hands of the Nazis, and trampled underfoot wreaths which they had found there. These attacks echoed demonstrations carried out ten years previously in the same district and were duplicated in other parts of the country.

The activities of the fascist groups were not only directed at the relatively small number of Jews who live in the city, but in true traditional fashion they were also aimed at left-wing groups. To older Italians they revived the memory of the castor-oil brigades and murder squads of the black-shirted gangs of toughs known as *squadristri* in the 1920's when Mussolini was riding to power by skilfully exploiting the divisions amongst the parties on the left, a weak Government, a hesitant and docile monarchy and Vatican, and a prevaricating army and police force.

Young socialists laying a wreath on the memorial to Giacomo Matteotti, the socialist deputy murdered by the Duce's thugs in 1924, were attacked and beaten up. Any doubts about the identity of the attackers were dispelled when two members of the MSI were arrested after the same marble memorial was removed in 1960.

Para-military groups raided communist party offices and there was an attack on the home of a communist chief in Rome. In July 1960, in Milan, bombs were thrown into the garden of the

Soviet Trade Office and attacks were made against communist premises in the same city.

In spite of the noisy and provocative electoral activity in Rome in the middle of 1962, the MSI did not gain many new supporters and only slightly increased their percentage poll to about 16 per cent of the total votes cast.

To understand the significance of these events, it is necessary to go back to events immediately after the war when Italians were finding some difficulty in adjusting themselves to the re-introduction of the unusual practices of democracy. The country had to face serious economic and social hardships, and the people were depressed by defeat and by the loss of their overseas possessions.

It was therefore hardly surprising that large numbers of Italians turned to political extremes which perhaps explains why the Communist Party in Italy became the strongest in the Western world. But in a Catholic country there were many Italians who could not stomach undiluted Marxist ideology and some of them gravitated to the extreme right and found a home in the 'Uomo Qualunque', or 'The Movement of the Ordinary Man' founded by Guglielmo Giannini, a writer who had achieved considerable fame in the field of literature.

Not long after—in 1946–1947—the right-wing section of the 'Ordinary Man' decided that its leader was not extreme enough, and split off to form the Movimento Sociale Italiano. This organization soon showed its fascist character although today it takes some pains to point out that its fascism is not of the pre-war variety. It claims, for instance, that it is not at all a racialist party despite the excesses of some of its followers. Mindful of its public image, leaders of the MSI repeatedly claim that it was the German Nazis who were responsible for the concentration camps and the mass murders and that Italian fascists never condoned these activities.

The MSI attracted one and a half million votes in 1953 and two years later was represented by twenty-nine Deputies and nine Senators in Parliament.

In the 1958 election the party had a set-back losing one seat in the Senate and four in the Chamber. But these losses were made good in April 1963 when the MSI increased its number of seats in the Senate to fifteen and in the Chamber to twenty-seven.

The MSI has consistently followed three lines of policy:

(1) To revive memories of the fascist period and the glories of the Duce's leadership;

(2) To discredit the system of democratic government by blaming it for all the ills of present-day life in Italy, both on the domestic front and in matters of foreign policy;

(3) To fight communism, claiming that their movement is the only force to prevent a communist régime being set up in the country.

This propaganda proved successful and the party has gained considerably since the early formative post-war years. As well as increasing their voting strength the new fascists have obtained ample financial support from Italian businessmen who are alarmed at the 'opening of the left' and the threat of communism, and see in the MSI the bulwark to ward off even 'mild' socialism.

The party also finds friends among the wealthy land-owning class who believe that they are being threatened by the liberal-minded or leftist trend in Italy.

Because fascist movements from other countries see in the MSI one of the most promising instruments for gaining power, it is claimed that they have not hesitated to pump funds into the coffers of the Italian party leaders. But these operations are always carried out with the utmost secrecy and there is no means of checking the authenticity of these reports.

In the early post-war years the Vatican did much to help the growth of neo-fascism in the country; it seems to have panicked in the face of what it deemed the communist menace and proposed the establishment of a fascist and anti-communist front. Only vigorous efforts by Alcide de Gasperi, Italy's post-war Prime Minister and other Government leaders who at the time rejected Vatican proposals prevented this move gaining momentum.

The most pressing demands on de Gasperi took place in April 1962 when Father Lombardi, an emissary sent by Pope Pius XII, tried to force the Prime Minister to accept an alliance with the MSI.

'The Pope would prefer seeing Stalin and his Cossacks in St Peter's Square than seeing the Italian Communists gain control even of the Rome City Hall' was the startling message he conveyed to the de Gasperi household.

Monsignor Montini, then in the Vatican Secretariat of State

and the present Pope, paid a call on one of de Gasperi's colleagues the very next day to reinforce the Pope's demand to bring the fascists into the Government fold.

'The Pope's decision to support the right-wing coalition is irrevocable,' he said, and, later, after de Gasperi had stoutly resisted this Vatican pressure he was told by Montini of the Pope's anger.

Even today the fascists in Italy make strenuous efforts to win over the Catholic Church to their cause and enlist the aid of the Vatican in their 'crusade' against bolshevism.

In January 1963 it became known that a 600-page volume containing rabidly anti-semitic writings of all ages, together with other racialist and anti-communist 'facts', had been distributed to the participants of the Ecumenical Council gathered in Rome.

Entitled *Plot against the Church* and written by a certain Maurice Pinay, the book was divided into such sections as 'The Secret Engines of Communism', 'The Hidden Power of Free-masonry', and 'The Jewish Fifth Column in the Clergy'.

The compilation and editing of this 'encyclopaedia' is believed to have been organized by the 'Ordine Nuovo' (The New Order) —the Italian fascist group which has connections with similar movements in Spain, Portugal, Belgium, France, West Germany, Egypt and South Africa.

The object of this immense work of crude racialistic propaganda was clear. Extreme right-wing movements were alarmed at the growth of a liberal spirit in the Vatican inspired partly by Cardinal Bea, head of the Vatican Secretariat, and of course by the late Pope John himself.

Fearful of what they considered to be the potential loss of such a powerful ally, these right-wing movements call liberal Catholic clergy part of the 'Jewish fifth column'. The purpose of their book, which gave every indication of having been compiled with great urgency and some expense, was to try and arrest this liberal trend by frightening the delegates to the Ecumenical Council.

A German version of this book was later published in Spain and distributed in various European cities. The Bonn Government eventually banned the work which bore so much resemblance to the crude medieval bigotry and 'theology' of the Nazi, Julius Streicher.

Council delegates later received a racialist pamphlet signed by fourteen reactionary groups from France, Spain, Portugal, Germany, Austria, Italy itself and several Latin American countries. The churchmen were told: 'Many Popes had the courage of adopting strong anti-Jewish measures to prevent Christianity being replaced by a Pharisaical theocracy.

'If the Church deplores the persecutions and outbursts of anti-semitism which always occurred throughout the centuries, she will end by condemning herself.' Bishops were then accused of submitting themselves to 'Jewish pressure and allowing themselves to be sold to Jewish gold'.

The growth of the fascist-style MSI party in Italy can be partly explained by the heritage which Mussolini left in his wake that fascism can be equated with social progress. The Duce launched gigantic social welfare schemes and land reclamation projects which enable many Italians today, especially those of the poorer classes, to claim with a certain amount of understandable sincerity that 'Mussolini was for us.'

They have not forgotten that the fascist dictator ruled in the proud days of the Empire and that he introduced colonization schemes which relieved unemployment by reducing surplus population. Italians like the theatrical atmosphere that goes with the mass rallies, the rhetoric, the heroic posturing which is echoed by MSI propaganda. There is also a certain bitterness over the loss of the country's possessions such as Eritrea, Albania, North Africa and Istria—the area behind Trieste.

Favourite Mussolini phrases such as *'posto al sole'* (place in the sun) and *'spazio vitale'* (vital space) are trundled out for the nostalgic-minded and for those who wish to revive the memories of former colonial glories. At the same time the MSI claim that their present-day fascism is merely a nationalistic policy run by a truly National Party. Unlike the communists they do not take orders from 'foreigners' in Moscow or elsewhere.

The MSI has found a valuable friend in the much-decorated midget submarine commander, fifty-six-year-old Prince Valerio Borghese, whose violently anti-British views are echoed by some Italians. Accepting the post of President of the MSI in its earliest years, Borghese immediately won over many supporters to the party. He was, and still is, considered a great war-time hero in Italy for his daring and highly successful exploits against British shipping in Alexandria harbour, Malta and Gibraltar.

At the end of the war Borghese was commander of the Tenth MAS Unit (Italian naval motor-launch battalion) and had been charged with the set purpose of preventing Trieste from falling into Yugoslav hands. He was captured by the Allied armies and handed over to the Italians.

Borghese, who is often referred to as the 'Black Prince' or the 'New Duce' was tried in 1949 for collaborating with the Nazis and was also charged with co-operating with the Germans after the Italian armistice and with making attacks on partisans. He was sentenced to twelve years' imprisonment, but because he had already been in jail for four years while awaiting trial he was released.

A tall, still youthful figure, almost Prussian in bearing, Borghese has a certain romantic air about him. Many admiring Italian youths decided to join the MSI in the wake of their hero, and he was also backed by an influential group of landowners, businessmen and industrialists who supply much of the necessary financial support.

Borghese is resentful not only of the British, but also of the Americans, and is bitter about what he considers Italian humiliation over Istria and the lost colonies. Boldly the Black Prince tells his followers: 'We are fascists, but we believe in a new kind of fascism.'

With the passage of time and in conjunction with the National Monarchist Party with whom election pacts were made, the MSI grew into the fourth most powerful group in Italy. The leader of the Monarchist Party at the time of the agreement with the MSI, which involved co-operation in the parliamentary, political and labour fields, was Alfredo Govelli.

This collaboration was particularly effective in the South where the combined strength of the two parties enabled the MSI to infiltrate into many municipalities.

The first real chance for the fascists of the MSI to exploit their strength occurred when the Christian Democrat Prime Minister, Signor Tambroni, tried to rule with the support of their deputies in the Italian Parliament. This was in 1960 and it was the first occasion since the war that a Government found the need to rely on fascist backing to remain in power. As predicted by many people, it resulted in violence and upheaval.

Immediately the MSI began flexing its muscles more openly and one of its more aggressive acts was to attack the headquarters of the Radical Party. But perhaps the most provocative step of all came when the MSI, its confidence strengthened by the fact that it felt that it was part of the Government, convened a congress to be held in Genoa in July 1960.

There is no place in Italy where the forces of anti-fascism are stronger than in the northern industrial city whose municipality had been awarded a gold medal for its resistance to the fascists and Nazis during the war. To call a meeting in Genoa was of the same type of deliberate provocation as that exercised by Sir Oswald Mosley in Britain when he organized meetings in the East End of London.

What inflamed anger more than anything else there in the hot month of July, when in any event political passions normally run high, was the fact that the chairman of the proposed fascist congress was to be Carlo Basile, who had been Prefect of Genoa after Mussolini's downfall in 1943 and who was instrumental in deporting many workers to Germany during the war. Basile had been sentenced to death, but was released under an amnesty.

A protest meeting was arranged and wreaths were laid on the memorial to the city's resistance fighters. Later there were violent clashes with the police and a general strike was called which led to the cancellation of the MSI congress.

The former resistance fighters in the city as well as democrats throughout Italy were aroused, for the MSI had the same ultra-nationalistic outlook as the old fascist party and the same belief in the gospel of violence; the same pretence that only fascism could save Western civilization from the force of communism. The incidents at Genoa gave an indication of the outcome to be expected should the MSI ever seize power.

In other parts of the country there was a feeling of restlessness and alarm as the Italians watched the MSI gain strength, and on the 7th and 8th of July there were riots in the 'red-belt' city of Reggio Emilia where the police opened fire with sub-machine-guns on armed demonstrators. Five people were killed and scores injured. Other casualties occurred as a result of disturbances in Rome and other Italian cities up and down the country during the same period. The communists took full advantage of the situation by calling out their supporters into the streets and making capital out of the fact that the fascists were being used to maintain the Government in power.

The extreme left, however, was not the only target. Fascists in Reggio Emilia, on the eve of the riots there, set fire to the house of a former leader of the war-time resistance, Arrigo Boldrini, who was president of the National Association of Italian Partisans. Another incident, which was a direct result of MSI activity, was the attack on one of their deputies, Giorgio Almirante, who held a provocative gathering in Piedmont with a crowd of three hundred fascists to back him up.

Almirante, who is believed to have many supporters among police officers, is considered the real founder and one of the brains behind the MSI. He is chief of the extreme, head-cracking black-shirt element in the movement. Other personalities include Augusto de Marsanich, a Trieste nationalist, and Arturo Michelini, an insurance man who became party political secretary. Marsanich represented the MSI in Parliament, as did Pino Romualdi, who claims to be a natural son of the Duce.

Many of the leaders of the Italian fascist movement come from the 'cream' of the upper class who sometimes find it distasteful to have to rely on supporters from the poorer and ill-educated elements of society. (One of the hot-beds of fascist activity in the country is the squalid 'Quarter of the Virgins' in Naples.) Among the younger generation of MSI supporters are many youths who come from University circles and from families of old-time fascists and Mussolini supporters.

In October 1965 an arms dump consisting of forty heavy pistols, fifty machine-guns, and a host of other small arms and ammunition was discovered in the luxurious Rome villa of a wealthy and high-connected young Italian. This hoard was destined to be used by terrorists in the Alto Adige region. And as a result of information gleaned from documents in the villa further police raids were carried out in other parts of Italy.

One of the top men in the MSI is Filippo Anfuso, a former fascist ambassador in Berlin from 1943 until the end of the war and now also a party deputy. An important official of the Italian Foreign Office under Ciano, Anfuso was tried and sentenced to be shot in the back at the end of the war, but later he was re-tried and amnestied.

With these former fascists sitting in Parliament representing a party whose policies are similar to pre-war fascism—despite a law on the statute books forbidding any such revival—it was hardly surprising that in January 1955 on the death of seventy-two-year-old Marshal Rodolfo Graziani, Mussolini's last-ditch fascist commander, a hundred thousand sympathizers flooded the streets of Rome to pay homage to his flag-draped coffin.

Singing fascist songs and chanting 'Italia-Italia' in the high-low cadence with which Mussolini's supporters used to sing 'Duce! Duce!' they gave Graziani a great farewell. His body was cloaked in the old 'Sahariana', the uniform of his North African campaigns which had been stripped of the medals he lost in a 1950 war crimes trial that found him guilty of treason. Finally, amidst great tumult, his coffin was sent to its resting place at Affile, a mountain village some fifty miles from Rome.

In their thousands these fascist supporters quite openly shout 'Duce! Duce!' at election meetings, give the open palm fascist salute and walk about in black shirts, the illegal symbol of Mussolini's régime. They flock to his tomb at Predappio, visit the peasant house where he was born and gaze with awe at the slightly preposterous life-sized nude statue clutching a sheaf of wheat labelled 'to the Duce' before buying postcards and 'holy' ornaments.

The same extremists were responsible for incidents like the desecration of a synagogue in Genoa in 1955 with the slogans 'long live Nazism' and 'death to the Jews' scrawled on the walls, and the occasion two years later when swastikas were daubed in red paint on a monument commemorating Jewish martyrs, also in Genoa.

Another MSI supporter is the Padre Zucca, a Franciscan in Milan, who after underground fighters had shot Mussolini and his mistress and had hanged them up by their heels in a gasoline station, helped bury the body in a secret grave. The man who stole Mussolini's corpse before its second interment, Domenico Leccisi, became party secretary for the MSI in Milan.

Following the revival of fascism in Italy came the newspapers and journals supporting the extreme right-wing movements. In 1951 a weekly, *Popolo d'Italia*, under the editorship of Luigi Garganese, made its appearance and bore a striking resemblance to Benito Mussolini's old paper, even to using the same title-head. In fact, it was so similar to the Duce's former mouth-piece that within twenty-four hours the editor was charged with making 'an apologia for fascism'. He had said in a leading article: 'Fascism has written the finest and most glorious page of national life.' Other contributions were violently anti-British and anti-American, and there was the inevitable reference to Trieste and Istria 'which shall return to the mother country'.

By 1956, the new fascist paper, *Il Secolo d'Italia*, had become a daily. Other similarly-minded publications continued to flourish as well, and the *Asso de Bastoni* warned angrily: 'Tomorrow the defence of our Italian seas will be entrusted to Tel Aviv rabbis.'

On the 9th of December 1961, Dr Giovanni Durando appeared before a tribunal in Genoa for having insulted the Jewish religion and casting slurs upon Jews in his journal *La Voce della Giustizia* (The Voice of Justice) in which he said that the Jews did not have the right to try Eichmann. 'They are responsible for the crucifixion of Christ and therefore they do not have the right to judge people of other races.'

The same article said that the Jews were of a doubtful morality and should be considered as the 'killers of God'. The accused, himself a magistrate, was acquitted.

The editor of *Il Secolo d'Italia* was charged with contempt following an article by the MSI leader, Almirante, who described a projected celebration of the resistance movement by its members in Rome as 'harmful and politically crazy'. A campaign was run by the MSI and similar right-wing extremist movements which aimed at preventing this resistance rally—in 1957—from taking place in the Italian capital. So fierce and persistent were their propaganda efforts that the Government eventually prohibited the former partisans and underground fighters from holding their gathering in the Holy City.

The previous month—November 1957—Count Vanni Teodorani, a nephew of Mussolini and publisher of a fascist paper, was sentenced to eight months in prison for saying: 'We used to burn Jews in ovens.'

In December 1963 *Il Secolo* was taken over by the MSI and Michelini became editor. The outgoing owner, Franz Turchi, said proudly: 'Our newspaper has succeeded in becoming recognized as the one genuine fascist voice in the wide world. It will continue to be an instrument in the service of the idea which moves us, and which has moved us, above all in the great hours of the fatherland and of fascism.'

Another notable fascist demonstration in the streets of Rome was one which resulted in a fierce fight breaking out between the police and crowds of black-shirted fascist supporters who were following the cortège of Roberto Mieville, a fire-brand fascist leader and Italian deputy who had died in a car crash. He had been captured by the American forces in North Africa at the end of the war and had been kept in prison for three years.

In May 1966 violent clashes between left-wing and fascist students were witnessed at Rome University as a MSI deputy Raffaele Delfino led his supporters in an attack on liberal and socialist groups in the campus buildings. Disturbances stirred up by small groups of extremist fascist students spread to universities in Naples, Genoa and other parts of the country. One student died before the Rector of Rome University, Professor Ugo Papi, who was accused of having a fascist past, resigned.

Far smaller than the MSI but certainly more virulent in its fascist outlook is the 'Ordine Nuovo' (New Order) or 'Centro di Ordine Nuovo', which is based in Rome. Publishing a monthly review which is described as 'the journal of revolutionary politics', the movement also issues a bulletin called *Informazione*, which is sent to newspapers and magazines. Far more telling than any policy statement, the activities of this movement speak for themselves. In January 1960 police seized bazookas, pistols, ammunition, swords, bayonets, field telephones, Nazi flags, banners and racialist leaflets when they raided the premises of an offshoot of the international 'The European New Order' in Milan and arrested twenty of its members. Arms and propaganda material were also found in the flat of Professor Antonio Monaco, the leader of the Milan group. And following a raid by the fascists on the Italian Students Union in Genoa, police arrested fifty of the attackers including Franco Petronio, a member of the city council.

In a bid to 'revenge' the murder in the Congo of thirteen Italian airmen, members of this same movement assaulted an American Negro in the streets of Rome while they shouted: 'Out with the Jews and Negroes.'

Composed of many dissident members of the MSI, the 'Ordine Nuovo' is imbued with the spirit of Nazism and has among the members sitting on its national management committee Clemente Graziani, Rutilio Sermonti, Stefano Mangiante, Dr Giulio Maceratini, Nini Fanelli and Pino Rauti, who is national secretary of the movement.

In Rome the constitution of 'nuclei of corporate action' within the 'Ordine Nuovo' was established with the set purpose of creating underground cells throughout the country. Today local groups of the 'Ordine Nuovo' are to be found in Milan and dozens of other Italian cities.

The movement had particularly close links with fascist organizations in other countries and its review, *The New Order* (*L'Ordine Nuovo*) carries articles written by well-known foreign fascists like Amaudruz of Switzerland. Connected with the 'European New Order', it has acted as host to international gatherings of this movement.

In February 1965 some two hundred members of the 'Green-shirts'—another extremist group which also broke away from the MSI because its policies were too 'moderate', were arrested following a bomb plot against the Rome headquarters of the Christian Democrat party. Some of the jailed men were accused of taking part in a bomb outrage in Austria in which a policeman was killed and twelve people injured.

Right-wing groups in Italy played a prominent part in the hey-day of the OAS campaign in France. Secret underground army men found refuge in Italy where they collaborated with leaders of the MSI in a bid to establish a powerful international organization.

Jacques Soustelle received a number of Italian politicians at a villa lent to him by a friend near Rome; and he made his way to Italy in February 1964 when he was expelled from Switzerland. The following month fascist youth of 'Ordine Nuovo' tried to hold a mass meeting to be followed by a religious service in church in memory of Colonel Jean-Marie Bastien Thiry, executed in Paris for trying to assassinate de Gaulle. But church authorities barred the ceremony as riot squad police stood by.

The Italian authorities, who were somewhat embarrassed by the comings and goings of men wanted in France, did their best to expel Georges Bidault of the CNR (Council of National Resistance) from the country. It was known that Bidault was making strenuous efforts to organize all the extremists in Europe into one coherent organization. It was for this purpose that Bidault, who was eventually expelled from Germany where he had established his headquarters, made extensive journeys throughout Europe—including two such trips to England.

CHAPTER V

France

AT DAWN in June 1963 the crack of bullets from a French firing squad brought to an end the life of Lt-Colonel Jean-Marie Bastien Thiry. The execution of this thirty-six-year-old leader of an OAS assassination squad caused a stir throughout the country. Some Frenchmen were angry and indignant—others shrugged their shoulders and said justice had been done to the terrorist who had so narrowly failed in a bid to kill President de Gaulle at Petit Clamart in August 1962.

But the bullets did more than end the life of Bastien Thiry. The echo of the shots struck a blow at the Secret Underground Army and its ambitions of seizing power in France. And ranging further afield, the sounds of the execution squad's rifle-fire were a set-back to the fascist-inclined extremists all over Europe who had pinned great hopes on the OAS overthrowing the Government of France.

The death of the Secret Underground Army leader—the fourth to perish at the hands of a firing squad—came a few months after two other events which could be interpreted, superficially at least, as indicative of the triumph of democratic ideals in France.

On the 10th of January 1963, the former Nazi SS General Karl Oberg, known with good cause as the 'Butcher of Paris', and his deputy, Colonel Helmuth Knochen, who between them had been responsible for mass murders, brutal tortures and the deportation of many thousands of people in the best Nazi traditions, had been freed from Mulhouse Prison. These two Germans, who had been sentenced to death twice since the war and reprieved on both occasions, were the last of the Nazi war criminals detained in France. With their return to Germany it seemed as though the scourge of war-time fascism had been wiped clean from the face of the country.

The other sign of the defeat of extremism was the way in which the far right-wing parties had suffered severe reverses in the elections of November 1962. No Poujadists were returned and out of eighty deputies who directly or indirectly had supported the OAS, only five emerged victorious at the polls. With the country enjoying a full flood of prosperity, it seemed as though France had little to worry about from anti-democratic forces wishing to impose their will on Paris.

But fascism still simmers beneath the present-day calm surface of French life. And it lingers strongest in the hearts of the men who had been roused by the circumstances which gave birth to the OAS.

This secret army, dedicated to overthrowing the state, was formed in Madrid in 1961 when different wings of the 'activists' among the European settlers of Algeria and in the French army merged into one body. Generals and other high-ranking officers, as well as scores of other army, navy and air force men, flocked to the cause which reached the zenith of its strength and influence in Algeria in the period before the country was granted independence. Among its supporters was General Salan, known as the 'mandarin' because of his secretive imperious methods when serving in Indo-China, and General Edmond Jouhaud who, like Salan, ended up in prison after being caught and sentenced to death.

Not only did military men join the ranks of the OAS. Civilians such as Jean-Jacques Susini, the fair-haired president of the 'Students Association' in Algiers, and a dedicated national-socialist, became one of the movement's leading lights. So did Jean-Jacques Soustelle, a fervent right-wing extremist, and thirty-six-year-old Pierre Sidos who had been a leader of the fascist 'Jeune Nation' group. Hundreds of other supporters, including top aristocratic names like that of Lt. Bougrenet de la Tocnaye, were violently opposed to the concept of Moslems in Algeria having a full say in the running of their own affairs.

In February 1966 Susini was sentenced to death in his absence by a French court for making yet another attempt to kill de Gaulle. The former Algerian leader was also wanted as a witness in Spain's inquiry into the mysterious death of the Portuguese opposition leader General Delgado.

Appealing to the self-interest of the settlers who were fearful about losing their homes, jobs, and privileged position in Algerian society, the OAS won mass support among the million European 'pieds-noirs' in the country. The leaders of the secret army, following the traditional line of fascist groups elsewhere, declared that 'communism' was the chief enemy—and that the real fight was to prevent the country going 'red' under the rebelling Moslem FLN nationalist leadership.

The fascist weapons of violence and terror were exercised to their logical and brutal conclusion in the bitter months of 1962 when thousands of innocent men, women and children—both Arab and European—died at the hands of 'killer commandos' and in the inevitable revenge attacks of the FLN.

The importance of the OAS lay in the fact that it was a movement dedicated to gaining power and installing in France a totalitarian régime of the extreme right. It encompassed within itself the worst aspects of racialism and nationalism and threw up in its wake a disturbance which rippled round several countries in Europe and more than any other single post-war force helped create a pro-fascist climate in the West.

The symbolic figure of the OAS was the tough, romantic French paratrooper. This camouflage-uniformed warrior with his swash-buckling ways, his glorification of war for its own sake, and his supreme physical arrogance, took the place of the discredited and out-of-fashion storm-trooper. Fighting against the hordes of 'communism', he was, and still remains, the hero and great white hope of every fascist and Nazi organization in the world.

Defeated at the polling booths, and failing utterly and disastrously to live up to its boast of keeping Algeria part of Metropolitan France, the OAS, and now its political successor, the CNR (Comité National de la Résistance) is still active with ample funds at its disposal. It sprays out extremist propaganda in the form of information sheets like 'France Presse-Action' and plots and schemes to achieve its aims in France and over Europe.

In November 1963 one of the movement's bulletins described the aims of the secret army political group as:

(1) To overthrow the Gaullist régime, and

(2) To create a Government of public safety whose primary objects would include:

(a) the bringing to trial of the leaders of the present régime who were guilty of treason, and

(b) the setting up of a régime opposed both to big Capital-
ism and to International Communism, which would restore
French links with Africa, build Europe and restore
France's vocation within a West proud of it.

The new links with the African states 'will be those of a confederation, once the Marxist dictators and kinglets had been
eliminated.'

The bulletin refers to General de Gaulle as 'the madman of the
Elysée' and says once he and 'the old witches' have been eliminated, 'Eurafrica will be able to begin to be that young giant
capable of opposing the two materialisms, the Marxist and the
Capitalist.'

The OAS also at the same time warns civil servants, judges and
policemen considered to be too zealous in carrying out the
Government's orders against its supporters, that it would be
without pity for them 'after the disappearance of the tyrant'.

That the 'ideals' of the Secret Underground Army still have
the sympathetic backing and potential support of numerous army
officers, as well as half a million or more 'pieds-noirs' now dis-
contentedly settled in France, is evident. Under its new leader,
Captain Sergent, it carefully plays upon the bruised nationalistic
emotions of many Frenchmen who wholeheartedly supported
the cry of 'Algérie Française' while at the same time it keeps alive
the ambitions of groups who would like to see an end to the de
Gaulle régime.

Written off as a 'lost cause' the remnants of the OAS still at
liberty consider themselves far from beaten and in 1964 launched
a new weekly journal, *Jeune Révolution*. Fanatically dedicated to
their cause, they have set up their hiding places all over Europe,
and plot the downfall of the present French Government.

Georges Bidault, the one-time French Premier who joined the
ranks of the OAS, may be out of action as an exile in Brazil, and
hundreds of active members may crowd the French prisons, but
the movement still has plenty of life. In July a two-man commando team, Serge Fabre and Jacques Ferrari, were arrested
after they had crossed the Spanish frontier to try and launch yet
another attempt—the tenth—on the life of de Gaulle.

When the French President visited Mexico in March 1964
immense security precautions were taken as Louis de Conde, one
of the OAS men who had taken part in the abortive Petit Clamart

assassination attempt, arrived in the country from Brazil where he had taken refuge.

Only a few days before this the leader of the underground army's youth section, 'OAS Métro-Jeune', together with twenty students were arrested in Paris together with their illegal printing works. In the same month a Security Court jailed a Swiss-born legionnaire, Hans Husseinforder, and six Frenchmen for various underground activities including a plot to assassinate Georges Pompidou, the Prime Minister.

The various efforts to assassinate the French President may seem futile, but they are still taken seriously by the security services of the country who guard de Gaulle with a tight ring of armed might. For the men of the OAS believe that they are only a razor's edge away from seizing power—the difference between a bullet going astray or reaching its target.

They understand only too well that de Gaulle has built up an apparatus whereby a would-be dictator could so easily take over the reins of supreme power. Should de Gaulle die, or relinquish control, the right-wing extremists, backed by the army, believe that they will be in a position to seize the country in the resulting political vacuum and confusion. It is this thought which keeps their ambitions alive and enables them to find the strength and support to keep their campaign going.

Despite its spectacular debut on the political scene in France, the OAS was not an isolated movement, but rather a link—albeit a very large one—in the chain of fascist activities which started before the war and which is still alive today.

The underground army's predecessor was a movement called 'Jeune Nation', which was founded in February 1950 with the aim of 'restoring to youth the taste for morality, for loyalty, for honour, for sacrifice and for civic duty by taking as an example the life and work of Napoleon.' These 'noble aims' masked sinister intentions and the movement soon showed its true colours.

It was animated by the brothers Jacques, Pierre and François Sidos, whose father had been executed after the liberation, and it gathered together a number of militant-minded young men. The group ran into trouble in May 1958 and was disbanded by the authorities for 'threatening the security of the State'.

This did not stop its members from continuing to operate

clandestinely and publishing their violently racialist organ, *Jeune Nation*, which is also regarded as the journal of the outlawed right-wing 'French Nationalist Party'. The movement continued to hold secret meetings where fascist and anti-semitic ideas were proudly proclaimed.

Several of the members of 'Jeune Nation' who were involved in the Algiers plot at the end of January 1960 were caught and convicted. At the beginning of July 1962 Pierre Sidos was arrested at Neuilly-sur-Seine when, in possession of a forged identity card, he was organizing attacks on Moslems who he claimed were members of the FLN.

Directed at the time by Maître Jean-Baptiste Biaggi, a Corsican —which may explain the movement's obsession with Napoleon— 'Jeune Nation' has for its emblem the Celtic Cross. It believes that if only a truly nationalist state opposed to the democratic principles of the 1789 Revolution could be installed in France, it would have the effect of a chain reaction throughout Europe. 'The continent would then be strong enough to resist the communist and coloured menace' say the followers of 'Jeune Nation'. They add: 'The re-awakening of the white peoples is a salutary reaction against the Negro, Arab and Asiatic enemies of Europe. It is also a safeguard against the massive invasion of hundreds of Jews of double and triple nationality without roots in race or country, embittered, revolutionary and destructive.'

Another group founded in 1954 by Biaggi was the 'Revolutionary Patriotic Party' which attracted ex-paratroopers and young men, chiefly students, with the aim of overthrowing the Government. It had about 10,000 members and supporters with shock-troops for street demonstrations. Dedicated to the defence of 'Algérie Française' by the use of methods borrowed from the communists and above all from the teachings of Mao Tse-tung on guerrilla warfare, this party aimed to seize power in France. It was dissolved in May 1958.

It is not only the right-wing extremists in France or the bitterly disillusioned North African Europeans who support fascist movements in the country. There is a large section of the middle class which no longer trusts democracy. Caught between the rising living standards of the working class who are virtually on an economic level with them, and the impossibility of ever attaining the status, power and wealth of the upper class, they turn in despair to men like Pierre Poujade who was so successful that he won sixty seats ten years ago when he launched himself into the political life of the nation.

This provincial stationer, whose avidly-read monthly journal *Fraternité Française*, edited by Jacques Tauran, is strongly racialist in outlook, fully realizes the potential support to be gained from the discontented Algerian settlers in the country, as well as the small-time native shopkeeper and artisan class. Poujade proposed that a national popular front be established in which his supporters, who it is claimed number over 100,000, will form the spearhead. Now retired from politics, there is little doubt that Poujade will make a come-back if conditions are ripe.

As in any country after it has lost an 'empire' or suffered what many consider a defeat, there arises a wave of angry jingoism which skilled orators and propagandists can whip up in times of economic strain. Should there be an economic set-back in France, then this latent force will be fully exploited by movements such as that led by Poujade.

On a slightly higher intellectual scale, fifty-six-year-old Maurice Bardèche, author of anti-semitic and fascist literature, has established himself as one of the spiritual leaders of the 'new' type of fascist.

In his book entitled *Qu'est-ce que le fascisme?* (What is Fascism?) in which he openly admits that he is a fascist, Bardèche develops the theme, echoed by his British counterpart, Sir Oswald Mosley, that fascism is not responsible for the crimes of Nazism, the errors of Mussolini, the hypocrisies of Francoism or Vichyism. He goes on to explain that modern-day fascism is not really opposed to the Jews but strives for the coming of social justice and the creation of a united 'independent' Europe.

The policy of toning down anti-semitism is part of the 'new-wave' fascism, and the attack is shifted on to the national-socialist position of 'cleaning up corruption and rottenness in the press and high-finance controlled by international bankers.' These 'international bankers' are, of course, a euphemism for the Jews, and the various fascist and right-wing periodicals—both old-fashioned and modern varieties—made a great to-do when Georges Pompidou, one of the directors of the Rothschild bank, was appointed Prime Minister of France. *Rivarol*, with its 45,000 circulation which makes it one of the more important weeklies in

France, said in April 1962: 'The setting up of Rothschild on to the throne of France is a heavy blow. We shall not fail to be present at the march past of conscience still bleeding from this heavy blow to the chin, from this kick of heavy boots. . . . But we are not discontented by this audacious promotion of M. Pompidou who is an omnipotent advertisement of homeless people and super-capitalism (i.e. the Jews). What better argument is there for our theory which we have never abandoned, namely, our national-socialism.'

The less sophisticated readers of *Appel de la France*, the CNR–OAS journal, are told quite simply: 'De Gaulle=Pompidou=Rothschild.'

Another right-wing publication, *Charivari*, which claims an 18,000 circulation, makes frequent references to 'Judeo-Communism'. It took up the Pompidou theme begun in *Rivarol* when in June 1962 it stated: 'We live under the reign of the golden calf. The heart of France has been for ever replaced by the coffers of a son of Zion.' Henry Coston, in *Lectures Françaises*, uttered the following thoughts: 'This promotion of the Rothschilds' first clerk to the functions of Prime Minister of the Republic only surprised the innocent. . . . From now on all is clear—the Fifth Republic may well be called the Republic of the Rothschilds.'

This was but one of the numerous racialistic accusations made in *Lectures Françaises* which also tries, as do many other fascist publications throughout the world, to play down the cruelty of the Hitler régime and to minimize the number of Jewish and other victims who perished in the German concentration camps. Henry Coston, the editor, is a professional racist and was sentenced to forced labour for life for collaborating with the enemy after the war. Later he was pardoned on the grounds of poor health. The author of numerous works, such as *L'Europe des Banquiers* and *La République des Rothschilds*, Coston pours out a constant stream of extremist 'literature'.

Maurice Bardèche may now wear his fascism with a benevolent air, but his views in the past have landed him in trouble and more than ten years ago he was convicted of justifying war crimes and was sentenced to a term of imprisonment. In addition, his book *Nuremberg or the Promised Land* was confiscated by order of the Court of Appeal.

Sentenced to death after the last war as a collaborator and then pardoned, Bardèche has never changed his views. He has attended scores of international fascist meetings during the past fifteen years in various European cities.

Bardèche sees fascism as a form of direct confiscation of 'unjust wealth' and the elimination of social 'parasites'. There is a call for fascist internationalism in the form of a united Europe (a third force with its own army and a means of defence unconnected with military alliances with either East or West)—a neutral state between Communism and Capitalism. And he comes to the conclusion that President Nasser of Egypt is the ideal post-war fascist prototype.

Despite the efforts of Bardèche to promote modern fascism as a new whiter-than-white idealistic creed, his programme still concentrates on the themes of authoritarian rule, strident nationalism, anti-communism, anti-Negro prejudice and a vague 'physical cleansing of youth' (whatever that means).

The various public manifestations of right-wing extremism which have taken place in the country since the end of the Second World War can be traced back to pre-war fascist movements such as 'Action Française' whose heirs may now be found grouped round such journals as *Aspects de la France*. This newspaper, which has a circulation of some 27,000, is edited by Xavier Vallat, a former Commissaire of 'Jewish Questions' from 1941–1942 after France was overrun by the Germans.

Another fascist organization in France is the 'Phalange-Française' created in 1955 by Charles Gastaut (Charles Luca), nephew of Marcel Déat, the Nazi-saluting Frenchman who stood high in state councils when Hitler was in France. It does not have a large membership—believed to number only eight hundred active supporters in Paris with others in the provinces—but it is a group which distributes racialist and right-wing pamphlets and posters.

The members wear black uniforms and they have a monthly journal called *Fidélité*, the editor of which is Luca: it is called the fighting organ of the 'Mouvement Populaire Français', professing an undiluted Hitlerian faith. It also published a duplicated bulletin, *La Vague*, which was discontinued in May 1958. This group was one of the many connected with the Malmoe International.

Then there is Georges Sauge's 'Civic Committee' which professes anti-communist aims and is extremely nationalistic. This movement has contact with high-ranking army officers and leaders in Catholic circles. Sauge, who is the director of the 'Higher Centre of Social Psychology', is an expert 'on the psychological methods to be used in the conquest of masses'. He has held joint meetings with Poujade.

The Catholic hierarchy in France has often condemned Sauge for the doctrine adopted by his movement and his influence is described by many churchmen as 'pernicious'. The 'Cité Catholique'—an organization whose objects are not far removed from the 'Higher Centre'—is also heavily influenced by Sauge. At meetings of these groups the fascist-propaganda-style statements like 'intrinsically perverted communism' and 'stateless finance' are freely bandied about.

The 'Movement of Peasant Defence' is inspired by the Vicomte Henri d'Halluin, better known under the pseudonym of Henri Dorgeres, who was accused of pro-Nazi activities during the occupation of France and who in 1957 with Poujade and Antier formed the 'Green Front' which only lasted a few months. Financed by Vichy, Dorgeres created a special militia, 'Les gardes-messieurs', whose job it was to persecute maquisards. He has written over two hundred articles against the Freemasons and resistance leaders. After the liberation of France, the Vicomte was sentenced to ten years' loss of civil rights, but was subsequently reprieved when he claimed he had carried out acts to help the resistance.

There was also the 'National Revolutionary Movement' which had European-wide ambitions and maintained relations with similar right-wing groups in Italy, Germany, Switzerland, Spain and Portugal. This group was dissolved in 1961, but many of its members joined other organizations with similar views.

Its two initiators, industrialist Max Baeza and bookseller Jean Daspre, professed militant anti-semitism and were sympathetic towards neo-fascist activities. M. Baeza previously belonged to another extreme rightist organization, 'Union des Français Nationaux'.

Most of these movements were supporters of, or were actually engaged in, the activist wing of the OAS in Algeria. In Marseilles, for example, where more than half of the repatriates are gathered, and where relationships between the newcomers from North

Africa and the local population are still tense, attempts have been made by extreme rightist organizations to capture the 'pieds-noirs'. Chief of these is the 'Afonoma' led by Colonel Bettesti, which calls upon the refugees to unite and press for the blocking of financial aid to Algeria until repatriates have been fully compensated for their losses.

There are a number of students scattered among these various fascist and neo-fascist movements, but 'Jeune Nation' and 'Phalange Française' are the groups specifically catering for the right-wing young men and women. The followers of 'Jeune Nation' were considered the direct descendants of the pre-war 'Camelots du Roi' and the 'Action Française'. The 'Federation of Nationalist Students', which in 1962 held its second national conference in Paris behind closed doors, takes a racialist and anti-semitic political stand. Some professors in provincial universities have supported these students and declared their 'wish to see the victory of French nationalist ideals in French universities'.

The right-wing publication, *Écrits de Paris*, has prospered since its birth in 1947 when it concerned itself with whitewashing the Vichy régime and attacking the practice of eliminating collaborators from public life. It claims that the real war was not against the Germans, but against communism and it still maintains that Nazism was justified by the Treaty of Versailles and the 'Communist danger'.

C'est à Dire, which had an irregular life, has praised Franco and all fascist chiefs in general. Its editor, Jean Ferre, counted among his contributors journalists from *Rivarol*.

Charivari has published various anti-semitic articles including one by a man who worked for the Vichy Government and who was arrested after the war but later released, and who has hardly changed the tone of his convictions since the Nazi occupation of France. Ten pages of one of these articles were devoted to the 'Jewish Diaspora', and among other comments this thought occurs: 'The Jews sometimes mix their blood with that of Christians. They change their names while continuing to be masters of the banking and finance world.'

Bardèche also edits a monthly called *Défense de l'Occident*.

It was estimated in 1965 that these various right-wing and fascist journals have a total circulation of more than 200,000. Some of these periodicals and the movements they represent are recommended by the Brussels-based fascist monthly *L'Europe Réelle*.

The international outlook of the various extremist movements in France was emphasized by the way in which the OAS operated through its network in the surrounding countries of Spain, Italy, Belgium, Germany and Switzerland. This network called 'Résurrection Patrie', which is in particularly close touch with Spaniards who were behind terrorist activities on the Iberian Peninsula in 1964, counted among its members a number of Poujadists. One of these is Marcel Bouyer, sentenced to twelve years' criminal detention in July 1962, and another is Paul Vidart who in turn received eight years.

The number of actual war-time Nazis in France does not seem to be more than 3,000. Many are former members of the 'Charlemagne' Division of the SS which was the last unit to fight the Russians in the Berlin underground railway. Today these survivors, wearing their uniforms, meet in small groups, exchange memories and drink beer in damp, seedy cellars while singing Nazi songs.

These old soldiers would in normal circumstances be expected to fade away. But their ideas live on. In January 1965 the police in Calais uncovered a 'National Socialist Proletariat Party' whose members were mostly teenagers. These young fanatics were busy preparing lists of Jews in the town when arrested and at their homes, arms, ammunition and photographs of Hitler were brought to light.

Six months earlier a number of Nazis belonging to the French section of the 'World Union of National Socialists', led by the American Rockwell and Britain's Colin Jordan, were arrested in a nation-wide police swoop. Explosives were found at the homes of one of the members and the leader was found to be a former Waffen SS volunteer. The membership of this group numbered no more than a hundred, but an interesting aspect of its activities was the close affiliation it maintained with other European Nazi bodies.

Documents and letters headed with swastikas and the German eagle emblem showed in particular the links with British Nazis. Colin Jordan's wife, Françoise, the niece of the late fashion king, Christian Dior, was asked by French police to appear at an inquiry into the activities of the arrested French extremists.

Another Nazi group headed by prospective 'Fuehrer'—Jean Claude Monnet—made its appearance in January 1965. Preparing a new version of *Mein Kampf*, Monnet predicted boldly that he would be in power 'by 1975'.

A number of racialist books have been published in France. One such volume is *Le Mensonge d'Ulysse* by Paul Rassinier, who describes the 'enviable' treatment the Jews received in Nazi concentration camps.

Repeatedly the author tries to minimize the number of victims, quoting references of pure fantasy, and speaks of the inmates as being 'office-worker prisoners' in the camps. 'These deportees supplied us with our Governments, our censors and our judges,' says Rassinier. 'They constitute the most fabulous collection of history's trash.'

The author also claims in his *Ulysse Trahi par les Siens* that 'recent evidence' has been discovered which establishes the 'truth' about the fake deaths of the millions of Jews in the Nazi camps. In another work entitled *La Mauvaise Conscience*, Vivien Martignac says that he has instituted a psychological study of those who applied the racial laws and writes about 'the horrible Jewish notions which corrupt and debase all that is best in us.' Xavier Vallat in *Le Nez de Cléopâtre* defends himself for being a racist.

Despite the attempts of the more 'progressive' fascists of today to play down racism in France and elsewhere, anti-semitism and anti-coloured sentiment is constantly employed either directly or indirectly by various right-wing groups to win support among the less enlightened members of French society. For instance, the 'Jeune Nation' urged that France be purified of 'alien' elements, namely Jews, Arabs and Negroes. It condemns the location in Paris of the Jewish Memorial dedicated to the victims of Nazism (The Unknown Jewish Martyr) which, in May 1959, was desecrated by hooligans.

The same year a large number of slogans, such as 'Death to the Jews', appeared on the walls of buildings and in the Métro, and there have been a number of swastika-daubing incidents in Paris and in provincial cities. In one of his speeches, Pierre Poujade demanded the removal of Jews from the commercial life of the country. The reference was obviously meant to win praise from the highly overcrowded shopkeeper class who are still among his most faithful supporters. Many of these small-time traders would welcome the removal of some of their competitors whether on racial or any other convenient grounds.

A number of incidents showed that the police force is by no means immune from fascist sympathies. Anti-Jewish remarks were made at a demonstration by several thousand police outside the National Assembly. A more serious incident occurred when police attacked a Jewish café in the 'Pletzel' Jewish quarter in Paris. 'We prefer Algerian terrorists to you', 'Hitler did not kill enough of you', and 'We shall liquidate all Jews in France', were some of the insults hurled at the people crowded inside the café as the police got to work on them with their clubs and batons. Several were injured and the following day protests were made which resulted in two policemen being suspended.

Although the OAS was supported by many Jews in Algeria, the movement has strong anti-semitic streaks. For example, in October 1961, Mlle D. Weill, the mathematics mistress at the Lycée La Fontaine in Paris, received a threatening letter from the secret army accusing her of the double crime of being both a communist and a Jewess. Professor M. Gurwitch of the Sorbonne, who was on the Gestapo list because of his lectures on the 'methods of the Nazi propaganda machine in France' at Strasbourg University before the war, also received threatening letters. One communication informed him: 'We shall not tolerate the fact that you influence young Frenchmen. You are not really French yourself, for you came here from the depths of the Black Sea and from the Jewish market, a wandering Jew who had carried his bundle through all the countries of Europe.'

Despite the multiplicity of the fascist organizations in France, the number of active extremists is relatively small.

The present economic buoyancy provides relatively stony ground for their theories and ideas which need upheaval, disturbance, unemployment, riots and uncertainty in which to flourish.

But should the situation in any way deteriorate, the danger of fascism taking hold in France is a real and powerful one. For the country is no longer controlled by the bureaucrat, but by the modern technocrat who is not interested in the social and political problems of ownership and is concerned only with attaining technical efficiency.

France, more than any other country in Europe, has seen a

major change in the way power is exercised. Instead of following tradition, business, industry and the Government are controlled less and less by men from the 'right' class and the 'right' background. Their place is being taken by the intelligent, highly trained group of administrators and industrial managers turned out by France's excellent 'Grandes Ecoles'—such as the 'Ecole Polytechnique' and the 'Ecole Normale Supérieure'.

The young men who are admitted to these institutions, where the standards are extraordinarily high, are not chosen because of their parents' wealth or the social background of their ancestors, but purely by ability.

Generally springing from the middle class, the 'polytechniciens' as they are known, and there are 11,000 of them in France, are respected and held in awe by both manual workers and the wealthy. These modern-day mandarins are renowned for their intellect as well as their cultural and scientific qualifications.

They are to be found in boardrooms and in the top administrative ranks in every branch of the French economy ranging from nationalized industries to private concerns and from Government ministries to commercial organizations. These highly trained men believe firmly that technology is the key to human happiness. Their concept of a 'modern technocracy' visualizes control of the economy as a whole by themselves. And they are convinced that only with their superior training, intellectual capabilities, technical knowledge and their administrative skills, can France's potential be fully realized.

These super-technocrats feel that they are above politics, above Government and work not so much for individual profit, but for the country as a whole. Apolitical, disinterested in the fruits of power as such, these men who now form a distinctive class believe firmly in the concept of a planned economy.

When working ideally, this concept can be of immense value and happily marries capitalism with socialistic planning. As seen, for example, in the Renault car factory, it has produced a highly effective, efficient and liberally-run organization.

On the whole the technocrat is a desirable development in a modern highly complex, industrialized country which aims at expansion and the all-round raising of the standard of living. But there are dangers, too, in a system dominated by pure technocrats. For one thing it could become tyrannical if men on the factory floor are regarded simply as units of production in a massive blue-print. And in a country like France where many major industries are nationalized or partially controlled by the State, where the proportion of investment over which the authorities can exercise direct control is more than 50 per cent, then other dangers become self-evident. For where the Government can interfere directly, then the temptation for any extremist political leadership which gains control to exploit the system for its own ends could well become irresistible. The strength of the technocratic élite could easily be manipulated to by-pass normal democratic procedures and crush trade union resistance.

In France today on the one hand we have this immense power concentrated in the hands of trained scientific administrators, and on the other hand there is the officer corps of the French army which has neither forgotten nor forgiven its ignominious defeat in the past. Then there are the discontented, the soldiers and former 'paras' who cannot adapt themselves to civilian life, who are nostalgic for violence and who are no longer needed by their fellow citizens now that there are no more colonial wars to be fought.

Add to these the uprooted 'pieds-noirs' who feel that they have been betrayed and, despite their claims to be French, find themselves now living in France as in an alien land. Joining these ranks are certain segments of the lower middle class, artisans and small shopkeepers who no longer feel secure and find themselves being overtaken economically by the industrial worker. Together with the unruly violence-prone peasants and farmers who feel that they have been left behind by the higher living standards of the city workers, these various groups form an immense reservoir of potential trouble.

In addition a certain amount of racialism of the Smethwick type has been provoked by the presence in France of over a quarter of a million Algerian workers. Quick to seize on the propaganda value of this colour prejudice, extremist journals like *Défense de l'Occident* stated (January 1965): 'It is legitimate to resent certain quarters of our cities being turned into refuse grounds of all the races of the earth, for race mixing has a disastrous effect both on the mind and the spirit.'

Another publication, *Europe Action*, added: 'We proclaim the supremacy of our race.'

The host of fascist and extreme right-wing sympathizers in France were attracted to the banner of the colourful defence counsel, Jean-Louis Tixier-Vignancour, who championed their cause during the 1965 presidential election campaign. Masquerading as a 'liberal', Tixier is cast in the traditional reactionary, racialist mould and played a major role in the defence of OAS colonels and generals when brought to trial. In the early 'fifties, Tixier was associated with Maurice Bardèche in setting up a 'European People's Movement' aimed against communism, Jewry and freemasonry.

A former Vichy Minister, the Maître fought his campaign against de Gaulle as a champion of the 'Atlantic Alliance' opposing the 'Communist menace'. To prove his anti-red belligerency, the would-be dictator of France paid a visit to Saigon to see how the 'anti-bolshevik' crusade was getting on in Vietnam. But, alas for this self-appointed 'defender of the faith'. The American authorities in Saigon, who were about to be patted on the back for their campaign against the Viet Cong, were issued with strict instructions not to receive the Frenchman.

Little wonder. Tixier made his extremist views clear in the monthly *Découverte* where he violently denounced democracy as 'the régime of the nineteenth century and no longer applicable to this age.'

Coming out strongly in support of Tixier is *Europe-Action*, a journal launched by former OAS sympathizers such as Dominique Venner. These extremists believe in the 'global nationalist revolution' which they hope will defeat the Marxists' 'world revolution'. Although *Europe-Action* was not hopeful of the Maître's chances against de Gaulle it believes that 'something must be made of the electoral opportunity to prove that radical nationalism is not a museum piece but a vibrant political power'. In the election Tixier polled five per cent of the vote.

A somewhat picturesque nationalist movement has sprung up in recent years in the Basque area around Bayonne and Biarritz. Demanding independence for the Basque provinces from both France and Spain, the leaders of this movement have busied themselves scrawling slogans on walls and distributing their tracts. It comes as no surprise to discover that among its leaders are to be found war-time Nazi collaborators.

Neither the opposition of Tixier-Vignancour nor the motley

collection of fascist and right-wing movements is likely to worry President de Gaulle. But the matter takes on a new perspective when one realizes that the General has, through his policies of weakening parliamentary rule and boosting all things French, provoked a strong sense of nationalism in the country. This is highly dangerous, for tremendous power has been concentrated in the hands of one man—and although de Gaulle has used this power in the main benevolently, democratic principles have been steadily whittled away.

There are numerous examples of this. For instance, a law to curb strikes in the public sector has been passed in Parliament despite the concentrated opposition of the trade unions and the Socialist party. An American television programme featuring ex-President Eisenhower which might have been hostile to de Gaulle's Common Market policy was banned from French screens.

A series of strikes was launched by the staff of the state-controlled radio and TV network as a protest at the increasing interference by the Government in news and political programmes. In March 1964 the staff, after yet another stoppage, issued a leaflet which claimed that there was a 'process of degeneration' on the radio. The Government, stated the leaflet, considered the radio 'as the most formidable instrument for indoctrination that had ever been invented.'

'The Government wants to impose censorship, cheating and lies on the RTF. It is always the Government representatives that the public see and hear. Working-class, students', and peasants' demonstrations are misrepresented or passed over in silence. There is no balance in the programmes,' claimed the striking radio and television men.

When de Gaulle goes, whether peacefully or violently, an immediate vacuum will be created in France. Uncertainty, perhaps chaos and upheaval may well result. There are many men, organizations and sections of French society who will wish for this and who may even provoke it.

The prize of success looks glittering, for there is now in existence the perfectly shaped saddle of concentrated power ready for an extremist to leap upon and lead the country into a full-scale fascist dictatorship.

CHAPTER VI

Belgium and Holland

BELGIUM

As a country with a liberal tradition, it seems somewhat paradoxical that Belgium is today one of the centres of European
fascist activity. But recent internal developments, together with
the OAS influence spreading from France, and the disastrous
experience of the Congo, have created an unhealthy climate in
the country. A climate which is an ideal hot-bed for the growth
of extremist right-wing movements.

The events in Leopoldville in 1960 when Patrice Lumumba
panicked the Belgian Government into granting independence to
this rich but unprepared colony acted as a catalyst, precipitating
fascism in Brussels. There was world-wide criticism of Belgian
actions which seemed to most people a cynical attempt by
Brussels to hang on to the copper and other bountiful mineral
mines of Katanga without any thought for the welfare of the
inhabitants of the Congo.

The chaos and upheaval in Leopoldville was felt like a shock-
wave throughout Belgium where the population had been led to
believe—by the means of skilful, but misleading propaganda—
that all was well 'down there'. The wounded surprise provoked
by the world pointing its accusing finger gave way to guilty
resentment and feelings of offended national pride.

To add fire to the widespread anger, the disgruntled Belgian
colonists, like the Algerian *pieds-noirs* who flocked to Marseilles
as refugees, were bitter and resentful. They accused the Government of having 'betrayed' them—conveniently forgetting the
economic and political injustices they themselves had perpetuated
against the people of the Congo—and were eager listeners to
political agitators who wanted to exploit them for their own
ends.

Out of the ground-swell of seething indignation and anger

caused by the loss of the Congo, there sprang up the 'Comité d'Action de la Défense des Belges d'Afrique' (CADBA) which was joined by the 'Rassemblement Congolais'. The leaders of these two groups brought out a newspaper called *Belgique-Afrique*, which gave way later to another movement with much wider support called the 'Mouvement d'Action Civique' or more simply the MAC.

Because Belgians have always been keenly interested in French politics, the influence of the OAS spread across the frontier and was warmly welcomed by the members of the MAC, who defended the political doctrine of the secret underground army as close to their own. And although the supporters of the MAC deny that they are a fascist movement, they find it difficult to justify the fact that there are large numbers of former collaborators in their ranks.

One of the group's leaders is an optician, Jean François Thiriard, and another man in the forefront is Dr Teichmann. Thiriard, who writes under the name of 'Jean Tisch', was a former member of the AGRA (Amis du Grand Reich Allemand— Friends of the Great German Reich).

In one of his journals, *Nation Belgique*, published in Brussels, Thiriard follows the trend of modern-day fascists by claiming that he is not anti-semitic and he even issues a call to the Jews to join the 'common struggle against communism'.

At the same time Thiriard finds it difficult to break from old habits and does not hide his movement's sympathy for Leon Degrelle and the French collaborators of the Third Reich whose participation in the fight against the 'red menace' is constantly praised. 'Jeune Europe' is the youth section of the MAC organization and it publishes a newspaper of that name. 'Jeune Europe' has information bureaux in many countries including Austria, Denmark, Spain, Italy, Portugal, Holland, Switzerland, South Africa, Brazil, and the United States. In particular it maintains close relations with the French 'Jeune Nation' run by the Sidos brothers.

Thiriard's journals, for which a circulation of 10,000 is claimed, are distributed throughout Europe. Their close links with the OAS were emphasized when 'Jeune Europe' announced the reappearance of the *Quarterly Bulletin* of the 'National Secret Army' which 'fights clandestinely in France'. This 'National Secret

Army' was an offshoot of the OAS itself. In the issue of *Jeune Europe*, in August 1962, Colonel Argoud—one of the top leaders of the French OAS, who was later kidnapped by the secret branch of de Gaulle's security services—wrote an editorial 'Until Victory' which made it clear that he was ranging himself alongside all those in Europe, Latin America, and South Africa, who 'cherish the memory of Hitler and who wish to further the aims and ambitions of the Nazi dictator.' Freely sold in Brussels, this journal is distributed secretly in France.

Besides the usual right-wing and racialist propaganda, the publications directed by Thiriard have also been strongly critical of the role of the United Nations in the Congo and were pro-Tshombe. *Nation Belgique* takes a keen interest in French affairs and when Pompidou became de Gaulle's Prime Minister it published a sneering article entitled 'The Dictatorship of the Rothschilds'.

Leon Degrelle, who was chief of the 'Rexists'—the pre-war fascist movement in Belgium—and a member of the SS Wallonia, collaborated with the Nazis during the occupation and fled the country after the Hitler régime collapsed. Like many another Nazi, he made his way to Spain where he was befriended by Franco, and despite repeated representations by the Belgian Government to send him home, Degrelle has lived there ever since. In justification the Spanish Government claims that hostilities took place a long time ago and are 'best forgotten'.

Degrelle continues to have contacts with collaborators in Belgium and in particular with the former Waffen SS officer, Jean Robert Debbaudt, a political prisoner for several years after 1945, and who now directs an openly Nazi journal called *L'Europe Réelle*. Debbaudt is also a member of the executive of 'Jeune Légion Européenne' whose chairman is a German, an ex-SS man, Jean Baumann. In 1959 Debbaudt tried to convene in Brussels a two-day 'First National Congress of the Mouvement Social Belge', but vigorous protests by Belgian resistance fighters prevented the meeting from taking place. Debbaudt had hoped to form a Flemish section of the movement at this congress.

Showing that he, for one, had not fallen for the new 'reasonable' line of modern-day fascists, Degrelle in *L'Europe Réelle* insults and vilifies various personalities in Belgium in the crudest terms. Perhaps understandably worried about his own future, he warned rather apprehensively that 'the Jews are going to try a kidnapping act in Spain as they did with Eichmann in the Argentine.'

L'Europe Réelle ceased publication in December 1961, but re-started five months later in May 1962, announcing that it was fighting for a New European order and demanding the free expression of all opinions 'which are not dictated either by the Talmud or by Karl Marx'.

In July 1964 the paper explained away the existence of the concentration camps as 'propaganda started by Eisenhower'.

During the past eighteen months *L'Europe Réelle* has reprinted dozens of articles culled from French, United States, Spanish, and Hungarian *émigré* fascist journals and set up correspondents in various European and American cities.

Commenting sadly on Senator Goldwater's defeat in the United States presidential election, the paper in January 1965 said: 'The American decadence continues.'

'If the United States, that great bulwark of the white race, is to save itself, she must have a third party. In view of the growing demands made by the Negroes, we hope that American nationalist groups will steadily gain in weight and vigour.'

The journal advertises various fascist works such as *Tel fut Hitler* by H. A. Sabarthez—a hymn of praise for the German Fuehrer—and *Degrelle m'a dit* by Louise, Duchesse de Valence, in which the admiring lady author champions the Belgian.

Degrelle's latest book *Les Ames qui Brûlent* was also advertised by *L'Europe Réelle* in July 1964 as a 'purely spiritual work'. In Belgium, however, where they still remember Degrelle as the man who was lauded by Hitler, who said, 'If I had a son I would want him to be like you', the book was banned. Private copies are still available, however, by writing direct to the paper.

L'Europe Réelle is also the organ of the 'Mouvement Social Belge' which is built on SS lines and is the Belgian branch of the European Social Movement. It has repeatedly tried to help bring about a more co-ordinated Nazi organization in Europe. In October 1954 it convened a congress in Brussels which attracted fascists from all over the Continent, but the authorities expelled from the country twelve delegates, including SS men from Germany.

The 'Mouvement Social Belge' has contacts in various cities all over Europe and maintains close liaison with the Malmoe head-quarters of its parent body as well as with the MSI in Italy. In 1961 it published an article glorifying one of the 'grand chiefs of the OAS', Roger Degueldre, who was a former leader of the 'Rexist' youth, and a volunteer officer in the Wallonia Legion which fought for the Nazis on the Russian front. Degueldre, who eventually became a paratroop officer in the French Foreign Legion, was shot by a firing squad in Paris in 1962 for his OAS terrorist activities.

The MAC also has a wide network of agents and sympathizers. It maintains good relations with Poujadists in France and active links with the fascist movements in Europe which have adopted the Celtic cross as their emblem. Under the direction of its leaders an international 'Jeune Europe' organization was established at Forschhausen near Frankfurt. One of the major instigators of this movement was a Dr Walter Loewen from Hanover.

Previous to this, in 1956, a thirty-five-year-old Brussels businessman, Roger Chevalier, founded the small Belgian Poujade movement.

Connected with the OAS in Spain and France, and with various fascist groups wherever they are to be found, the MAC has the closest liaison with the 'Ordine Nuovo' in Italy, the 'Junges Europa' in Germany and 'Ataque' in Portugal. A military arm of the MAC, known as the 'Charlemagne' group, drew up a detailed plan for an 'International Brigade' to be based in Spain with the aim of 'fighting communism'.

Of late the comings and goings of fascist leaders like Thiriard have been on the increase as they strengthen their international links. The MAC, for instance, was strongly represented at the gathering in Venice in 1962 where the National Party of Europe was established.

Were it only for the activities of these relatively small numbers of fascist-minded men and their supporters, the threat of strong extremist movements gaining ground in Belgium would not be rated very high. The chief danger that the country today might fall into the control of right-wing demagogues stems from the deep social and linguistic cleavage which shows every sign of becoming more and more intractable.

This has its origins in the clash between the Walloons and the Flemish sections of the community. Broadly speaking, Belgium can be divided into three separate linguistic and even racial areas. In the south, there is the Walloon region where French or the

Walloon dialect is spoken, while in the north there is the Flamand Zone where Flemish is the dominating tongue. Then there is the central Brabant with the capital Brussels, where French is chiefly spoken, but where a small minority use Flemish as their main language. In many areas, and in particular in Brussels, Flemish was relegated in the past to a minor position. French was considered the only civilized tongue worth speaking.

After the First World War a Flemish national movement sprang up which aimed at giving the Flemish language equal status with French. But it was not until the 1939–45 war was over that this objective was finally achieved, at least in the administrative sense.

Brussels still has a French-speaking majority, many of whom do not take kindly to Flemish, which they feel is being rammed down their throats. The French-speaking people of the country resent having to learn Flemish, which they find difficult and unattractive, and as a result when bilingual posts have to be filled the jobs usually go to the Flemish Belgians who take quite easily to the French tongue.

The more moderate of the Flemish-speaking nationalists in the country do not want to stir up racial trouble in the land, and confine themselves to asking, reasonably enough, that civil servants should be able to speak both languages. But the extremists in their ranks—known as 'flamignants'—who belong to such bodies as the 'Flemish Action Committee for Brussels' will accept no compromise with their aims of turning the Belgian capital into a wholly Flemish city. And it is this linguistic conflict which is causing bitter economic and social antagonism between the two communities.

In the past the Flemish areas have been the most backward segments of the country. Their economy was chiefly agricultural in contrast to Wallonia which with its rich coalfields played an important part in the Industrial Revolution in Belgium. But since the Second World War, this situation has changed dramatically with Walloon industry gradually declining.

There are now some 5,000,000 Flemings in the agricultural north and west of the country, and only 4,000,000 French-speaking Walloons in the south and east. And as a result of the rising birth-rate of the Flemish population, employers have found themselves with a large and cheap labour supply which partially accounts for the rapid growth of industry in the Flemish areas.

In the face of this 'threat', the Walloons now demand that something be done about their own industrial future and the more extreme elements speak about a 'Federalist' solution to the racial problem in the country. At Namur such federalists have already set up a militant body to fight the issue with 'all means at our disposal'.

The widening of this gulf between the two chief elements of the population may well open the way to conditions which will irretrievably split the Belgian nation, and could lead to economic upheaval. It is in these conditions of unrest and disturbance that fascists and neo-Nazis see their opportunity of spreading their gospel and making a bold bid for power. Already among the extreme wings of the country's two Nationalist movements are to be found ex-Nazi and fascist elements thriving in the atmosphere of latent violence and racial sentiment.

This is particularly true among the Flemish population where 'combat groups' have been established. The men who collaborated with the Nazis during the war, and who have either been freed, thanks to amnesties, or who have completed their jail sentences, are now joining the 'Volksunie' ('People's Union'). And because of the application of the law granting remission for good conduct, the ranks of these freed Nazi collaborators have increased considerably in the past few years. As a result the 'Volksunie', which gathers to itself the most extreme elements of the Flamand nationalist movement, has gained in numerical strength and vehemence of view. It is hardly surprising that this party is more and more emphasizing the racial aspects of its nationalist policies.

Led by 45-year-old lawyer, Frans Van Der Elst, the Volksunie has its home in Antwerp. It demonstrated its growing strength in 1965 when it increased its seats in Parliament from five to twelve in the elections gaining seven per cent of the vote. Every Sunday in the summer coachloads of the movement's agitators and bully-boys with their black Flemish lion flags and emblems are sent out all over the country terrifying French-speaking villages and beating up opponents in the best Hitler youth tradition. The commandos of the Flemish Popular Movement, the militant wing of the Volksunie, wear uniforms of blue shirts, short leather trousers, boots and belts—some with the old SS motto 'Gott mit uns' engraved on the clasp.

It therefore comes as no surprise to hear that among the Volksunie M.P.s are men like Dr Hector Goemans, a war-time Nazi collaborator. Two other representatives in the Senate were also war-time collaborators.

Recently, acts of terrorism associated with this language conflict have been on the increase. There have been riots and running fights with the police as demonstrations and counter-demonstrations were held in the streets of Brussels and other Belgian cities. In June 1963, at Wemmel, five gendarmes were injured and had to be taken to hospital after a demonstration of some 7,000 Flemings who had been brought in specially by motor-coach from Antwerp and other Flemish districts.

A month later, the tomb of Belgium's unknown soldier was blasted by a bomb. The main damage was done to a bronze door in the base of a 100-foot-high 'Column of Congress' topped by a statue of King Leopold the First—the country's main monument to national unity. The explosion extinguished the flame which had been burning on the tomb since the end of the First World War and shattered windows in the surrounding square. The police acted swiftly and arrested a Belgian-born former Nazi SS trooper who was suspected of being behind the attack.

The double symbolic blow—to the unity of the country, and to the men who had fought against the Germans—was echoed by Flemish nationalists up and down the country on the same day during celebrations in the annual commemoration of the 'Battle of the Golden Spurs', a victory in 1302 for the free Flemish cities over French feudal knights.

These 'festivities' were accompanied by several anti-French incidents—such as the smearing of paint and tar on cars with French inscriptions and the puncturing of tyres. At Brussels airport notices in French were blotted out. At Courtrai, Flemish extremists invaded the garden of a Government Minister, M. Albert de Clerck, and smashed windows in his house because they felt that he was being too 'liberal' in his approach to the language dispute.

In August 1963 a grenade was thrown into a Brussels bar, wounding forty people including fourteen teen-age Belgian girls and a number of Congolese students. The assailants were believed

to be members of a right-wing extremist group who call themselves the 'Damocles network' who were angered by the way
Belgians were treated in the Congo, and also as a warning to white
girls not to mix with Negroes.

In a communiqué the leaders of this group said: 'For every
Belgian who falls into the hands of the Congolese Gestapo, three
hostages will be executed.'

The same month witnessed a further clash of Walloons and
Flemish nationalists travelling to Ostend in a procession of
more than five hundred cars, vans and coaches. The latter were
campaigning for their claim that the sea-front is Flemish
territory.

So serious has become this lingual problem between the two
communities, that in July 1963 Theodore Lefevre, the then Prime
Minister, handed in his resignation to King Baudouin. The
trouble arose over a split in Lefevre's coalition Government of
Catholics and Socialists over the question of bilingualism in and
around the capital. The resignation was rejected by the King to
avoid a national crisis and a compromise was reached.

The settlement aroused the anger of both the Flemish and the
Walloon extremists. The Flemish nationalists immediately announced that 'wide popular agitation' would be launched and a
march to Brussels was called for by the right-wing 'Volksunie'.

In October 1965 riot police had to break up a Flemish nationalist
demonstration in the seaside resort of Knokke. Earlier in the year
nine policemen were badly injured when Flemish and French-
speaking extremists clashed outside Ostend's main church.

The fight broke out as a result of Flemish protests against the
use of French in the evening service in the Church of St Peter and
Paul. An interesting facet of the riot was that two West Germans
who were found to be members of a Nazi group were among the
fourteen people detained.

Their excuse that they were mere 'tourists'—shades of 1939!—
was rather weakened when the police discovered that the two men
had daggers hidden in their clothing.

Repeated riots and other disturbances have continued to disturb the country. Yet another example was a riot in Brussels in
November 1965 when ten people were injured and twenty arrested
following a clash between rival mobs of Flemish and Walloon
extremists.

In January 1966 two miners were shot dead in rioting after a mob of three hundred Flemish blue-shirted extremists came to the 'aid' of striking miners in the Zwartberg area. In Parliament the Interior Minister complained bitterly that the Volksunie and another extreme movement had incited the discontented miners. Members of a foreign subversive group entered the country and were identified among those who attacked the police in the rioting, said the Minister.

In May of the same year there was rioting at the University of Louvain after Flemish student extremists protested at a decision to continue using French as well as Flemish as a medium of instruction there. Shops and French-speaking student club premises were sacked by Flemish toughs who flocked to the city from all over the country to stir up further unrest.

The deadly earnestness of the Flemish extremists to precipitate violence was underlined in August 1966 when Belgian police found nine men fitting fuses to time bombs in the attic of a Brussels suburb. The arrested men admitted that the bombs were to be used in countryside raids in a bid to start a full scale uprising of Flemish citizens.

Bedevilling the whole Walloon versus Flemish language issue is the religious aspect of Belgian life. The Walloons are generally liberal or left-wing in outlook, while the Flemish communities are staunchly Catholic and conservative. This means the electorate has always had the choice of voting either for the anti-clerical block of parties (Liberal and Socialists) or for the clerical party, the PSC (Christian Social Party) which contains the various strata of the Catholic population.

To complicate matters the PSC has both a progressive and conservative wing, a Flamand and a Walloon section, and gathers to itself the Catholic middle class, the majority of the farmers and a large proportion of the Flemish industrial workers. It is constantly under stress because of divided loyalties among its supporters, but it has never manifested racial tendencies and before the Second World War expelled Degrelle for holding extremist views. The PSC also condemned the widespread wave of swastika-daubing in 1959 and 1960.

The Christian Social Party suffered many defections in the past due to the diversity of its members. For example, there was the 'Rexist' breakaway in the 1930's, and the leaders also had to face

the loss of the Flemish wing. From the end of World War One the
PSC was abandoned by the extremists of the Flemist Nationalist
Movement who found a home in the 'Vlaams National Verbond'
(Flemish National Union). These were the ideological heirs and
pupils of the 'activists' of the 1914–1918 war, whose leader,
Auguste Borms, had at the end of hostilities been condemned to
death for collaboration with the enemy. Borms was reprieved,
but he did not take the lesson to heart and was again condemned
to death for the same crime at the end of the Second World War.
This time he was executed.

It was this 'Vlaams National Verbond' organization which
supplied Nazi occupation forces with their most fruitful source of
collaborators. One was Jean Funcken, a Belgian war criminal,
who was sentenced to death in 1945. A 'Rexist' leader during the
German occupation and responsible for the death of many resistance fighters, Funcken fled to France at the end of hostilities,
but eventually gave himself up. Another was Robert Jan Verbelen,
who was arrested in Austria in 1963 where he had been living
since the war.

This fifty-four-year-old former Nazi collaborator had been
condemned to death in his absence by a Belgian court on charges
of treason and murder. Assuming the name of 'Jean Marais',
Verbelen had maintained contacts with Belgian fascists ever since
the war and worked closely with Austrian extremists involved in
terrorist activities in the Tyrol. He has also taken part in gatherings of fascists all over Europe, including a meeting at Malmoe
in Sweden in 1962. Verbelen was head of the Belgian Nazi
security service during the war and also acted as deputy to
Degrelle who at one time was commanding officer of a Belgian SS
Division. With its stiffening of men of the calibre of Verbelen it is
the 'Volksunie' which is today taking over the role of the war-time
'Vlaams National Verbond'.

The international link-up of all these organizations is again
underlined by the fact that the terrorists who had been active in
the South Tyrol had been trained in Antwerp at the expense of
the OAS and the MAC. The tutors of these bomb-throwers of the
Tyrol were colonial officers from the Congo and former Belgian
SS men. In August 1961, on a visit to Vienna, Thiriard made
further contact with Austrian fascists.

The Flemish community has also thrown up a small group of

'Anciens du Front de l'Est' (Former Soldiers of the Eastern Front) and who seem to restrict their activities to financial assistance for Flemish ex-members of the SS. This group is in contact with 'Hinag', the Dutch ex-Waffen SS organization. The Antwerp youth organization, 'Lebensbom', is in contact with German extremist youth organizations. Another group, the 'Mouvement National Flamand' (VSB) (Flemish National Movement), which was founded in 1952 and which for a time published the periodical *Opstanding*, no longer seems to carry out activity in the open.

On the Walloon side, there is the Liège 'Jeunesse Nationale' whose chief, Pierre Joly, was closely connected with the Algerian extremists. He collected money for the OAS and acted as spokesman for Ortiz, one of the fanatical leaders of the French settlers in North Africa.

Another group which had close associations with the activities of French extremists is the 'Centre d'études et de formation contre-révolutionnaire de Tournai', whose founder was General Emil Janssens, head of the Congolese army before independence. Embittered by his experiences, Janssens backs the extreme rightwing, has spoken on the MAC platform, and writes articles for magazines and journals with fascist tendencies.

Supported by Janssens and other former colonial officers, the 'Centre' contains a number of active agitators and is led by a dentist, José Delplace, and a mathematics student, Jean-Claude Absil. Its programme is militant anti-communism and antifreemason, and the group admires the authoritarian Portuguese dictatorship of Salazar which advocates the idea of a 'strong corporate central' state. This group ran into difficulties with the Belgian authorities when it was discovered that they were using a powerful transmitter hidden in the back of a café to keep contact with OAS men who had taken refuge in Spain.

There were clashes between Belgian fascists and the police in a number of centres in November 1953. Over two hundred demonstrators, including two Dutchmen who were later deported, were arrested at Ghent and Louvain. And at least four hundred armed students and other fascist sympathizers were arrested when trying to stir up trouble before a rally at Dixmunde where former members of the resistance movement were holding a protest meeting against the release of war criminals. One of the arrested men was Bob Maes, a well-known Rexist leader. (Forty-one-year-old Maes is now the undisputed leader of the Volksunie militants.) At another meeting ex-members of the Flemish SS parading in uniform caused a number of disturbances. In centres near the frontier swastikas were daubed in red paint on road signs and notice-boards.

Another group called the 'Vlaamse Militantorde' (Order of the Flemish Militants) has recently sprung into existence. Wearing grey shirts and black trousers, the intentions and philosophy of its members are quite clearly undiluted Nazism.

As can be seen, Belgium today has a hopeful and growing active fascist nest in its midst. Exploiting the remnants of colonial bitterness and the tension between north and south, right-wing extremists know that an atmosphere of economic or social upheaval is fertile ground for the mass propagation of their political views.

Operating through the extremist wings of the jingoistic movements like the 'Volksunie' and combining with groups like the MAC, war-time Nazis and their present-day successors are making a calculated bid for increased influence and ultimate power in the country. Their ambitions were boosted by gains made by both the 'Volksunie' and the French-speaking 'Front Démocratique des Francophones' in recent elections.

HOLLAND

Holland has no language dispute to split its people into two warring camps, but the Dutch today are finding that their own native fascist movements are drawing support from the young University student who is proving susceptible to extremist wooing, and from the war-time veterans whose Hitlerian convictions have not changed with the passing years.

That some members of the present-day student population should have been attracted by the racialist propaganda sent out from Berlin in the 1930's, and still heard re-echoing in many places today, is not all that surprising. After all, some 50,000 young people from Holland joined the German armed forces during the war to fight under Hitler—a figure which must have pleased the Fuehrer who was not having quite such success in other countries which he had conquered. Whereas at the beginning of 1944

Norway had provided just under six thousand volunteers for the SS, Holland had produced eight times as many targets for the Russian guns on the Eastern Front.

At the end of the war many of these young people did not forget their war-time convictions and tried to keep in touch with similarly-minded people in Germany and elsewhere.

One of the groups which these former Nazi volunteers belong to is the 'Hinag', the Dutch branch of the West German organization of former SS members. So concerned is the parent movement with its Dutch followers that it runs a special supplement of its mouthpiece *Der Freiwillige* (The Volunteer) for their benefit. Normally one would have thought that the activities of such a group would have diminished with the passage of time—after all the war ended twenty years ago and even former SS men must fade away. But the 'Hinag' flourishes as never before, and in 1961 three hundred Dutch and West German former SS men planned to hold a meeting at Naarden in Holland under the auspices of 'Hinag'. The object of this gathering was to discuss ways of strengthening their organization. The two men behind the meeting, J. Hartman and B. Hofman, both members of the Dutch Volunteer Corps of the SS who are now living in Amsterdam, make frequent journeys to West Germany where they meet Herr Caspar Serno, who is the representative in the Bonn Republic of the SS Grenadier Division of the 'Landstorm Nederland'. Hartman is the chief representative in Holland of the periodical *Der Freiwillige*.

It was intended to hold the meeting in the country restaurant 'Oud-Valkeveen', owned by two former Dutch Nazis, but the get-together was forbidden by the authorities.

It is not only war-time veterans who are keeping alive the spirit of Nazism. Students are also participating. Incidents involving the 'Dachau Game' in Dutch universities reached such a pitch in September 1962 that the police were forced to intervene. The most publicized event occurred when hundreds of semi-naked students were forced into a cellar during an 'initiation ceremony' organized by the Amsterdam Students' Corporation—the oldest and most fashionable all-male students' organization in the Dutch capital.

During the ceremony several young people fainted because of the lack of air, and students were subjected to physical violence and verbal abuse reminiscent of playful storm-trooper behaviour. The 'game', which lasted all night, consisted of insulting the freshmen with racial abuse and letting loose a pig stuffed with castor oil among them. Several of the students protested that their parents had perished at Dachau, and the repercussions of the incident reached the Dutch Parliament where Dr Cals, the Minister of Education, described the game as 'simply disgusting'.

Two prominent older members of the 'Students' Corporation' —one of them the son of a well-known member of Parliament— had, during the 'game' forced some of the freshmen present at this higher centre of learning to sing anti-Jewish songs. It was then revealed that this was not an isolated incident, for the 'Students' Corporation' in Amsterdam has had a racialist reputation for many years, while similar incidents had occurred at the Universities of Leyden and Delft.

The post-war revival of Dutch Nazi organizations was first brought to the attention of the public in 1953 when it became known that a group of fascists was behind the escape of seven Dutch war criminals from Breda Prison to West Germany. During the same year the National European Social Movement (NESB) was formed by Paul van Tienen, a former Dutch SS officer. This group soon ran into trouble with the authorities and its news-sheet *Alarm* was seized by the police. The movement was disbanded when van Tienen and fellow-leader Dr Jan Wolthuis received prison sentences (later quashed). It was alleged that this new group was simply an extension of the NSB, the old Dutch Nazi movement founded by Anton Mussert.

Van Tienen, who had served on the Russian front during the war, brought out an eight-page *Social Weekblad* journal which called itself the 'National European Information Journal and Organ of the National Opposition'. In this publication van Tienen tried to white-wash Dutch Nazis by saying that they had nothing to do with the German Nazis. But at the same time this former soldier now turned publisher advertised German books which explain that the 'crimes' which had been committed by the Nazis during the war were not crimes at all. And that if they were crimes they had been justified by events, or else exaggerated by the Allies.

In May 1957, the *Social Weekblad* gave way to a monthly called the *Nederlandse Archieven van de Conservatieve Revolutie*. Tienen

continued as an editor, and besides acting as the Hague representative of the 'Hinag' movement, he also founded a military
book club which solicits subscriptions from among the armed
forces of the country.

Among other extremist organizations in Holland are: 'The
Netherlands Fascist Movement' and the 'Foundation of former
political offenders' run by Wolthuis. Both maintain contacts with
the European Social Movement as well as with other SS groups.
There are two youth movements, 'Europese Jongerenorde (EJON),
run by L. Logger and which has *Jong Europa* as its news-sheet,
and the 'Heel Nederlansche Jongerenbeweging', which maintains
contact with the youth section of the Swedish-based European
Social Movement.

CHAPTER VII

Germany

BUT WHAT of Germany today? The land which threw up Hitler?
The Germany of the concentration camps, the gas-chambers—
where the creed of national-socialism and racialism-gone-mad
reigned supreme?

Even today—two decades after the ending of the Nazi régime
in Europe and the crushing defeat of the German armies—so
much emotion is aroused by the subject of Nazism in the Fatherland that it is extremely difficult to view the matter with
dispassionate objectivity.

Has the menace of Nazism been wiped out? Or does it still
linger in the hearts and minds of the race who accepted Hitler and
his sadistic racial theories? What does one make of the constant
unearthing of Nazi criminals in all walks of society—including
some in very high places? Are these unavoidable remnants of an
historical aberration in German history, or are they symbolic
of a rottenness which has eaten deep into the structure of the
land?

Take a few incidents. In Kiel Grand Admiral Karl Doenitz, the
Nazi leader after Hitler committed suicide, turns up at the
Geesthact Grammar School and says that as a soldier it would
have been morally wrong if he had refused to obey orders from
his superiors during the war. The implication by the man who
was sentenced to a ten-year prison term as a major criminal by the
Nuremberg Tribunal is quite clear. The three hundred pupils
were being told that the atrocities committed by Nazis were
unavoidable, for the men who committed them were only 'acting
under orders'.

At Bad Windsheim, one thousand former members of the Nazi
élite 6th Mountain Division held a private reunion. Later they
marched in silence through this small Bavarian town to a war
memorial for a ceremony in memory of fallen comrades. In Bad

Godesberg, near the capital of Bonn, German veterans who were awarded the Nazi's highest military honour—the Knight's Cross —during World War Two held their own annual gathering, but denied that neo-Nazis had permeated their ranks.

Over in Flensburg we have Martin Fellenz, a Free Democrat city councillor, a leading member of the 'European Union' and the organizer of a 'hands-across-the-seas' association between his city and the English town of Hayes and Harlington in Middlesex. Fellenz, a wealthy and respected citizen, loved nothing better than leading local choirs in peaceful singing activities. But one day it was revealed that Herr Fellenz had a guilty past—he found himself facing allegations in a German court of having murdered 40,000 men, women and children in the Cracow area of Poland during the war. He was sent to prison for seven years.

And if Fellenz is held to be an exception, what about Herr Georg Heuser who until 1959 held the post of Chief of the Rhine-land Palatine State Police? It appears that Heuser was a high-ranking Gestapo officer in the war with something like 70,000 murders on his hands. The police chief's accomplices included a technical instructor, a customs inspector, a draughtsman, a clerk, a school teacher, a salesman, a butcher and a bookkeeper—all worthy, established members of German society, all men who had played their part in the building up of the new democratic post-war Germany.

Heuser has since been sentenced to fifteen years' imprison-ment, but what about the scandal of the Chief Public Prosecutor, Wolfgang Fraenkel, who was sacked from his post because in his unsavoury Nazi past he acted as one of Hitler's prosecutors?

The trial of twenty-two former Auschwitz concentration camp guards revealed the horrors of the Nazi régime, but even more revealing was that the guilty men, and they included wealthy businessmen, a salesman, dentists, a doctor, a gynaecologist, a farmer, a carpenter, and ordinary workers, had been allowed to live quite openly in Germany without the authorities ever investigating their war-time activities.

The lawyers at the trial said that most Germans were opposed to such judicial procedures and that they had had difficulty in getting local co-operation for arrests to be made. One of the witnesses, restaurant owner Karl Seefeld, from Stuttgart, who had given pre-trial evidence against the accused, refused to testify in the court-room, saying: 'I must be just an SS man. My customers don't like this trial. It is a shame on our country and it gives us a bad reputation abroad.'

In his moving testimony at the trial, one of the former concentration camp inmates said: 'This machinery of murder could never have functioned if there had not been tens of thousands who were ready to operate it.'

One could think of these indicting words and of the thousands upon thousands of Nazi criminals of one sort or another who are free today, in many cases holding high Government posts, and claim that the spirit of Hitler and the Nazi philosophy must surely still be rampant in the so-called democracy of Western Germany. It is estimated that at least 120,000 former Nazis, including many war criminals, are living with false papers and identities in the country.

Something like 85 per cent of the top-ranking and middle-rung Nazis are enjoying full pensions for their service to Hitler while more than a million victims of the Nazi terror are still waiting to be compensated. Many of the Germans who have something to be guilty about in their pasts are protected either openly or by silent accomplices in high Government places who know all about their war-time record.

This was strikingly illustrated by the circumstances which eventually led to the trial of the men involved in the Nazi 'euthanasia' programme. Many doctors and other high officials who were involved in the so-called 'mercy-killing' of some 200,000 mentally ill or physically handicapped adults and children under Hitler's orders, were never brought to trial. Most had resumed their normal activities at the end of the war with the help and complicity of their fellow German citizens.

One of the leading figures in the 'euthanasia' project, which incidentally served as a blue-print for the eventual mass killing programmes in the concentration camps, was Dr Werner Heyde, who was a pre-war professor of medicine at Wuerzburg University. For twelve years after the fall of Hitler he masqueraded as a doctor in the North German city of Flensburg and rose to become medical adviser to courts in the State of Schleswig-Holstein under the name of Dr Fritz Sawade.

Heyde and four other men were arrested and charged to stand trial at Limburg. But Heyde committed suicide in his cell in

February 1964, and another accused, Friedrich Tillmann, fell to his death from the eighth floor of a Cologne police building.

Tillmann, who had been Heyde's assistant, had spent the post-war years as a director of a Cologne orphanage and a warden of a Roman Catholic hospital in the Ruhr.

The third man who failed to put in an appearance at the trial was Dr Gerhard Bohne, who jumped bail in July 1963, and fled to the Argentine from Duesseldorf. Another of the 'mercy-killing' men who skipped the country was Reinhold Paul Robert Vorberg who was arrested in Spain in 1963 and extradited to Western Germany. He is to be tried separately. In fact the only man to face the judges at Limburg, where the trial was originally scheduled to take place, was Munich bookshop salesman, Hans Hefelmann.

Commenting on the suicides of two of the accused, the prosecutor, Fritz Bauer, said: 'The suspicion has never left me that there is a silent agreement and conspiracy by all involved that the trial should not take place.

'There are many doctors who are interested that their names and work during the Third Reich do not become public property.'

The prosecution also believed that Bohne's escape to Latin America had been financed by sympathizers who were not very anxious for his evidence to be heard. Bauer claimed that a former co-prisoner of Dr Heyde, Goetz Wicke, was promised £2,000 to help free the former Nazi and smuggle him to Brazil or Egypt, 'with the assistance of a large organization'.

As a result of evidence presented to the court, cases against ten other doctors practising in Germany were launched.

Schleswig-Holstein, northernmost of the German states, has been the hiding place of an unusual number of Germans wanted on war crimes charges. So widespread was the silent complicity of many leading figures there, that Herr Otto Osterloh, a prominent West German Christian Democrat politician, helped set up a state parliamentary committee to inquire into the protectors of Dr Werner Heyde who had for so long lived in the area before giving himself up in 1960. Twenty-two prominent citizens who knew all about Heyde's past were named by the committee.

Osterloh, who was very active in his opposition to former Nazis, was also responsible for the suspension of Lothar Stielau, a

Luebeck schoolmaster who wrote that he doubted the authenticity of the Anne Frank diaries. He also launched an inquiry into the circumstances surrounding the invitation of Doenitz to address a school. Strangely, Osterloh, who was the Minister of Education and Culture in Schleswig-Holstein, committed 'suicide' in February 1964. Another man who was reported to have taken his own life during the same month was Ewald Peters, chief bodyguard to Dr Erhard. Peters was recognized by former Nazi victims and accused of killing civilians in Russia during the war.

As late as 1962 the widows of Goering, SS chief Himmler, and Heydrich, the 'butcher' of Czechoslovakia, were drawing pension cheques from the Bonn Government. Yet when the widow of General Sack, who was executed for his resistance movement activities against Hitler, applied for State assistance, she was refused any help.

The number of police officers in Germany who have recently been found to have had a hand in the brutal killings by Nazi squads during the war has been startling. In January 1964, two chief inspectors of the Hamburg police, Wolfgang Hoffman and Julius Wohlauf, were suspended on suspicion of having taken part in war crimes. In May of the previous year, Josef Uhl, who had been personnel chief of the Southern Bavarian police until his arrest, went on trial with a police constable and tax inspector for murders in Russia.

In December 1963, Commissioner Werner Meyer became the sixth police officer to be arrested in Schleswig-Holstein since 1959 and charged with complicity in war crimes. And Captain Wilhelm Doering, who was head of the criminal police in Siegburg near Bonn before his past was discovered, was sentenced to four years for his part in massacres in the Soviet Union. Also arrested was Dr Georg Fleischmann, CID chief in Ludwigshafen.

Then there was the stir caused when it was revealed that Professor Theodor Oberlaender carried a loaded revolver on him when attending Parliament. He was the same Oberlaender who had been a Nazi SS Captain before becoming one of Dr Adenauer's cabinet ministers. The Professor resigned his post as Refugees Minister in 1960 when it was alleged that he was involved in a war-time massacre in the Ukrainian city of Lvov. But he was cleared, and then returned to Parliament as a deputy—still toting his pistol.

And so the tale could be continued of how Nazi criminals have avoided justice; of how in Western Germany there are dozens upon dozens of neo-Nazi movements, with a host of banners, symbols and publications representing their extremist fascist views. To add force to the critics of the West German Government and its claims to be democratic, there was the unsavoury incident of the '*Spiegel*' case. Journalists on that news magazine who had so fearlessly exposed the faults of the Bonn authorities found themselves in prison without even the opportunity of getting their point of view heard in open court. This state of affairs evokes echoes of the past when all critics of the régime were ruthlessly eliminated.

But is it not significant that the scandal of the arrests and the outcry over the attempt to suppress the freedom of the press brought about the resignation of Defence Minister Franz Josef Strauss in 1963 and shook the Adenauer Government to its foundations? And that day after day, week after week, Nazi criminals are ferreted out and brought to trial by the Ludwigs-burg Centre for the investigation of Nazi crimes? Is it not significant that the German Government asks for the extradition of war-time criminals whenever they come to light in Spain, Egypt or Latin America? And that the authorities in Bonn refuse to grant an entry permit to Per Engdahl, the Swedish extremist, because of his activities in furthering the cause of the post-war fascist international?

The Justice Minister of Baden-Wurttemberg, Dr Wolfgang Hausmann, expressed the view of many German officials when he said that courts throughout the country should proceed with-out delay in order to 'convince world opinion that the Federal Republic was making every effort to bring those guilty, the really guilty from the period of arbitrary rule, to rightful punishment.'

In Frankfurt, in January 1963, a West German court ruled that the local University had acted correctly in depriving Josef Mengele, the former chief doctor at Auschwitz concentration camp, of his doctoral degree because of the inhumane experi-ments he had carried out on his innocent victims.

A month or two before this particular incident, four leaders of a Nazi movement received prison terms ranging from four to nine months for 'spreading ideas directed against Democratic order'. Two others—under age at the time of the offences—were given one month in a youth detention home after being convicted of the same charge. They belonged to the 'German National Youth', a small group which has been banned because of its pro-Nazi aims, and were arrested following the wave of swastika-smearing late in 1959 and early 1960. They were also accused by the police of the unfurling of a Nazi flag at a midsummer night's celebration.

In March 1963, a twenty-one-year-old student, Hans Juergen Bischoff, a member of the banned Nazi terrorist movement, the 'National Students' Bund' was killed while making a bomb in his home in West Berlin. The 'Bund' were believed to be responsible for sixteen explosions along the Berlin Wall and the bombing of the Russian Intourist travel agency a few days before the accident to Bischoff. Western officials in Berlin were concerned for they feared that the anti-Wall incident was being used by extreme nationalists just as the Nazis gathered support by their campaign against the German frontiers set up by the Versailles Treaty after the First World War.

But the fact that the Nazis *are* being dealt with in the courts, that the '*Spiegel*' affair roused the whole nation, that Nazi-minded youths are being punished, is an indication that democracy has made some progress in digging in roots in the Germany ruled so long by Hitler. As Harold Wilson, the British Labour Party leader said in March 1964: 'The achievement of democracy in modern Germany is one of the historic developments of the post-war world. . . . The new men and the new philosophies in Germany deserve our support and our encouragement.'

His words were echoed by the West German Minister of Justice, Ewald Bucher, who said that the growing demand for an amnesty for war criminals would be firmly resisted. 'In the next five to eight years a further five hundred Nazi war crimes trials would be heard in Germany,' he said.

In 1957 the play based on the diary of Anne Frank, who more than any other single person has come to symbolize the guilt and inhumanity of the Nazi past, was presented in more than sixty-two German theatres and a million copies of the book were sold. In 1958 some 2,000 Hamburg youngsters made a pilgrimage to Bergen-Belsen, the concentration camp in which Anne Frank had perished. The following year some 8,000 young people joined similar trips to concentration camps to commemorate the victims. 'We do so in mourning and shame,' said the words on the wreath deposited at Dachau by a group from Munich.

Modern Germany has two faces which it presents to the world. Firstly, one sees a land riddled with Nazis and the proliferation of fascist-minded movements, and secondly the country presents itself as filled with democratic-minded citizens who are determined to prevent the re-birth of a new Hitler or the spread of his pernicious and extremist views.

To determine which is nearer the truth, it is important to examine the Germany which produced Hitler and to see whether the conditions for the revival of another 'fuehrer'-type figure exist today.

The basic difference between the two Germanies lies in the fact that now there is prosperity whereas the great economic depression and mass unemployment of the inter-war years paved the way for the seizure of power by Hitler. Nobody can be absolutely sure how the fifty-eight million West Germans would react if they were suddenly faced with six million out of work. But with today's highly developed social security structure, it is highly unlikely that the despair of the middle classes which acted as one of the most important factors in the rise of Hitler will be reproduced.

Secondly, the weakness of the Government which prevailed then is not matched by the situation in Bonn now. With the defeat of Hitler, the German people had to face the disillusion-ment of disaster and the loss of life and property on a gigantic scale which would hardly encourage them today to follow blindly another 'fuehrer'. In the Weimar Germany there was a genuine boredom with democracy and nostalgia for old-style glory. All this plus bitterness over the harshness of the peace treaty was sharpened by the economic uncertainties of the age.

Whereas between the wars the German people associated the democracy they knew with unemployment, depression and chaos, today the same political force has given them an 'economic miracle' which has made the country one of the strongest and most prosperous in the Western world. The rabble-rousing of a Hitler is not likely to appeal to people with full bellies who have the security of a welfare state to lose. The country would have to be cast into a mood of national despair and economic disarray before the threat of another dictator on the same scale could become serious.

It is interesting to note that a survey made in Germany in January 1964 showed that only 10 per cent of the population thought that the Hitler era was the greatest of this century. This contrasts with a percentage of forty-two out of every hundred who thought thirteen years ago that the Nazi period was best. Now, 62 per cent of all Germans believe that the present time cannot be bettered.

There are those who claim that only Germany could have produced the concentration camps, gas-chambers and sadistic horrors of Nazism and that there is a flaw in the German soul which craves a strong leader to lead them to world domination. There are those who say that the arrogance and militarism, the ingrained sense of blind obedience of the German race will always throw up dictators and compel the Germans once again to go marching against the rest of the world.

But these characteristics are not the sole prerogative of people born in Germany. We do not have to go back very far to examine the methods of the British in Ireland, or the French forces in Algeria, to find that there is a certain breed of man who in certain circumstances will descend to the most bestial of behaviour when given a free hand in dealing with 'opponents'. What Nazism did do was to give the sadist and pervert the opportunity to exercise his sordid talents to the full. Who can with full certainty say that the same type of man born in another country will not enact similar crimes if given similar unhampered opportunities?

An important difference between the 'thirties and today is that the European nations have been growing together, thus helping reduce the importance of frontiers and the force of nationalism. The Common Market may help to create a new belligerent European nationalism, but it also presents one of the most hopeful solutions to Europe's problems and if developed along liberal and outward-looking lines it is perhaps one of the major defences against a Hitlerian dictator springing up in Germany—or for that matter anywhere else on the continent.

But there *are* Nazis loose in Germany and there *are* a large number of right-wing organizations who believe in fascist ideals. The danger lies in ignoring them and treating them as of little importance. On the contrary, they should be closely studied for they reveal the presence of a certain poison in the minds of men.

The outbreak of swastika-daubing on walls throughout Germany at Christmas-time in 1959 and other manifestations of Nazi activity indicated that sections of German youth had found German democracy a dull and uninspiring force and looked for inspiration to the 'heroic' feats which had been performed under Hitler's generals. There were young men who admired the 'green devils'—parachutists of Ramcke, and the air ace Hans Rudel who was once a national hero and who makes political speeches at meetings of the Reich Party. The same Rudel who had fled to Latin America after the war to become an Argentine Government official under Peron.

However, there is the other side of the coin. Shortly after the swastika incidents, the 'Bundesjugendring'—an organization of six million German youngsters in fourteen religious, sports and youth groups—published a statement asserting that the transgressors had nothing in common with German youth. In 1960 the student councils of the major universities voted to expel all those who held anti-semitic or Nazi views.

As in Holland and other countries, so in Germany today there are two main groups who are drawn into neo-Nazi movements or who indulge in fascist activities. One group consists of men who lived during Hitler's years of power and were completely imbued with his racialist ideals. Some of these men served the Fuehrer in humble ways, others became the leaders of Nazi Germany and were guilty of major war crimes. Many still live and work in the country either under disguised identities or with the silent complicity of those around them. They harbour secret thoughts and bear nostalgic memories of the 'glorious past'. Many participate in extremist activities.

The other group consists of young people who were born too late to know much about the Nazi reign of terror in Europe and who do not believe the evidence of the concentration camps in which millions perished. They are attracted by the semi-clandestine nature of the neo-Nazi movements and are indoctrinated by their leaders.

Many of these Nazi followers belonged to the 'Deutsche Reichspartei' (German Reich Party), which in the spring of 1959 won important successes in local elections in Rhine-Pflaz and the Niedersacksen areas. With their fanfares, and flags, they held a wide variety of meetings and rallies all over the country and won the admiration of many younger Germans.

A new poster showing an eagle and a new version of the swastika was drawn up for the party, but following the outbreak of swastika incidents at the end of 1959, party rallies were forbidden. It gives some indication of the mood in Germany today that the party dismissed the two members who had painted the swastikas and slogans in Cologne, and declared that it was not an anti-semitic movement.

The Reich Party, which merged with other right-wing groups to form the 'National Democratic Party' (NPD) in December 1964, runs a number of youth sections with evocative names such as 'Young Storm-troopers', 'Young Vikings' and 'Ring of Youth'. Members wear a uniform of brown shirt, black knickerbockers, peaked caps and buckled belts. Their martial music and marching songs are all aimed at introducing the spirit and atmosphere of the Hitler period. When the young boys fall into disgrace, disciplinary action is taken from an old Hitler youth movement book of rules, *The Steel Hat Handbook* of 1927. The 'Last Letter of Hermann Goering' is read as part of their training.

The youth leaders include the former SS officer Dr Karl Ganser, and Karl Lehmann-Teja who was jailed for five months in 1954 for neo-Nazi activities. Another leading figure in the movement, Adolf von Thadden, said that about a quarter of the 16,000 party members were former Nazis. The group's chief, Wilhelm Meinberg, a former Nazi and SS Brigade Commander and a member of the Reichstag, was imprisoned by the British after the war. Now he says: 'We are the party of the future'. Van Thadden is a former Chairman of the German Reich party.

The party has its own newspapers, *The New Reich* edited by Heinrich Heartle, formerly secretary to Alfred Rosenberg, the notorious Jew-baiter, and *Reichsruf*, renamed Deutsche Nachrichten.

The NPD vigorously carried forward the pre-war Hitler doctrine of racialism. 'Still piping their old tunes of hatred,' was the headline comment of a German newspaper following a meeting called by the NPD in March 1965 to discuss 'the Middle-Eastern crisis; Judaism and Zionism.'

'The murderous hordes of Zionists who have formed an international conspiracy . . .' was the sort of rhetoric heard at the meeting. One of the speakers, former Nazi Erwin Schonborn, attacked the Social Democrats for supporting Israel's claim to diplomatic recognition. 'This simply furthers the cause of Bolshevism' he told his cheering audience.

The founder of another NPD branch, Professor von Bormann, boasted of his Nazi past. 'I am proud of having done my bit in the days of national awakening,' he said in March 1965. Social Democrats and local trade unions protested. 'How much longer can Germany allow self-confessed fascists to poison the minds of the young?' they asked.

The movement calls on its members to 'love the Reich' and demands the return of the Sudetenland and East Germany. There is a strong distrust of pacts with the West and links with NATO. That its leaders are as ambitious as ever was indicated when a new youth group called 'Junger Kameradschaft' was launched. At the same time another youth movement called 'Bund Deutscher Jugend', which uses as its emblem one of the Nazi runes, was formed in Essen by Alfons Holler.

The *Reichsruf* magazine published articles which attack Poland for 'murdering 50,000 Germans in September 1939, in order to provoke the Second World War . . .' Former Chancellor Dr Adenauer is criticized for 'proffering reparations to the Western powers' and attempts are made to absolve the Nazis of any part in the burning of the Reichstag. The journal also makes elaborate excuses for Richard Wagner's latent anti-semitism and commends the Waffen SS for its part in the defence of the West under the inspired leadership of Heinrich Himmler.

In September 1964 the *Reichsruf* blamed Britain for starting the Second World War. The works of the French fascist, Paul Rassinier, also receive warm praise in this journal.

During the German elections in the late summer of 1965, the NPD campaigned hard to win votes and several of their rallies attracted mass audiences. In Nuremberg in September the biggest hall in the city was filled to overflowing and thousands listened outside as the party leaders' voices over loudspeakers proclaimed their Hitlerian faith.

Franz Winter, Chairman of the Bavarian section, laid a wreath on the graves of Nazi criminals hanged by the Allies, and he then called the dead men 'innocent victims of justice'.

When a Munich lawyer, Dr Erich Bohrer, started legal action

against the wreath-laying on the grounds that it 'glorified' the Hitler criminals, he received numerous anonymous telephone calls and letters telling him that 'soon we will be putting a wreath on *your* grave.'

Throughout the election campaign yard-high swastikas, SS signs and 'Heil Hitler' slogans were found daubed on posters and house walls in a number of cities including Koblenz and Konigswinter near Bonn.

In Bamberg a Jewish cemetery was desecrated, while in the same town the walls of United States army buildings were painted with anti-American slogans such as: 'Immoral U.S. army thugs.'

Although this Bavarian town has only a tiny handful of Jewish inhabitants, scores of people rallied to their side by placing wreaths marked 'forgive us, brothers' on the desecrated graves and turned out in their thousands in pouring rain for an open-air meeting of prayers of atonement. The mayor told the gathering: 'We want to show the world that the events of the past few days have filled us with great pain and genuine sadness.'

Others volunteered to reinforce police patrols to prevent further trouble.

Dr Erhard, the Chancellor, denounced the 'phantom swastika painters', but the NPD continued to preach their virulent national socialist programme.

'We are fed up with sitting in the pillory while the world throws rotten eggs at us. The people who ought to be in the pillory are those who betrayed the Fatherland and went abroad during the war to help the enemy,' said one of the party's leaders before Germans went to vote.

Although party chairman Fritz Thielen has denied that the NPD is Nazi, old Hitlerian songs are heard at meetings, Nazi ideas spread and war criminals glorified. The movement attacks the continuing trials of Nazi criminals and racialism is whipped up by attacking 'foreign workers' in Germany. At a mass rally at Karlsruhe in June 1966—the largest extremist right-wing gathering of its kind since the Nazi régime ended—Thielen's speech calling for a 'New Order' in Europe was a carbon copy of those that Hitler and Goebbels made when they were on their path to power.

Indeed two of Thielen's deputies, Wilhelm Gutman and

Heinrich Fassbender, were Nazi party members. Out of eighteen members on the executive, twelve were active Nazis under Hitler.

The Minister of the Interior, Hermann Hoecherl, estimated that in 1964 there were 112 right-wing organizations in the country having a total membership of 27,000. Forty-six newspapers and periodicals with a known circulation of nearly 200,000 are published by these groups. In 1965 it was revealed that a further sixteen new extremist groups had started up in business, but twenty others ceased to exist.

In addition, many of the international organizations outside the country make a particular point of keeping in close touch with their German counterparts. For instance, the 'Deutsche Soziale Bewegung' (DSB) regards itself as the German branch of the Swedish-based 'European Social Movement'. And during 1964 and 1965 seventy-eight different racialist broadsheets and brochures were regularly sent into Germany from Britain, Sweden, the United States and Egypt. One of the most active groups to dispatch its 'literature' to Germany was Rockwell and Jordan's 'World Union of National Socialists'.

In November 1965 anti-Nazi resistance fighters calculated that neo-Nazism in West Germany was supported by 123 organizations and publishing houses with about 25,000 members.

In the early post-war years the Nazi 'Socialist Reichs Party', led by Major-General Otto Ernst Remer, attracted support, but it was later banned by the authorities for its fascist propaganda. Remer was sentenced to a term of imprisonment for racial slander and fled to Egypt to join his ex-Nazi colleagues who had taken shelter there. It was Remer who, as the Berlin guard battalion commander, helped put down the 1944 revolt against Hitler. He was arrested in Soltau, South Germany, in 1963 and charged with fraudulently obtaining £23,000 by falsifying agricultural machinery statements.

One of the most important groups which has connections with fascist movements in other lands is the 'Nation Europa'. This organization publishes a monthly journal with the same name in the North Bavarian town of Coburg. Copies are distributed all round the West. Run by former SS leader Arthur Ehrhard, *Nation Europa* considers itself the organ of international fascism and the Malmoe movement. It claims a steady rising circulation.

The first issue appeared in January 1951 with the sub-title 'Monthly for European Regeneration', and counted among its directors the Swedish Carl Carlberg and Arthur Kogel of Chicago. It takes articles from men like Sir Oswald Mosley and former German Nazi officials. And like fascist publications in other countries, *Nation Europa* claims that its fight is 'against the Communist menace'.

In the December 1962 issue an article praised the Nazi measures of 1933 which aimed at sterilizing the 'unfit'. 'Whereas in former times those seriously ill died at an earlier age they are now kept alive by hygiene and medical science and are thus able to procreate,' it said in explanation of its views.

Another writer in the same issue deplored the 'invasion of our Nordic territory by millions of foreign workers most of whom are utterly alien by nature. Italian labourers are dirty and lack discipline, are dishonest and show a tendency to theft.' Angrily the author declared that many German girls married these foreigners with the result that a 'Eurasian-Negroid' race would arise.

Italians and Negroes are not the only targets, for the Jews, too, are held to be 'responsible for the troubles of the past'. The editor quotes widely from a pamphlet, *Vajoel Moshe*, by a Jerusalem author, Joel Teitelbaum, who is quoted as saying: 'Auschwitz was for years knowingly and systematically prepared by the Zionist movement' and that 'The Zionists prevented the rescue of Jews'.

Even after the revelations of the Auschwitz trial, *Nation Europa* declared in May 1965 that the deaths of six million Jews in the concentration camps were a myth. 'It is the other side that has first trampled on international law,' blandly says the editor of this journal. Echoing the smear tactics used so successfully by Goebbels, *Nation Europa* states: 'The thirteen million Jews in the world through their influence in the United States companies exert great influence also on the German economy.' And gravely the journal warns its readers that as a result 'The Jews have a great influence on the world press and on West Germany's political decisions.'

In the 1964 'Christmas Issue' of *Nation Europa* the editor once again turns on the full blast of racialism. 'The mixing of unduly differentiated races gradually throttles the will to self-preservation on both sides and not only disrupts the biological foundations of any specific racial civilization, but also makes any further evolution impossible.'

Mein Kampf seems to come alive again as he continues: 'We Europeans may claim that the self-surrender of the White nations will constitute a particularly grave disaster for humanity. Stringent racial selection in the course of the natural processes has been responsible for the fact that, for centuries, the Europides were the chief architects of world history.'

It is interesting to note that among the shareholders of 'Nation Europa' appears a Herr Otto C. Jaeckel of Windgates, Ireland.

The German neo-Nazi parties keep close links with other fascist groups in different parts of Europe and delegates from Germany travel freely to attend the various international conferences and congresses of these extremist elements. Karl Heinz Priester, who was formerly press and propaganda chief of the 'Hitler Jugend' and an SS officer, was a member of the 'European Social Movement' run by Per Engdahl. Former members of Hitler's crack Waffen SS, among them European SS volunteers from Belgium, Holland, France and Denmark also meet frequently. Such a gathering took place in the middle of 1962 at Moenchen Gladbach under the auspices of HIAG, the ex-Waffen SS friendly society. Their spokesman, Herr Steindorfer, stresses that 'our common bonds are sealed by blood and hallowed by the graves of comrades.' He also denounces the 'Distorted view of historic events which was responsible for the continuing vilification of the Waffen SS.'

'One day,' boasts Steindorfer, 'history will prove that the idea of a united Europe originated with the Waffen volunteers.'

Throughout 1965 the HIAG journal *Der Freiwillige* was still asserting that the Waffen SS were 'not really Nazis at all . . . We were conscripted and given no choice.'

Late in 1964 an international committee of experts who were gathered to find ways of combating neo-Nazism asked the West German Government to dissolve the HIAG as it was the 'backbone of the international neo-Nazi movement'.

Their plea was given force by a further gathering of over 1,200 members of the Waffen SS who came to Rendsburg, near Kiel, in October 1965 to celebrate the eleventh annual HIAG rally. Hitler's war-time veterans from all over Europe flocked to this Schleswig-Holstein town to sing their marching songs and cheer the leaders who told them: 'We were only soldiers who served the Fatherland. The entire German people should be ashamed that we have been held collectively guilty and treated continually as second-class citizens now that the war is long over. The gruesome crimes of the concentration camps cannot be held at our door.'

Nine hundred former victims of the Nazi régime thought otherwise, for together with a number of young Germans they also turned up at Rendsburg and paraded outside the meeting hall with banners proclaiming 'Auschwitz' and 'Dachau'. Protests against holding the gathering flooded in from not only all corners of Germany but from many other countries as well. But the town council refused to ban the meeting after Prince Friedrich zu Schleswig-Holstein interceded on behalf of the HIAG 'in the name of humanity and comradeship'.

The 'comrades' who flocked to Rendsburg gave an indication of their 'humanity' when they termed the soup they drank at their dinner 'Cracow-style soup'. To outsiders who do not quite understand this little 'joke', Cracow was the site of a Jewish ghetto during the war and situated less than fifty miles from Auschwitz concentration camp.

Members of the HIAG organization operate under the veneer of legality by claiming that they are a 'welfare society'. Repeatedly they claim that they were 'soldiers' doing their duty. But in fact the Allied War Crimes Tribunal in Nuremberg condemned the Waffen SS as a criminal body. And there is no doubt that the members of the HIAG who now proclaim their innocence belonged to the same SS which came under Heinrich Himmler's orders to carry out such activities as concentration camp atrocities.

Even more blatant in its propaganda than the HIAG journal is the *Deutsche Soldaten Zeitung* published under the editorship of Gerhard Frey in Munich. Early in 1963 it was renamed the *Deutsche National Zeitung* and in July 1965 was estimated to have a circulation of over a hundred thousand. The publication persistently attacks the 'Bonn democracy', the 'Western powers' and the 'West German authorities' in sneering tones. It has also accused Willy Brandt, Mayor of Berlin, of a 'dereliction of duty' for not using 'naked force' against the communists, and has demanded the replacement of the Allied garrison by a purely all-German army.

Another of the paper's enemies who is attacked with venom is Air Marshal 'Bomber' Harris for his 'ruthlessness' in bombing German cities. 'Allied murderers in the hundreds of thousands went scot-free, were even decorated for their foul deeds' is the theme running through the January 1965 issue when defending German atrocities.

In 1964 the same newspaper, which greatly admires President Nasser, was favoured with official Egyptian advertisements. *Nation Europa*, as well as the Austrian Nazi journal *Der Trommler*, also advertises its wares in the *Deutsche National Zeitung*. This paper is engaged on an ambitious expansion programme and has bought up extremist journals on all sides.

The increasing boldness of this periodical provoked a strong protest by fifty-seven leading intellectuals, two Nobel Prize winners, authors and university professors in the spring of 1965. In a plea addressed to the President, the German parliament and other bodies, the signatories described their growing apprehension over the fascist and racial ideas propagated by the newspaper.

Undaunted, the journal smeared their attackers as 'communist fellow-travellers, knaves and misguided professors'.

In March 1965 the Social Democratic M.P. Doctor Adolf Arndt said during a Bundestag debate: 'We cannot yet say, alas, that the past is not repeating itself when periodicals like the *Deutsche National Zeitung* are still published here in Germany, reeking of poisonous anti-semitism in every line.' 'What is written in the newspaper is the language of tomorrow's potential murderers,' he added.

A feature of West German life is the extremist 'book club' or library movement. Literally hundreds of publications are pumped out by over forty of these neo-Nazi publishing houses. The nationalist Stahlem has a book club in Bonn; there is the Waffen SS lending library, Wiking Ruf in Hanover, and the Breinlinger book club operates from Berchtesgaden.

Another book club which sends out its own speakers for discussion groups and seminars is run by Helmut Sundermann, director of the Druffel publishing firm. Sundermann, who is the author of the anti-British book *Old Enemy, What Now?* and *The Third Reich* which was published to 'correct certain misconceptions' about Hitler's régime, also turns out works by a large number of leading Nazis and members of the SS including editions of Rudolf Hess's letters to his wife.

A deputy Reich press officer under the Hitler régime, Sundermann is a prolific writer of typical Nazi propaganda, more particularly of the violently anti-semitic kind. In November 1940, for example, he published an article entitled 'Twilight of European Jewry' where he described the 'healthy European nations' struggle against the rotten blood which had forced itself into their body, poisoned their minds and menaced their lives. . . . The time is approaching when the 2,000 years' disastrous invasion by the Jewish bastards into the nations of Europe will be no more than an evil memory.'

Although various German publications like *Der Spiegel* have turned down attempts by Sundermann to advertise his wares, the *Times Literary Supplement* rather unwittingly carried publicity for four of his 'documentary' books on Germany in September 1963. The former Nazi made the most of this to boost his image by sending out circulars which announced: 'For countries outside Germany, we advertise in *The Times Literary Supplement*.'

There are many tens of thousands of Eastern Europeans in Germany who are bitter about the fact that their countries are 'under the communist yoke'. Although not all of them are fascist in outlook, many are eager listeners to the speeches of the right-wing extremists who constantly play upon their anti-Russian sentiments.

One such gathering consisting of hundreds of Germans, Austrians, Iron Guard Rumanians, Arrow-Cross Hungarians and Hlinka Guard Slovaks, in 1962, heard Sundermann say: 'The German collapse in 1945 was not only a catastrophe for Germany but for all the countries directly or indirectly concerned, especially for those bordering on the Danube. Europe must become strong enough to enforce a revision of the 1945 settlement.'

The reference was meant to feed the strong beliefs held by many Germans and expellees living in the country that the original borders of the Fatherland should be restored. A Bulgarian, Dr Dimiter Weltschaff, who also addressed the gathering, said: 'Eastern and South-Eastern nations smarting under Russian domination demand their liberation.' Roundly he declared: 'Self-abasement and self-incrimination must stop. The so-called redemption of the past must never be purchased with the destruction of Germany's future.'

A number of the expellee parties, including the All-German Party and League of Expellees joined the NPD at the end of 1964. In fact twenty-eight per cent of the 20,000 membership of the NPD are men who come from communist dominated Eastern Europe.

There are other publishing groups such as the Abendland Verlag in Wuppertal which produces anti-Western books and the Plesse Verlag in Gottingen under SS man, Wolfgang Schutz. There is also the Gottinger Verlagsanstalt which has published a biography of Hermann Goering portraying this Nazi bully as one of the friendliest of men.

In June 1962 the thirty-nine-year-old publisher, Helmut Cramer, complained that police had seized from his office in Seiburg, near Bonn, thousands of copies of the memoirs of Otto Skorzeny, the former SS officer now living in Spain as a prosperous businessman. In all, 21,000 books were confiscated from Cramer—himself an SS officer. Another volume seized was a fictionalized biography of a young Nazi officer on the Eastern front. The authorities blacklisted this work as it was considered a danger to youth for 'idealizing Nazi attitudes'.

The object of books such as those written by Skorzeny are quite simple. They try to build up the legend that the German army had an honourable and clean fighting record and that all the blame for the cruelties of the concentration camps rests squarely on the shoulders of the few 'Nazis'. In this book, *We fought—We lost*, the former SS man says: 'It is a malevolent twisting of the facts to pretend that the Waffen SS had anything to do with the concentration camp horrors.'

In April 1965 Cramer fled to Egypt after a German court had charged him with subversive activities. The publisher managed to smuggle out over 20,000 books which had been banned by a Cologne court. After Cramer's escape the court warned the public that 'it is a punishable offence to sell or acquire these books.'

A number of extremist publishers, including Helmut Sundermann and Dieter Vollmer who maintain links with Nazi *émigrés* in the Argentine, formed the Society for Freedom of Publication in 1960 to help whitewash the Nazi past.

It was this group which awarded a £1,200 prize to the American David Hoggan in the spring of 1964 for the publication of a book, *The Forced War*, in which the author claimed that Hitler was an excellent fellow and the war was Britain's doing. Another 'prize' given to the American was a teutonic candelabra which the Nazis used for their Nordic race ceremonies.

Hermann Hoecherl, the German Interior Minister, agreed that the book was a 'gross outrage' and the Rhine-Ruhr club notorious for its ex-Nazis reluctantly cancelled a lecture that Hoggan was due to give to them.

Hoggan, who teaches at San Francisco University, ran into such a storm of protest over his inaccurate historical work that a lecture tour to Vienna, Linz and Graz was banned by the Austrian authorities.

Another extremist group, the reborn German National People's Party, was founded in Kassel in 1962. The former pro-Nazi Deutsch-Nationale Volkspartei (DNVP) won notoriety under the late Hugenberg for its 'extreme opposition' to the Weimar Republic. A prominent member of the executive, Heinrich Fassbender, who was one of the founders of the original DNVP, said that the chief task of the party was to 'restore German self-confidence' and to 'imbue the nation's youth with respect for the greatness of the past.' Fassbender is now a leader of the NPD.

A speaker at the initial meeting of the People's Party was Otto Karl Dupow, a prominent journalist who supports various other right-wing splinter groups. He pleaded for the 'creation of an army in the Prussian tradition, pre-military training in the schools and the formation of a new *élite* based on character, virtue and performance.' Other speakers hit at the trade unions whose 'terror has to be broken'.

The capture of Adolf Eichmann in 1960 caused Germans to look closer at their own past, something which many of them had not really done since the ending of the war. In schools, universities and other spheres the history of the country under Hitler, and certainly his racialist excesses, had been glossed over. But the action of the Israeli secret service men brought all this out into the open.

There was very little activity from the right-wing and neo-Nazi movements in the country as the trial proceedings revealed in horrific detail the crimes of the former leaders of Germany. But the country was flooded with literature coming from the Argentine, Spain and the Middle East which bitterly attacked the

Israelis for kidnapping the former Nazi chief. One result of the
Eichmann trial was that the careers of several other Nazis were
closely examined and the number of war-crimes trials were
speeded up.

The Germans became more sensitive about the pasts of the
men who had prominent positions in public life. For instance,
in January 1963 there was fierce controversy over the proposal
to put up Dr Max Frauendorfer as a parliamentary candidate.
Frauendorfer was adjutant to Heinrich Himmler, a leading party
official and the holder of the Nazi Party's Golden Order as
well as a former editor of Nazi indoctrination pamphlets for
schools.

His name had been put forward by the Bavarian branch of
Chancellor Adenauer's Christian Democrats as a prospective
representative. The party said in its official journal, in answer to
numerous critics, that every citizen had the right to readjust his
views and that the enemy of today was not dead Nazism but living
communism.

Attention was also focused on Dr Hans Globke, West Germany's Secretary of State, who was said to have deprived Jews
of citizenship and property under Hitler and who helped frame
some of the racial laws; Dr Ernst Achenback, a pre-war diplomat
who was accused of recommending in 1943 that 2,000 Jews
should be shipped to the East as a reprisal for an attack on two
Nazi officers, also found himself in the public gaze. After the war
Achenback had become adviser to industrial millionaires in the
Ruhr.

At a propaganda 'show trial' in East Berlin in July 1963 the
communists claimed that Globke had worked on a Nazi law for
the 'protection of German blood and German honour' and that
he had been praised by the Nazi Interior Minister, Wilhelm
Frick, for his 'quite outstanding participation in the Nuremberg
race laws of 1935'. These laws included 'the protection of the
healthy stock of the German people and the changing of family
and first names of Jewish citizens to make them unmistakably
Jewish.' All Jewish men had to bear the additional name of
'Israel' and all Jewish women the name of 'Sarah'.

Dr Globke has denied these charges, but the court in East
Berlin sentenced him in his absence to 'hard labour' for life.

The spotlight was also turned on Lieutenant-General Reinhard

Gehlen, who was chief of Hitler's intelligence staff. This Nazi was taken over by the Americans and became known as the 'United States' number one spy' abroad. At the biggest espionage trial in Western Germany since the war in July 1963 it was revealed that Heinz Felfe, who was accused of working secretly for the Russians, and who had been one of the top men in the 'Gehlen' organization, had also been a leading Nazi during Hitler's régime. Another West German standing trial with Felfe was Hans Clemens who admitted that he, too, was a former Nazi, an intelligence major with the SS who had led an execution squad which massacred three hundred and thirty Italian hostages near Rome during the war.

Also heatedly discussed at the time was the case of Dr Herbert Dittmann, a West German diplomat who was implicated by evidence regarding the mass deportation and liquidation of Jews in the East. He had become an Under-secretary of State and in 1960 was appointed ambassador to Brazil.

In February 1963 the Central Council of Jews in West Germany criticized the appointment of Dr Ludwig Martin, a member of the Nazi Supreme Court in 1939, as West Germany's chief prosecutor. Dr Henrik George van Dam, chairman of the Central Council, said that the Nazis must have considered Dr Martin a good man to appoint him to their Supreme Court. Refugees Minister in the Bonn Government, Hans Krueger, was suspended from duties after it was revealed that he was a Nazi Party official and judge in occupied Poland.

The list seems endless, but the important fact remains that there are still a large number of Nazis guilty of major war crimes who are today living and working in Germany. There are also a number of Nazi-minded young people who see the fascist movements around them as capturing the 'exciting' military spirit of the past.

These numbers are comparatively small in comparison with the vast bulk of the population who are indifferent or apathetic to racialism and want nothing better than to be left in peace to enjoy the present stability and affluence.

This was emphasized by the mere two per cent of the vote won by the NPD in the 1965 Bundestag elections. But although the climate of today is not the climate of Hitler, the fact that 658,000 Germans did vote for the evocative nationalism preached by

Thadden's candidates is an indication that there are many who hanker for something other than democracy.

That the NPD was gaining strength was demonstrated in local elections in 1966. In Hamburg the party polled 3.9 per cent of the votes, thus more than doubling its previous best in the city. At the municipal elections in Schleswig-Holstein the NPD share of the vote was between six to ten per cent. The same pattern was repeated in Bavaria, birthplace of Hitler's Nazi party.

In the late summer of 1966 the revolt of some army generals against civilian control and their subsequent resignation was yet another indication that the old school of military men are less than enthusiastic about doing away with the pre-1939 Prussian spirit.

Coinciding with the rise in the support of the NPD came a new wave of anti-semitic and anti-democratic incidents. A Jewish community office in Berlin was blasted by a bomb; gravestones in Jewish cemeteries in several towns and cities were overturned and swastikas painted on walls. In Rendsburg a memorial to Germany's war dead was damaged.

The Interior Ministry warned that Nazi and extremist right-wing activity was on the increase. Membership of extreme right-wing parties, the circulation of their newspapers and acts of terrorism and distributing pamphlets had trebled in 1965, said a Government report.

But despite these manifestations of a disillusionment with present-day democracy and a return to extremism, all the evidence points to the fact that as long as Western Germany is part of the new prosperous Europe, and as long as the new prosperous Europe remains an outward-looking community avoiding the excesses of nationalism, then it is highly doubtful if the men and women of Western Germany will have anything to do with a new dictator breathing fanatical extremism and promising dangerous military adventures. For the immediate future at least it looks as though Bonn has established itself as one of the pillars of democracy in the West.

CHAPTER VIII

Austria

BENEATH the calm surface of life in Austria today there is a more significant fascist undercurrent than there is in Germany.

Why this is so is not quite clear—perhaps it has something to do with the fact that the full blast of world opprobrium at the end of the war was directed on Germany, and as a result the Germans —unlike the Austrians—had to take positive steps to try and make amends for the past.

The German leaders in Bonn who took control after the war were determined to ensure that the terrible Nazi crimes were never repeated. Compensation was promised to victims and, despite the long delays, Nazis were sought out and punished in the courts of the land. Anti-semitism was frowned on officially and even fascist movements like the Reich Party had, publicly at least, to claim that its policies were not racialist.

Austria has never been in the limelight in the way Germany was; her citizens do not have to squirm uneasily as Germans do even today when war crimes trials implicate a whole generation. The Viennese do not have to face world suspicions about their political intentions, or doubts whether the Nazi spirit is really dead in the country. Its Government is not after all one of the major powers, and so Austria has been allowed to forget the murky part many of its citizens played in the Hitler régime.

Colonel Kaes, who was a member of the Austrian resistance movement, commented bitterly in May 1962 on the growing tide of fascist activity in the country. 'It does no good to minimize the damage done by the Nazis of today,' he said. 'Swastikas are being daubed up on walls, Jewish cemeteries are being desecrated and there have been numerous meetings of ex-members of Hitler's storm-troopers. The Austrian courts generally acquit war criminals, even when their crimes are proved.' The colonel explained that the state prosecutors had had to drop thirty out of forty-four cases of neo-Nazi subversion 'since there was no hope of obtaining convictions'. The two main political parties were also inclined to grant concessions to neo-Nazis, he added.

And at the same time, said Kaes, the Austrian Government 'systematically handicapped former resistance fighters.' He pointed out that even the ceremony at which he was speaking, marking the anniversary of the liberation of Mauthausen concentration camp where nearly 123,000 men, women and children had been killed, had to be privately sponsored because the Government was unwilling to support anti-Nazi meetings.

These were not simply the bitter words of a disillusioned wartime hero. *Die Furche*, a Catholic weekly of repute, had similar words to say in 1961 after it was discovered that Franz Novak, Eichmann's right-hand man and the Nazi responsible for the murder of 100,000 human beings, had been living in Austria under his own name for many years. 'A political climate had been created intentionally in Austria to the extent that any recollection of what happened in the past, and for which not a few Austrians bear a share of guilt, is being repressed. . . . Who knows here and who wants to know about the Nazi Gauleiter of Vienna, Odilo Globocnik, and his responsibility for the gas-chambers which the Germans set up in Austria?'

The journal, after analysing the political situation in Austria which had resulted in a recrudescence of Nazi activities, quoted from a 'gas-chamber' song of the Heimattreue Jugend, a Nazi organization which indicated that the memory of Nazi crimes was being cherished by a section of Austrian youth.

> 'The gas-chambers were too small;
> We shall build bigger ones;
> There will be room for all of you'

were the words being taught to young Austrians to sing as they went for their walks in the forests and mountains.

Commented the *Voix Internationale de la Résistance* published in Brussels: 'The peril of the growth of Nazism in Austria is greater than in any other country of Europe.'

Following the capture of Eichmann and his subsequent trial, Austrians were rudely reminded that at least one-third of his prominent collaborators in the 'Solution of the Jewish Problem' had been Austrian born.

One of the best known of these Nazis was Eichmann's former aide, Erich Rajakovitch, who was responsible for the deaths of over 100,000 Dutch Jews including possibly Anne Frank. This former Austrian lawyer served not only as head of the Dutch-Belgian Jewish 'special department', but also worked for a period as deputy chief of the Nazi security service in Berlin. Rajakovitch went into hiding in Austria and then the Argentine at the war's end. When unearthed in 1963 he had become the owner of a machinery trading business based in Milan which sold goods to East European countries. The Austrian Government arrested him and the former Nazi was sent to prison for some two years.

During the Auschwitz trial at Frankfurt in March 1964 it was revealed that the man who had built the concentration camp's gas chambers was an Austrian, and he recently built a church in his homeland where he had been living since the war. A war crimes trial against twenty-five former Austrian guards at Auschwitz is now expected to be held in Vienna.

A few days before this was revealed, Simon Wiesenthal, former head of the Jewish documentary centre in Vienna, said that he had given police the names of fourteen Austrians who were trained by the Nazis to gas people and burn their bodies. 'They are still alive and free,' he said.

'Gassing efficiency was taught at four schools to young men during World War Two,' added Wiesenthal. 'The leading school was at a camp in Upper Austria while there were three others in Germany.'

In addition to the fourteen men whom he had named, Wiesenthal claimed that 'many, many more who were trained as expert killers had disappeared. Some had been killed in the last days of the war, and some were reported to have committed suicide, but others were believed to be living as good citizens in Europe or overseas.'

It became more and more obvious that large numbers of men who had committed grave crimes during the Nazi period had been allowed to enjoy full freedom in Austria. These included Nazis who were responsible for the annihilation of thousands of men, women and children in Droholycz, Stryj and Stanislaw.

In November 1963 the Minister of the Interior launched an inquiry into the background of a Viennese police officer, Karl Silberbauer, who admitted that he had played a role in the war-time arrest of Anne Frank in Holland. The past of all members of Austrian police forces who served in the Gestapo or other branches of German security during World War Two also began to be more closely scrutinized, for Silberbauer had failed, as did so many others, to disclose his war service record in full when joining the police.

The proceedings against Silberbauer were later dropped as it was decided that he had played only a minor role in the arrest of the little girl whose diary is now world renowned.

The background of members of the Austrian police again came under question in June 1965 when it was revealed that an entire police battalion recruited in Vienna had played an important role in carrying out brutal 'pacification' purges and punishment operations in Poland, Czechoslovakia and Russia for the Nazis. The belief that many members of this battalion today hold responsible posts in the Vienna police caused a major stir in the Austrian capital.

Another example of a former Nazi who had been treated indulgently by the Austrians was the killer of the Jews in Vilna, Franz Murer, who had been given a leading position in a representative agricultural body.

In June 1963 Murer was acquitted by an Austrian court in Graz after being charged with the murder of Jews. Several hundred survivors from the Ghetto of Vilna protested in Tel Aviv. Wearing yellow 'Star of David' badges, they unfurled black banners proclaiming 'We will not rest until Murer is convicted' and 'The victims were our brothers.'

The demonstrators marched to the Austrian Embassy, handed in a memorandum calling for Murer's re-trial away from Graz and suggested that the judge and jury be screened for possible Nazi records.

A foreign war-time Nazi who sought refuge in Austria was the Belgian Robert Jan Verbelen who had arrived in Vienna immediately after the war. Despite requests by the Brussels authorities for his return, the Austrian Government dragged its feet over the extradition process. He was later acquitted of complicity in the war-time murder of seven Belgians by a Vienna court.

The growing tide of right-wing extremist activity in Austria has from time to time manifested itself in violence in the streets of Vienna. Explosives have been let off in front of the Italian

Embassy as a token of sympathy for the extremist terrorists in the Tyrol, and wreaths laid at the memorial of the Austrian freedom fighters have been stolen. Time-bombs have been discovered in the immediate vicinity of the Russian and the United States Embassies as well as the Austrian Parliament. Later this building was also raked by bullets from a fast-moving car.

In each case the culprits left nationalist literature and propaganda leaflets which in their virulence would have been admired by Hitler's Nazis in their days of victory.

Following the gun attack on Parliament, three young men were arrested. One of them, Gerd Honsik, aged twenty-one, was found to be the son of an officer of the Waffen SS who was killed in action, and the nephew of Ammon Goeth, commander of a concentration camp, who had been executed after the war. The others, Guenther Pfeiffer, aged twenty, and Rainer Burghardt, a student, had similar backgrounds.

At about the same time the Freiheitliche Partei Oesterreichs (The Austrian Freedom Party) demanded that a monument be set up for the glorification of the former deputy Landeshauptmann of Upper Austria, Franz Langoth. He was an SS brigadier who obtained his appointment in March 1938 when Hitler entered Linz. From then onwards Langoth never looked back. He became a member of the Reichstag, a leading light of the 'People's Tribunal' and Lord Mayor of Linz under the Nazis.

The Austrian Freedom Party has in its ranks extremists who are particularly 'nationalistically-minded' and a number of men who were former Nazis. In one of its journals, the *Kartner Nachrichten*, it attacks the men who are bringing Nazi war criminals to trial in Germany. 'There still exist among us Germans besmirchers of the German honour, who will vilify their own people in their subservience to communism. The day will come when the German people, conscious again of its honour and cultural mission, will dispatch these distorters of history to places reserved for the corrupters of the nation.'

'We should not criticize Hitler,' says the journal; 'nor should we decry his heroic endeavour to secure for Germany not only the leadership of Europe, but also the status of a world power comparable to that of the United States.'

Former Nazis of the Waffen SS have come together in the

Kameradschaft IV. Active in putting pressure on Austrian right-wing parties, these old soldiers keep in touch with their comrades in the German HIAG movement.

Various incidents showed that extremists in Austria do more than write fascist articles. A Jewish cemetery at Innsbruck was desecrated and forty-three tombstones were knocked over. Three students, Herbert Fritz, Roman Pilz and Hannes Schillinger, who were arrested in Vienna for singing Nazi songs in the Ringstrasse near the Government buildings, were charged with Nazi activities. Searches conducted by the police in the homes of the three men revealed that they belonged to a secret Nazi organization with cells all over Austria and with particularly strong support in Innsbruck and Graz.

Later, the leader of the Tyrol Avalanche Warning Service, Dr Otto Schimpp, was arrested in Innsbruck; while Thomas Bohn was taken to police headquarters in Graz for questioning. The importance of these arrests was that they gave the police some idea of the type of men who were supporting the campaign in the South Tyrol.

The Minister of the Interior, Josef Afritsch, said that Austrian courts had punished 120 young people for fascist activities, and he admitted that in Austria a certain Nazi revival had taken place. Christian Broda, Minister of Justice, also spoke about the existence of neo-Nazism in the country. Another Government official added that it was known to the authorities that terrorist groups were in existence.

Attempts to bring Nazis to court have been deliberately hampered by red tape and although 800 investigations are pending, during the past six years only fifteen cases have been disposed of.

In the March 1966 general election the Conservative Peoples Party increased its vote by playing on the anti-communist bogy and launching an anti-semitic campaign. The idea of a new 'Greater German-Austrian Reich' was aired.

With the opening of the Eichmann trial, there was a series of violent incidents provoked by extremist movements. The Austrian television service, which had been broadcasting reports of proceedings in Jerusalem, was sabotaged and fires broke out in some studios. Letters threatening death, signed by men who called themselves 'The Avengers', were sent to Mr Gerhard

Freund, the director of the service. Another letter, which contained part of a Nazi swastika flag, was sent to a Vienna evening
paper complaining that 'Jewish persecution is becoming unbearable and so we are taking action.' This one was signed 'Cell
20'. A plastic bomb was planted at the Republic memorial near
the Parliament buildings and the explosion shattered window-
panes in nearby houses. Another bombing incident occurred in
the Kaerntnerstrasse, one of Vienna's smartest shopping streets,
where a sulphur bomb was thrown through the window of a
jeweller's shop.

One organization known for its extremist views was run by a
Nazi called Theodor Soucek, who was sentenced to death by an
Austrian court after the war, but who was later reprieved. Calling
himself 'Chancellor' of the Sozialorganische Ordnungsbewegung
Europas (SORBE), Soucek claimed to be in touch with hundreds of
local and national associations throughout Europe. His right-
hand man, Lars-Erik Helin, often travelled abroad to maintain
links with international fascist movements and report back to
Soucek. The SORBE group maintained particularly close links with
the Scandinavian Rikspartiet.

Soucek, who was aided by a deputy 'Chancellor', Konrad
Windisch, was considered by the Nazi-minded youth in Austria
and Germany to be one of their future international leaders. But
to their disappointment Soucek emigrated to South Africa where
he ran into difficulties with the police and was deported. He then
made his way to Madrid.

The evidence of racialism and extreme right-wing views among
students gives the impression that there are more than just a tiny
handful who have succumbed to the ultra-nationalistic style of
propaganda so well developed by Hitler. As an example, thirteen
students' associations had to be requested by the Ministry of the
Interior to remove 'Aryan-only' clauses from their statutes. There
are, too, a number of extremist organizations for secondary school
pupils, such as Gotia and Scythia which foster racialism.

The Cartel of German Students' Associations, Germania, has
an ally in Johann Polnitsky of Vienna who co-ordinates the
activities of Austrian members. Also collaborating with this
German group is a Committee for German Union with headquarters in Vienna which aims at 'pan-Germanism'.

The 'Berg-Isel Bund' based in Innsbruck has branches in

several Austrian universities and trains its members to use fire-arms. In 1963 fourteen students in this group were arrested for supplying arms and explosives to the South Tyrol terrorists. The 'Bund' maintains close contact with fascist groups in Belgium.

There is yet another students' association group which rallies round the Sudetia movement and which is even more emphati-cally nationalistic in character than the others. It has contacts with the Federation of Youth Loyal to the Homeland and with the Association of National Students in Germany. In Austria these student bodies have close contact with Fred Borth's Legion Europa.

This Legion Europa is in fact a branch of the Jeune Europe movement active in other European countries. In addition, a number of organizations which have been disbanded by the authorities still maintain links with the Federation of Youth Loyal to the Homeland in Nuremberg.

Der Trommler (Fighting Journal of Patriotic Youth) was founded in Vienna by Windisch in 1955 before being transferred to the editorship of Fritz Danner. It is in close contact with the Tacuara in the Argentine and with de Louth in Australia as well as with Colin Jordan in Great Britain.

The tenth anniversary of the German-Austrian Federation of Nationalist Youth Associations (KNJ) was celebrated in *Der Trommler* in 1964. Windisch, who now leads his own Austrian League of Patriotic Youth (KNJ) maintains close liaison with the German Viking Youth and Eagle Youth League.

Windisch is in close contact with the Irish National Youth (INY) which publishes *The New Guard* edited by M. I. Reiss of Dublin. Articles on Sir Roger Casement written in Eire have been reproduced in Austrian fascist journals.

It is hardly a coincidence that major international fascist conferences should be held frequently in Austria. To name but one—The European People's Movement merged with the Social Organic Movement of Europe at a meeting which took place in Salzburg in December 1957. Vienna has also been the venue of several gatherings of the extremist Young European Legion.

The German Reich Party before its merger with other groups in Germany into the NPD late in 1964 had representatives in Vienna and also maintained links with the weekly *Echo* in the Austrian capital.

Worried about the lack of knowledge of the role played by the Nazis during the last war, a conference of history teachers in Vienna in April 1965 called on their colleagues in Austrian schools to 'see that their pupils should be made immune against all "Greater German" and racialist influences.'

The influence of the pro-Nazi movement in the country was emphasized by a professor at the Vienna College for Commerce who, writing in the Nazi journal *Nation Europa*, attacked 'intellectuals who welcomed the occupation powers as liberators.'

These various fascist movements have strong financial support from wealthy businessmen, both Austrian and German, and from Nazi sources in other European and Latin American countries.

In November 1964 a conference of former anti-Nazi resistance fighters in Belgium were told that 'neo-Nazi elements had infiltrated the Austrian Liberal Party represented in Parliament as well as the Turnebund Youth Society.'

Late in 1965 a group of thirty-one West German and Austrian skin-divers were refused permission by the Austrian authorities to continue a search in Lake Toplitz, in the Styrian Alps, for secret documents sunk there by leading Nazis a few days before the end of the war.

In the lake where 50,000 German-forged Bank of England notes were found some years ago, there are believed to be cases containing lists of bank accounts in Switzerland that would reveal the identity of Nazi leaders, such as Bormann, who fled abroad to re-start life under new identities.

The question asked was: 'What are the Austrian authorities trying to conceal?'

With some justification it is claimed by many extreme right-wing leaders throughout Europe that there is a strong chance of their friends in Vienna gaining in power and influence in the next few years. For unlike Germany where Nazi-minded men are usually propelled into the harsh gaze of world opprobrium, the Austrian authorities seem to have followed a policy of cloaking the fascists in their midst with discreet silence.

CHAPTER IX

Scandinavia

SWEDEN

ONCE a picturesque herring harbour, and now a thriving industrial seaport with busy shipyards and sugar refineries, the city of Malmoe in Sweden has earned for itself the reputation of being the spiritual birthplace of post-war fascism. Even today it is known throughout the Western world as one of the nerve centres of extremist activity, with a flood of Nazi literature pouring through its post office to Africa, the Americas and to most of the other countries of Europe.

But why Malmoe? Why has this city, founded in the twelfth century, become the hub of extremist activity with its spokes of fascist propaganda and ideas spreading out across frontiers, seas and continents? Not only have the men who still believe in the philosophy of Hitler flocked to Malmoe from all quarters of the globe at one time or another since the war, but it is also the home of most of the present-day Swedish fascist parties.

The answer is not a simple one, for it is partly coincidence that the city was chosen by extremists for their activities. It could easily have been any other of the country's major centres, and it is necessary to delve a little further to understand why Sweden has differed so radically from her neighbours, Norway and Denmark, in providing a modern home for the ideas formulated by Hitler in the early 1930's.

One important factor is the obvious one that whereas Norway and Denmark had the doubtful benefit of being hosts to Nazi forces during the war, the Swedes were not able to appreciate at first hand the full delights of the doctrine of national-socialism. Nor has Sweden had the salutary example—as had her neighbours—of seeing compatriots who believe in Nazism co-operate with an invading army and turn traitor on their fellow citizens.

Neo-Nazism is shunned by nearly everyone in Norway and

Denmark and its propagators meet with outright opposition from most people in these two countries. But the situation in Sweden is somewhat different. Unlike her two Scandinavian neighbours, the country has traditionally been bound up with Germany by close intellectual and commercial ties, and the connection with forces of Nazism can be traced back to the early 'twenties. In all, Sweden has produced more than ninety Nazi and crypto-Nazi bodies of varying size and importance including present-day organizations and splinter groups. One such movement was the Swedish National Socialist Party started up at Upsala University in the early days of Hitler in 1930.

Before World War Two these home-bred admirers of Hitler— who included a number of army officers—were mainly concerned with supporting the development of the German Nazi Party and its seizure of power in the Fatherland. They emulated their heroes by carrying out anti-semitic campaigns and even planned to grab power in their own land. Quick to seize on potential allies wherever they could, the Germans assiduously wooed their northern neighbours with money and moral encouragement. Journals, books and news-sheets destined for the edification of Swedes were printed in Berlin, and every effort was made to keep up and develop contacts throughout the country.

In July 1963 Swedes with access to the files of Nazi Germany discovered that Colonel Stig Wennerstroem, the Swedish Air Force colonel arrested for espionage on behalf of the Soviet Union, had been an active spy for the Germans during the war. He was a member of Nazi-inclined organizations in Sweden and had made repeated journeys to Germany with espionage very much in mind.

The war came and went without leaving the terrible scars so apparent in the rest of Europe. This lack of first-hand experience combined with the comfortable, but faintly aseptic welfare society which prevails in Sweden today, has produced boredom amongst many sections of the young people who are without ideals or a purpose in life. The urge to shock, to break through the dullness of their lives, is often satisfied by joining the ranks of Nazi organizations. Many of these young people make great play of their hobby of collecting war-time Nazi stamps, of parading in uniform and barking out strident commands in German. The idealistic vacuum noticed in modern society is heavily exploited by the men who dominate the Nazi movement in Sweden, and they are helped by the fact that the history of the Second World War is not taught in Swedish schools so that the young are left in ignorance of the deeds committed in the name of national-socialism.

One of these old-time fascists is the tall, thin, veteran Per Engdahl, a poet, who has been actively engaged in promoting his extremist political policies since his schooldays in the early 1920's. His war-time activities included the leadership of the Svensk Opposition, a coalition organization founded in 1941 which openly sided with the Quislings in Norway and Denmark and which wholeheartedly supported the aggressive German war policies. While the Wehrmacht was blasting its way across Europe, Engdahl contributed to many Nazi and Quisling publications and lectured at meetings.

Today, Engdahl follows the line of many 'modern' fascists by claiming that he is not racialistic, but he finds it difficult to explain away his war-time speeches and writings and the fact that his 'moderate' line is so often quite blatantly contradicted by his supporters and admirers in many countries. All his foreign contacts are neo-fascist, neo-Nazi and virulently racialistic, but Engdahl says that he does not like a man's past to be held against him.

Despite his protestations about being a man who is trying to save Europe from his bête-noire, the 'communist menace', Engdahl is forbidden to enter either Western Germany or Switzerland because of his collaboration with world-wide fascist organizations.

Undaunted by his numerous international commitments, Engdahl also runs the purely domestic party called the New Swedish Movement (Nysvenska Roerelsen). Through this movement he aims at getting a foothold in the universities of the country and has sufficiently wealthy backers to enable him to publish an eight-page periodical, the *Vagen Freemat* (The Way Ahead). A district leader and editor of this news-sheet is Yngve Nordborg, a sixty-two-year-old singing teacher and during the last year of the war an SS officer in Germany.

Composed of district federations, divided into 'circles' or regional sections, this movement keeps its membership and much of its activities under a close veil of secrecy. Its annual meeting in 1961 attracted over a hundred delegates including members of the

Volkspartei der Schweiz which, under its leading light Amaudruz, has a strong racialist programme.

Malmoe is also the home of a vicious racialistic journal called the *Nordisk Kamp* (The Nordic Struggle). This is the mouthpiece of thirty-four-year-old Goran Assar Oredsson, whose favourite dress is an old Nazi uniform decorated with a blue-and-yellow swastika armband. His movement was founded in 1956 under the name of Sveriges National Socialistiska Kampfoerbund (Swedish National Socialist Fighters' Union). It is now called the Nordiska Rikspartiet (Nordic Reich Party), has nothing to do with the modern, new-style fascism, and is quite bluntly full-bloodedly Nazi, peddling the most extreme anti-semitic propaganda. Called the 'Fuehrer' by his followers, Oredsson says that the Jews in Sweden have too much economic power and should be expelled from the country. He attacks Per Engdahl for 'watering down anti-semitism'.

Oredsson's journal, generously decorated with swastikas, proudly proclaims that it is the organ of the 'National Socialist Combatants' and carries articles from that prolific writer, von Leers, from Cairo. Understandably enough, Nasser is vigorously defended against the attacks of the 'Liberalist Marxist press'. One edition reproduced the speech which Hitler delivered at the Nuremberg party rally in 1937, and other issues quote chunks from *Mein Kampf*. The journal also carries advertisements for foreign fascist papers such as *Nordische Kultur Information* published by Otto Karl Dupow of Bad Godesberg in Germany. In turn Jordan's movement in Britain gives this Swedish fascist movement publicity in its own publication.

The Rikspartiet claims it has 15,000 members—a highly exaggerated figure—and it runs other papers such as the *Bohuslaens People's Newspaper* and *Norrbottens People's Newspaper*. Assistant editors are Sven A. Lundehall and Knut Andersson. Foreign correspondents John Alling from Copenhagen, Otto Braun of Vienna and Horst Nolte of Luneburg give an international flavour to these two publications dedicated to glorifying Nazi leaders like von Schirach who is regarded as a martyr and Rudolf Hess who serves as a 'hero' symbol.

In January 1958 a special section, headed by Allan Johansson and Sten Sundstrome, was set up in Stockholm to arrange for co-operation with foreign organizations. Close liaison has been maintained with the fascist group SORBE in Austria and with its extremist counterpart in France headed by Charles Luca.

The Rikspartiet states that it has widespread international contacts in Europe, Turkey, Jordan and Egypt, and calls for 'Scandinavian racial regeneration' and the 'breaking of the Jewish domination in the economic and cultural life of the country'. From Cairo the Government department of information sends the party racial propaganda material. And in August 1956 an Austrian 'World Union of National Freedom' was launched in Vienna under the leadership of Gelmar Fritjof, a German, in association with Oredsson.

'The people of the North must awake,' says Oredsson. 'Trust in Britain and France must be stamped out, alliances with them must end. We must help Germany to rearm.' And in 1960, to shouts of 'Heil Oredsson', the 'Fuehrer' said in the Stockholm Civic Hall (giving some respite to the citizens of Malmoe): 'Hitler is our master in the same way as Marx is the master of today's Social Democrats. I want to say that we have adopted all Hitler's ideas. In some instances we have improved his programmes. . . . If we gain power we shall expel all the Jews from this country. If necessary we shall go underground—we shall meet our enemies with terror.' Another speaker at this meeting was Robert Naslund, the party's Stockholm representative.

On the first day of the Eichmann trial, members of the Rikspartiet began a propaganda campaign putting up posters in Stockholm stating: 'We drift towards racial chaos. Our leader Oredsson needs you.' Other posters which included pictures of Eichmann were also plastered up on city walls.

Oredsson's movement has been amply supplied with funds from outside sources as well as from the man Swedish Nazis proudly called 'our millionaire', Carl Carlberg.

With funds which had been put aside with great secrecy in Sweden during the war by prudent Nazis, and with money from his own resources, Carlberg, described as the 'Swedish Hitler' before he died in 1962, helped support many of the Nazi groups in the country and made a particular point of directing his activities towards youth. His Carlberg Foundation became one of the most important centres of fascism in the country and in 1960 and 1961 young people gathered there to discuss political and ideological subjects. The youngsters were also subjected to open Nazi propaganda and efforts were made to imbue them with the spirit of Hitler's racial theories.

Carlberg, whose pet hobby-horse was 'Nordic purity', established an impressive library in one of his homes in Stockholm which included such works as the *Myth of the 20th Century* by Rosenberg; *Mein Kampf*; a large collection of Swedish and foreign fascist publications; and an extensive display of European and American pamphlets advocating racial segregation. Carlberg also ran a publishing firm, Svea Rike, in Stockholm and an illustrated Nazi paper, *Signal*, which was issued in fifteen different languages and distributed all over the West during the war. He produced hundreds of thousands of leaflets and maintained friendly relations with Sir Oswald Mosley in Britain and Maurice Bardèche in France.

In 1946 this pro-Nazi set up a relief committee for German officers in distress and wrote articles on his creed for *Nation Europa*. On one occasion he suggested that Rudolf Hess be awarded the Nobel Peace Prize.

By profession a civil engineer, Carlberg was fined 15,000 Swedish crowns (about £1,000) for having distributed in schools and universities anti-semitic pamphlets printed in Finland. His bookshop contained large stocks of left-over copies of Swedish editions of Nazi works printed before and during the Second World War. His shop and home with its extensive library acted as a shrine for both local and foreign Nazis visiting the country.

Another publisher in the same line of pro-fascist business as Carlberg is Einer Gustav Vilhelm Aberg of Norrviken near Stockholm. With no great financial resources of his own, Aberg seems to have run the Sveriges Antijudiska Kampfoerbund (Swedish Anti-Jewish Fighting League) as a one-man show since its foundation in 1941. He is backed with sufficient capital by international sympathizers and has the support of Carlberg to enable him to export large quantities of anti-semitic material.

An example of the type of literature he specializes in is indicated by one of his pamphlets, *The Truth to the People*, in which the revelations of a 'Dr Benedikt Kautsky' are reproduced.

The 'doctor', who is alleged to have spent seven years in concentration camps including three years in Auschwitz, says: 'I was in the big concentration camps in Germany. However, I must establish the truth that in no camps at any time did I come across such an installation as a gas chamber.'

Copies of this pamphlet were widely distributed in Europe, the United States and in South Africa.

Aberg has at various times been fined and sentenced to terms of imprisonment for infringing the Swedish press laws, but this punishment has not dampened his fascist enthusiasm. He maintains close contact with a Christian Arab, Antoine F. Albina, who writes racialist literature from the Jordanian sector of Jerusalem.

Despite Carlberg's death, the work of his movement went on, and in May 1965 thirty-year-old businessman, Bjorn Lundahl, was arrested with five fellow Nazis in a dawn swoop.

It was the largest police operation for many years and two arsenals of illegal arms including machine-guns and grenades added weight to the evidence that the group had been planning to try and overthrow the Government.

In the movement's headquarters resplendent with portraits of Hitler, Nazi flags and poison-gas canisters, documents revealed that Lundahl had appealed to Nasser for 'sabotage material and effective war gases with complete instructions concerning their use to be sent to us.'

'I apply for your consideration if it will be possible for us to send a small number of our men to Egypt in order to completely train them in secret agent work, sabotage and intelligence activity. This education must be communicated in English.'

Lundahl signed the document 'Svea Rike (Swedish Reich)— Legal Government of Sweden.'

It was revealed that the group headed by the would-be dictator aimed at seizing Stockholm, overthrowing the Government and setting up close relations with Egypt. The Viking section of the movement had been busy for several months undergoing rifle and hand-grenade practice on an estate near Upsala. Norwegian police visited Stockholm after it was discovered that a branch of the group had been formed in Oslo.

Also unearthed was evidence that the Egyptians had treated the venture with some interest, for a UAR embassy official held lengthy conversations with the Nazi group.

Lundahl in return for help was going to send '5,000 troops to fight Israel'. He aimed at seizing all Jewish property in Sweden and to liquidate the country's key Jews by injecting poison into them.

Later that month, two journalists who had exposed the activities of the Swedish Nazis received threatening letters: 'We have been partially exposed, but we have regrouped our leadership. The fight goes on. Heil Hitler. Swedish Nazi Party.'

Lundahl was acquitted in June. The following month former concentration camp victims who had settled in Sweden complained to the Prime Minister, Dr Tage Erlander, that they had received threatening letters.

This was not the first physical manifestation of fascist activity. Swastika-daubing outbreaks have been noticed in many parts of the country including the particularly well organized campaign at Christmas time in 1959. Seven years previously in August 1952 the synagogue at Gothenburg was desecrated.

And although it is an indictable offence to spread propaganda derogatory to any racial or religious group in Sweden, anti-semitic propaganda was contained in two broadcasts made over the state radio in 1963. In one programme a man who expressed anti-semitic views was allowed to remain anonymous, but Stockholm papers said that he was a notorious Swedish Nazi who deserted from the Swedish army during the Second World War and joined the Hitler SS corps, in which he obtained a commission.

In the programme, the man said it was not proved that the Jews were persecuted in Hitler's Germany, and claimed that reports of 6,000,000 Jews murdered in concentration camps was 'Jewish propaganda'.

Among other Nazi groups is the Sveriges Nationella Foerbund (Swedish National Union) under Ruetger Essen, the war-time foreign editor of the Nazi daily *Dagsposten* which boasted an 8,000 circulation. *Dagsposten* was later transferred into the periodical *Fria Ord* (Free Words), which in addition to the *National Tidning* (National Newspaper), is the press organ of Essen's movement. The National Students' Club is a parallel organization to the Swedish National Union.

Other student groups which are specifically connected with Engdahl's movement are:

(1) Studentklubben Reform (Students' Reform Club) in Lund,

(2) Studentklubben Det Nye Sverige (New Swedish Students' Club) in Upsala and

(3) Studentklubben Progressiv (Progressive Students' Club) in Stockholm.

These clubs are affiliated to the Neo-Swedish Students' Union whose president is Bernt Ohlin.

Two other members of the latter group are the Nysvenska Kvinner (Neo-Swedish Women) and Nysvenska Ungdom (Neo-Swedish Youth).

Yet another students' group is the Sveriges Nationella Student-foerbund (Swedish Students' Union) with Per-Olof Ihlefeld as its leader. This particular movement was founded in 1915 and is still going strong, although its aims have changed somewhat since the First World War. Ihlefeld also runs the Patriotic Front.

The *Fria Ord*, which appeared first in 1951, claims that it relies on public subscriptions to keep going; it has for its editor-in-chief a man called Theodor Telander, and makes its opinions quite clear in articles which describe the 'victors of the Hitler war as having descended into the lowest blood quagmire of inhumanity.' This particular article was reprinted in the German-based *Nation Europa* in a special Nordic issue. Both *Fria Ord* and *National Tidning* make use of a pro-Nazi press service run by the National-ist Information Bureau or Natinform, also published from the luckless Malmoe. One of the initiators of this 'news service' was a former British RAF officer, Hilary Cotter. This war-time pilot published a pamphlet *World Dictatorship* in 1955 which was dis-seminated in excerpt form all over Scandinavia by Aberg's Swedish Anti-Jewish Fighting League.

Mention, too, should be made of Sven Olov Lindholm, who after the war was arrested by the Stockholm police and accused of having received economic support from Nazi Germany during the war. The Nordic Youth Group who publish the journal *Patriotic Youth Union* was founded in 1957 and follows the line of Lindholm's pre-war movement.

A monthly review, *Fri Press*, is also published in Malmoe by Carl M. Bergh who was a pre-war supporter of Lindholm's fascist party. *Fri Press* is the organ of the Sveriges Nationella Frihetsroerelse (Swedish National Liberation Movement) whose leader is a man called Gottfried Lilja. This journal also carried articles by von Leers.

The fascist propaganda pumped out by the various extremist groups in Malmoe has certainly made an impression on youthful

minds. In March 1964, for instance, a student was arrested in
Malmoe when he was found carrying a Mauser rifle and fifteen
rounds of live ammunition outside a department store to be
visited by Soviet cosmonaut Yuri Gagarin.

Earlier the same day a visit by Gagarin to the store was post-
poned after an anonymous telephone call warned that a time
bomb had been placed in the building. About three thousand
shoppers and staff were evacuated, but no bomb was found.

Erhard Fliesberg is another vendor of racialist works. He
distributes from Sweden to Britain and Germany the Arab
League's anti-Israel pamphlets. Fliesberg maintains contact with
the fascist organization Ordine Nuovo in Rome and with
L'Europe Réelle in Brussels. In 1957 he set up his Centre for
International Co-operation through which he channels the post-
ing of his literature throughout Western Europe, concentrating
his efforts particularly in Germany. Calling his party the Nami
Partiet, Fliesberg, a civil engineer like Carlberg, prints the *Lands
Val* (The Country's Welfare), a four-page news-sheet appearing
at irregular intervals since 1954.

Another group is the Landsbygdens Samlingsparti (Coalition
Party of the Countryside). The leader is Gunnar Dalnaesm who
publishes the *Bygdens Baesta* (For the Good of the Countryside).
Dalnaesm has made various attempts to join up with the Rikspartiet of Oredsson, but without much success.

Yet another group called the Foersvarsfraemjandet (Promotion
of the Defence) was first established before the war as the '1939
ars foersvarsfoerbund' (Defence Alliance of 1939). It is a crypto-
Nazi organization and the chairman is Colonel Alf Meyerhoeffer.
The journals which it publishes are called the *People's Defence*
and *Effective Defence*.

Under the pretext of calling for defensive neutrality this
movement and its organs have been disseminating propaganda
since 1939. It claims to have 35,000 members, but the majority of
them joined during the war years prompted by a genuine desire
to participate in the country's defence, and not out of sympathy
for Nazi ideas. The German Officers' Relief Organization collects
money for ex-Nazis down on their luck.

A further racialist publication which has appeared since 1945 is
Den Enskilde (The Individual) which has its headquarters at
Ramloesabrunn in Southern Sweden, run by Richard Hejll. A

book club, Svenska Ibot-Norden or Svenska Ibot, originates from near Stockholm and is a centre for the distribution of neo-Nazi literature. It is headed by Ernst Karl Kupfrian, a bookseller who in 1943 came to Sweden from Germany where he had been an officer in the Hitler Youth. Ibot acts as a link with Scharnhorst-Buchkameradschaft der Soldaten, a Nazi militarist book club in Germany. And lastly there is the Central Union for Industrial Freedom, an older organization set up to break strikes which became semi-Nazi over the years. The office manager is Captain Carl-Axell Laurell, from Stockholm, who has been a member of numerous extremist organizations.

ICELAND

The Swedish 'fuehrer' Oredsson opened a branch of his movement in Iceland originally under a local 'gauleiter', Bernhard Haarde, who died in 1962. The work was continued by Danish-born John Holm who now heads the Rikisflokkurinn based in Rejkjavik.

The twenty-eight-year-old Holm is in close league with German-born Swedish fascist Walter Grun, who in October 1944 was expelled from Germany for his extremist activities.

Haarde's newspaper, the *Frjals Europa*, has now given way to the *Mjolnir* published by Holm. Many of the articles published in this journal are culled from the *Deutsche National Zeitung* (Germany), the *Foedrelandet* (Denmark) and the *Nordisk Kamp* (Sweden).

DENMARK

Unlike Sweden, where fascism has been kept alive, Denmark in the days following the ending of the German occupation saw very little activity from the men who admired the teachings of Hitler.

For one thing Danes are little interested in racialism, and one of the most humane acts of the last war was how the whole population combined right under the noses of the invaders in a gigantic and highly secret operation to help the country's Jews escape from the clutches of the Germans.

But even in a land like Denmark, men who found the creed of fascism attractive began to appear on the scene within a few years after the end of the war, and in 1960 Danish police were forced to

investigate the activities of the country's Nazi Party. Emboldened
by the passage of time, the leaders of this movement felt confident
enough to demand the return of their pre-war banners and swastika emblems from the police, and they complained bitterly when
this request was turned down.

In January 1961 the leader of the Danish Nazi Party, fifty-five-
year-old language teacher Sven Salicath, was sent to prison for
twenty days after being charged with offences against the
country's laws protecting racial minorities. By this date fascist
activities had been noticed for several years in Denmark. As early
as 1950 there was a meeting of 300 Danish SS men in Copenhagen where speakers told the gathering that Hitler was 'the
greatest creator and personality of our time'. Followers at the
meeting were also asked to repeat an oath of allegiance to Hitler.
And in 1953, as in 1960, there was an outbreak of swastika-
daubing in the country—memorials for patriots who died in the
war were painted over with the Nazi sign and fascist slogans.

During the past decade Danish extremists have held frequent
meetings where Nazi songs are sung and where traditional Hitler
salutes are freely swopped. Particularly close contacts have been
maintained with Mosley's Union Movement in Great Britain,
and Salicath's men also keep in touch with the extremist groups
in other Scandinavian countries.

The Danish Nazis dress in black boots and brown shirts, and
make a point of attracting support from young people by organizing 'schools' where philosophy, racialism and politics with a
peculiarly right-wing slant are studied. The man who is chiefly
concerned in this youth activity is a former SS officer Wagner
Christensen. Another Dane in the forefront of the Nazi movement in the country is Conrad Maier-Jensen who is particularly
concerned with keeping in touch with the Malmoe International.
But the most prominent figures are John Alling and Sven Salicath
—the latter edits the *Foedrelandet* (The Fatherland), the journal
of the Danish National-Socialist Labour Party (DNSAP).

This magazine calls for the 'economic and moral purification of
the Danish people on the basis of Nordic culture and pure race
principles'. It demands that its members carry on their fight
under the swastika banner—'that free and great symbol of our
co-operation with the other Nordic German people to whom we
are linked by ties of blood.' One edition of the *Foedrelandet*

carried a feature on the 'Protocols of the Elders of Zion', described as 'one of the most important documents for the modern historian'.

Besides being racialist in tone, *The Fatherland* is also anti-American and anti-communist. It was started up in 1951 under the title *Hagekorset* (The Crooked Cross). In the following year it took over the name of the pre-war Nazi journal *Foedrelandet*. Normally appearing monthly, it carries articles by foreigners including a Tom Graham of Sydney and Charles J. Schreiber, head of the Christian Patriotic Rally of Reseda, California. It also publishes articles supplied by the World Truth League of Jerusalem from Jordan. One such piece was entitled the 'Tragedy of Palestine'. Advertisements for German extremist publications also appear in this journal.

Foedrelandet served during the war as a propaganda instrument for the Nazis and their Danish supporters with some success, for 6,000 Danes joined the Waffen SS. But with the collapse of Hitler it was forced to cease publication until it was revived seven years later. Now it feels confident enough to make great play of commemorating Hitler's birthday with special issues. And like many other Nazi publications, and as though it were following some internationally laid down line, the paper tries very hard to minimize the horrors of the Nazi régime, and in particular claims that the number of Jews who died in concentration camps is grossly exaggerated.

The programme of the party, set out in its journal, is a five-point one: 'Denmark's honour; freedom and right; anti-democracy; anti-Jew and anti-communist.'

One of its contributors is Kai Normann of Norway who writes articles glorifying the activities of Quisling. Normann also writes for Swedish journals like *Nordisk Kamp* and considers himself a poet, having written verses praising German motherhood.

The Danish fascists pay particular attention to their international connections. Arthur Kielsen is a member of the European Social Movement while John Alling, who is also closely connected with the Malmoe group, is head of the Scandinavian Friendship Union which maintained close liaison with von Leers in Cairo. In May 1965 a new Nazi party under Bengt Irlov was launched in Copenhagen. The leader of the youth section of this National Socialist Party is a certain Arne Olsen.

Another publication which appears each month in Denmark is called simply 9 *April*. The title is derived from that date in 1940 when the Germans invaded Denmark. The paper explains that its movement has 'proof' that a secret agreement existed between the two countries which justified every form of collaboration during the war. Its politics are very similar to those of Poujade in France and it fights against the financial system now in existence in Denmark. The main figures in this movement are Jon Galster and Folke Trier Hansen, the director of an agricultural school.

As well as these openly fascist groups, war-time Nazis in the League of the former SS Volunteers and the leaders of the collaborators who were prosecuted after 1945 have concentrated their efforts since then in the economic and social spheres. There is, for example, the Union of Danish Front Fighters and the Norwegian League for Social Reconstruction who tried to obtain 'restitution' for the punishment their members received for war crimes.

NORWAY

In Norway, the home of Vidkun Quisling, whose name has passed into the West's vocabulary as synonymous with traitor, strenuous efforts have been made by local Nazis to try to clear the reputation of their infamous leader. In the October 1956 issue of *Nation Europa*, Helge Gronstad claimed that 'a team of world-famous Swedish professors of international and criminal law had given the view that Quisling had been denied justice and made a victim of repressed hate.'

Gronstad, who is secretary-general of the Forbundet movement, also claims bitterly that the Norwegian Parliament—the Storting—refuses to investigate and debate the claims made by these 'professors'.

The aim of the Forbundet is to make every endeavour to secure a 'revision of false judgements' against Quisling. Its members want him to be accepted as an honourable man and his pro-Nazi friends, who were punished by the courts after the war, to be fully reintegrated into society.

One effort to revive the pre-war Nasjonal Samling—the name of Quisling's fascist party which claimed at its peak a membership of 100,000—occurred in Oslo in May 1949 when the seventy-two-year-old lawyer Dr O. Lindheim issued a pamphlet saying that Hitler was the 'saviour of our country' and that the movement would continue with its policy based on 'International Fascism'.

The weekly journal of the Norwegian fascist party is called *Folk og Land* (People and Country) and the leader of the local branch of the Malmoe International is led by Einar Joentvedt. The membership of Nazi groups in the country consists mainly of former Quisling supporters and some young people who have been attracted to their ranks. In March 1964 Norwegian police unearthed a weapons hoard, including ten sten guns and forty pistols, which had been stolen by a Nazi group of nine youths. The police said that the youths, between seventeen and twenty, had formed a secret political movement, swore an oath to their twenty-year-old 'Fuehrer', brought loaded pistols to meetings and sang the Nazi Horst-Wessel song.

Meetings were held in a war-time German bunker, said the authorities, who discovered that a forty-year-old former Norwegian Nazi had 'advised' the young men.

The leader of the band called himself Reichs-Kommander Hess and on the premises were found Nazi emblems and literature.

On a different level, an incident which involved the Norwegian Minister of Justice, Jens Hauge, in 1955, gave an indication of how great is the interest shown by international fascist groups in each other's affairs. The Minister's downfall followed an appeal made by 183 civil servants who had been Nazi sympathizers during the war and who had been suspended from duty after the German collapse. These men claimed compensation for lost salaries—a claim which was backed by Hauge. Parliament rejected this move and Hauge resigned—a fact immediately seized upon by Mosley's British journal *Union* in November 1955. It praised the Norwegian Minister's 'political courage and foresight in opposing the vicious treatment of former members of the Nasjonal Samling, and went on to add that 'the enmities between Europeans should cease immediately. The enemy is now communism against which the Nasjonal Samling had a great record.'

Norway has also been the scene of international activity and *Folk og Land* spoke on one occasion of a project to organize a world congress of 'the victims of post-war persecution of all lands'. By this, of course, is meant men who had been imprisoned or who had escaped justice for the crimes they committed during the war years.

FINLAND

In Finland there is also some extremist activity among fascist organizations, such as the Finlands Nationella Ungdom (a youth organization) and Suomen Sociallinen Liike, one of whose leaders is C. Sillanpaeae. There is also the Finnish Association of Swedish Volunteers. Chairman of this group is former Colonel A. G. Nordsvan who served in the German Army.

CHAPTER X

Switzerland

IN THE days before the Second World War every conceivable method was employed to undermine the loyalty of the citizens of countries neighbouring Germany. And what better target was there than Switzerland, where large numbers of German-speaking people lived within yodelling distance of the frontier?

The situation for the Nazis was simplified by the fact that many of these German-speaking Swiss felt a natural sympathy—born of using the same tongue—with their German cousins in the Fatherland. Before the war admirers of Hitler in the various Swiss national-socialist organizations were actively plotting to incorporate Switzerland's military and civil powers into the Reich.

A Lucerne judge, in a summing-up following the trial of a fascist, commented: 'The incorporation of Switzerland into the Greater Teuton Reich was planned in the main office of the SS after 1940 by the Section Switzerland.'

After the war a number of other Swiss nationals led by the founder of the Union of Swiss Citizens in Greater Germany were found guilty in the courts of offences against the State.

The thread of post-war fascism was picked up by forty-three-year-old Gaston Armand Guy Amaudruz, one of the top names in international extremist circles and a man known in his own country as the 'Swiss Fuehrer'.

Now living in Lausanne, Amaudruz joined the international fascist movement in 1944; later he explained: 'I noticed how many followers of Nazism and Fascism began to change their allegiance, and I realized that new forces had to take their place. I was convinced that both these ideologies represented undeniable values.'

Amaudruz was one of the founders of the Malmoe Movement in 1951 which saw the rebirth of post-war fascism on an organized scale, but he became dissatisfied with the 'moderate' tone of his colleagues who were trying to give the tarnished reputation of their political creed a new image. As a result he started his own more extreme group which drew up the Zurich Programme in September 1951, following a meeting in this frontier city. A European Liaison Office was set up which led to the formation of the European New Order (ENO).

Under Amaudruz this organization in 1956 published the first 'Lausanne Declaration'. A host of meetings followed until October 1962, when another projected Congress in Lausanne was banned by the authorities. A Swiss administration court declared that the European New Order was comprised of 'foreign neo-Nazi elements who glorified Nazism and fascism and who sought to overthrow democratic régimes in Western Europe.'

At one of his meetings, Amaudruz explained that his congresses usually took place in Switzerland because 'the absence of liberty in the so-called democracies allowed no other choice'. He was commenting on the fact that the West German police had banned the projected 1962 conference from taking place at the original venue in Kassel.

Little information is available about the European New Order run by Amaudruz, for the movement is most secretive and not as publicity conscious as some of the other international fascist bodies. It is known to have had close contacts with the OAS but to what extent these two groups co-ordinate their activities is not clear.

The extremism of Amaudruz was encouraged by the wave of racialism and xenophobia which has been growing in the country during the past few years.

These un-Swisslike sentiments were provoked by the widespread immigration of some 800,000 Italian and Spanish workers who were attracted to the country. Needed by Switzerland's expanding economy, these foreigners, like immigrants to Britain and France, provoked hostility on the part of many 'pure' Swiss citizens who were anxious not to have their blood diluted by inferior stock.

In 1962 the racialist National Campaign against the Alien Penetration of People and Homeland was launched by a civil engineer, F. Meier. Under the motto 'So as to ensure that our grandchildren do not curse us, we must act now,' the movement denounced the 'intolerable invasion. . . . We are betraying the future of our Swiss youth and the heritage of our fathers,' proclaimed Mr Meier. One could almost hear similar words from Smethwick echoing in the Swiss Alps.

The movement evoked controversy with its call for 'an immediate stop to all further immigration' and that the constitution of the country be amended so that 'foreigners shall never exceed three per cent of the native population'.

In May 1965 a Swiss journalist writing in a Basle journal commented: 'Our behaviour illustrates starkly how the dormant seeds of fascism will, under favourable conditions, spring to life.

'All group hatreds are notoriously unpredictable as to the victims on which they fasten. Today's "Italians" can easily be tomorrow's "workers" or the "middle classes" or once more the "Jews". Not that one has to despair of the Swiss future, for our nation, level-headed, politically mature and eminently sensible, has the mental resilience to overcome the temptations of irrationality. At the same time it would be dangerous to underestimate our emotional susceptibility to the blandishments of fascism.'

The history of Nazism in Switzerland is mainly connected with the German-speaking section of the community, but there have been extremist elements in other parts of the country. For instance, Bernard Fay, a lecturer on French culture and civilization at the Institute Pratique de Français, which forms part of the University of Fribourg, has for many years been engaged in smear campaigns against Freemasons and Jews. Fay was made editor-in-chief of a periodical, *Documents Maçonniques*, published under the auspices of the Vichy régime, and he earned much praise from the Nazis for his writings. He was also one of the candidates recommended to Nazi Ambassador Abetz for the post of Director of the Central Office for Jewish Questions.

Because of his close collaboration with the German authorities during the occupation of France, Fay was sentenced by a French court to lifelong imprisonment but succeeded in escaping to Switzerland where he was able to re-establish himself. It was only in 1960 that he relinquished his post at Fribourg University when his activities in France during the war were brought to light.

The OAS also made its influence felt in the country and in

February 1964 three men were arrested and imprisoned following the burning down of two military installations and the blowing up of a villa and sawmill in the Jura area. The organization behind these terrorist attacks was the extremist Jura Liberation Front which had been campaigning actively for provincial independence for the French-speaking Jura area from the predominantly German language Canton of Berne.

Following the renewal of some nationalistic activities in Germany at the end of the war, Switzerland became one of the main centres of fascist publishing activities.

Défense de l'Europe, an extremist journal which published articles reminiscent of pre-war Nazi propaganda, made its appearance in Lausanne. There was also the *Neue Politik*, a German-language paper published in Basle. It spread Nazi propaganda not only in Switzerland but also in the American zone of Germany where hundreds of thousands of copies were distributed. The British, in their zone, prohibited the sale of the paper because of its racialist character. This *Neue Politik* conducted a vigorous campaign against the 'terrible treatment' meted out to the Germans. A Swiss Protestant pastor, Dr Karl Neck, wrote a book on the *Resurrection of Germany* in which he expressed the hope that there would be a Nazi revival. Dr Neck declared his faith in Adolf Hitler who was 'brave and faithful unto death'.

The publisher and editor of *Neue Politik*, Dr Wilhelm Frick, was the man who in November 1940 had signed the 'Petition of the Two Hundred' which demanded that the Swiss press adapt itself politically to Hitler's 'New Order'.

In the years following the war the Swiss magazine *Turmwart* published articles written by prominent Nazis such as General Ramcke. The editor of this journal was Dr Werner Meyer, an ex-teacher and leading light of the Swiss Nazi 'Front'. The *Turmwart* circulated widely in the countries to which Nazis had escaped.

Today, besides the *European New Order*, Amaudruz and Hans Oehler are also responsible for running the extremist *Volkspartei der Schweiz* and they publish two magazines, *Volksruf* and *L'Appel du Peuple*. These movements pay particular attention to maintaining contact with similar-minded bodies abroad, especially with the Malmoe Movement. Then there is the Nordic Alliance which has links with Sweden, Britain and other European countries.

In a new journal published in 1966 Amaudruz reprinted articles from the British National Party's *Combat*, Mosley's *National European* and the Sussex Racial Preservation Society's *Sussex News*. A feature, 'Is the Yellow Wave Coming?', from James Madole's *US National Renaissance Bulletin* was also published for the benefit of Swiss readers.

Movements such as the Young European Legion and a group at Winterthur keep in close touch with Austrian Nazis in the Soucek organization.

CHAPTER XI

Hungary

THE UPRISING of the Hungarians against the Red Army in 1956 and the heroism of the street fighters aroused the admiration of the Western world. And even if the rebellion was ill-advised, ill-timed and quite hopeless against the massive forces ranged against it, the deeds of the civilians who took on the Russian tanks in the streets of Budapest with their bare hands were magnificent.

A wave of sympathy went out to the men and women who fled from Hungary during this period. But there was a murkier aspect to this flight from Budapest, an aspect which has received little publicity—and understandably so. For among these *émigrés* who are now dotted over the globe, there were a number of war-time Nazis. One such man was Odon Malnasi, author of the book *The Hungarian Martyrs*, who had been a member of the fascist Arrow Cross in Hungary and who, after being brought to the United States, was later deported. Now living in Vienna, Malnasi writes for the *Nemzetor* (National Guardian), the Austrian journal of the right-wing group, the Hungarian Freedom Fighters, which is financed by Hungarians from New York and Washington.

There are something like a million Hungarians outside the communist countries and among them is a very active Nazi-minded extremist element which maintains strong links between the communities wherever they are to be found. They pour out a torrent of anti-semitic literature, express strong anti-democratic sentiments and are a constant danger to all democratic societies.

This point was driven home in March 1963 at the trial of fourteen men in Paris who were accused of attempting to assassinate President de Gaulle in August 1962 at Petit-Clamart. Among the OAS terrorists was twenty-one-year-old Lazlo Varga, a refugee from the Hungarian revolt of 1956, who was given ten years' hard labour for his part in the attack. Another Hungarian, Lajos Marton, a former member of the French Foreign Legion, was sentenced to death in his absence. And only a few days before, thirty-two-year-old Gyula Sari, also a 1956 refugee and OAS recruit, was charged with serious crimes against the State.

Among the leaders of the fascist-minded Hungarians is Lajos Marschalko, the editor of the Hungarian Nazi paper *Hidfo* (Bridgehead) and author of a book entitled *The World Conquerors* or *The True War Criminals*, published in London by Josef Sueli, which was described in the British parliament as the most extreme example of Nazi propaganda to be published since the war.

This book includes all the essential points of Hitler's teachings and claims that communism is a tool in the hands of the Jews and that the Jews are plotting to dominate the world. The book is often regarded as the textbook for present-day fascism. *The World Conquerors*, which was translated into English and put on sale in Hungarian bookshops throughout Europe, the Americas and Australia, claims that the accounts of the Nazi gas-chambers and the six million Jews who perished were all faked. The photographs and films of the death camps with their grim revelations of heaps of corpses were 'film trick photography put out as propaganda by the World Jewish Congress and similar organizations.'

Marschalko, who admits in the book that he is wanted in Hungary as a war criminal, complains bitterly about the Nuremberg trials and executions. 'World Jewry must be regarded as the sole war criminal of the Second World War,' says the Hungarian, and continues: 'It is the Old Testament and not *Mein Kampf* that must be studied in order to see that the gas-chambers were actually the invention of the chosen people.'

It is worth quoting from the introduction to this book, for it gives an insight into the thinking of men like Marschalko. 'It is our God-granted right and human duty to fight against the reign of terror exercised on a super-national level by a small fanatical nationalistic minority which has subjugated the world and driven mankind far along the road to total extinction,' says the author. He then goes on to lay the blame for the world's ills at the door of the Jews, from Moses onwards, and in case it is not known who the other Jewish leaders are, he adds the names of Roosevelt, Masaryk, Kreuger, Mann, Gide and Huxley to the list headed by the man who led the ancient Hebrews out of Egypt. Only a new, more thorough anti-Jewish crusade, he says, can save mankind: 'Anti-Jewish people of the world, unite before it is too late.'

Marschalko makes reference to old Nazi material, and also draws on articles written by von Leers in *Der Weg*, the journal published in the Argentine after the war.

Together with Ferenc Fiala, Marschalko has also written another book, *The Gallows Accuse: The Real Grave-diggers of Hungary*, which was sympathetically reviewed by the German Reich Party's weekly magazine *Reichsruf*. The two authors discuss the 'Hungarian tragedy' in this work, and by this they mean the period at the end of the war when the fascist régime was liquidated. The 'Indictment', based on the premise of fascism as respectable 'anti-communism', is directed particularly at Americans who are accused of having been under the influence of the 'communist secret organizations'. The Allies sought to 'extirpate the leading circles' in Germany and among Hitler's friends, so as to secure a free run for a final 'bolshevization'.

Again the 'martyrdom' of the executed Hungarian Nazis, who together with the Gestapo officers were in charge of the deportations of Hungarian Jews, is emphasized. The authors explain that in any case only 20,000 Jews were deported and not 500,000. And what is more, 'The Jews should be grateful for this noble treatment they received at the hands of the Hungarian people.'

Fiala, the book claims, was the 'last press chief of the non-communist Hungarian Government' and now lives in Western Germany. In fact, Fiala was sentenced to life imprisonment for his war-time activities but was freed by the Hungarian revolutionists and travelled to Brazil to edit a Nazi journal in Sao Paulo and to write another book, *Hungary in Chains*.

The magazine *Hidfo*, together with two other Hungarian fascist publications, *Cel* and *Hidverock* is distributed in more than a dozen countries.

Hidfo reiterates that it was a stupid crime to fight with Soviet Russia against Nazi Germany. What the West should have done was to have helped the Nazis against the 'Communist Menace'. It claims that the most reliable anti-communists in the West are the Nazis, and reveres as martyrs the executed war criminals. 'Communists must be attacked and destroyed immediately,' adds the magazine.

This propaganda is reinforced with the characteristic fascist argument that behind all the machinations of the communists there is a 'Jewish plot against the West and Christianity'.

This does not stop the magazine from quoting with approval the opinions of Jews which fit in with Nazi propaganda. For instance, Senator Barry Goldwater is praised for his anti-liberalism and his defence of Cuba's former ruler, Batista. Somewhat illogically, the Jews who are denounced as 'arch-communists' are also accused of being the 'arch-capitalists'.

Violently anti-American, due perhaps to the fact that Marschalko had been deported by the United States authorities, the magazine *Hidfo* joins the refrain taken up by the other fascist journals that 'Eichmann was the innocent victim of the Jewish conspiracy' and that the trial in the United States of a right-wing Hungarian officer, accused of having tortured Jewish slave-labourers, was another 'Dreyfus case'—this time staged by the Jews. This same clique of Jews, who turn up here, there and everywhere, in Hungarian extremist literature, is also accused of having been bribed by Adenauer and of being behind the enemies of Tshombe of Katanga. The late pro-fascist Hungarian Prime Minister, Gyula Gombos, and Senator McCarthy are included in the list of Marschalko's heroes, but the United Nations is called a 'pro-Communist conspiracy of the Wise Men of Zion'. Marschalko, incidentally, was the man who was responsible for propaganda during the war urging that Western prisoners of war in Hungary should be killed in retaliation for the bombing of Hungarian cities.

Hidfo shows in a small way how closely linked are these various Hungarian movements. Although published in London, it is printed in Munich. The founder and first editor-in-chief was Josef Sueli, who died in 1960, but his work was continued by his son, Levente Sueli, and Anna Aranyi. The London office of the magazine runs a lending library conducted on the same lines as similar Arrow Cross centres in many parts of the world including the USA, France, Australia, the Argentine, Belgium, Brazil, Canada, New Zealand and Spain.

Here is another quotation from the magazine to underscore the sort of line it takes: 'The reason why it is difficult to take up the struggle against the communist advance is that the directors of public opinion in the West are in the hands of sinister world conquerors whose first concern is the welfare of the Jews, their financial interest and their power position. It is in this interest that they carry out their pacifist and destructive activities against all other nations. Their cowardice is dressed up as phony humanism.'

The paper goes on to say with little logic that Khrushchev, 'the Red Tsar and an anti-semite', is 'kept on the leash by the Jews. This cunning Ukrainian knows well enough that the Jews are the best allies of the Slavonic Bolshevist world power.' (This was, of course, before the Jews "unleashed" the cunning Mr K.) In another issue of the journal the United Nations is abused as a 'world-conquering Masonic congregation under its banner of blue-and-white Zionist colours'.

'It is there that the world conquerors, the Bolshevik murderers, the spirit of the limping devil Roosevelt, the Stevenson-like eggheads and the African cannibals sit. And most of all, there sit the 2,300 leading officials of that institution, all of whom are equally at work day and night in the interests of the Israeli super-national Nazism.'

The paper goes on to say, 'The communist system has only one spiritual adversary—National Socialism,' and adds, 'a section of the Zionists and their allies, the Freemasons, plan to rule the world.' Even Castro, plus three of his ministers, the magazine claims darkly, are 'of Jewish origin'.

It is difficult to take seriously these wild and conflicting statements, but they are read and believed by tens of thousands. The theory, first enunciated by Hitler, is simple: people will believe a lie if it is big enough, wild enough and repeated often enough.

A major organ of the Hungarian Nazis is the *Szabad Magyarsag* (Free Hungary), a weekly journal published in New York and founded by the late Father Joseph Galambos of Cleveland, USA.

Galambos was the head of a small chain of Hungarian language papers printed in Cleveland which included the *Catholic Hungarians Sunday*, the oldest paper of its kind in America and the one with the largest circulation, and two monthlies, *Mindszenty's People* and *Hungarian Fortress*. This priest, before his death, raised sufficient capital to launch a major paper, and the *Free Hungary* was started in 1956. Kalman Rattkai, a former Hungarian Arrow Cross propagandist, was the first choice for editor. He was the author of a biography of Hitler, and in Budapest he edited the daily *Magyarsag* (the SS mouthpiece) in which he wrote front page editorials praising his heroes—Hitler, Goebbels,

Goering, Ribbentrop and Himmler. Unfortunately for the paper, the American authorities did not share the enthusiasm for Rattkai shown by Father Galambos and his other 'Christian' friends, and he was refused permission to enter the United States. Nor were the authorities eager to allow two other fellow fascists, Geza Alfoldi and Ferenc Fiala, into the country.

So Stephen Somodi, a Hungarian living in New York, became the editor of *Free Hungary*. And in a sense Father Galambos was not getting second best, for the man now running his paper had been editor of *Haro* (the Hungarian counterpart of the Nazi *Der Sturmer*) which viciously attacked Jewish journalists awaiting extermination in the concentration camps.

Somodi had been very active, too, in the campaign to rid Hungary of the contamination and influence of persons with 'Jewish blood' in the field of art and literature. As editor of *Free Hungary* he succeeded in obtaining the co-operation of leading Hungarian Nazi journalists and politicians who had managed to escape being caught and tried for their crimes after the war, or who had been liberated from prison during the 1956 uprising.

Marschalko writes articles for the *Free Hungary* as does Z. Fay, who at one time published anti-American works in Budapest. The magazine claims that American Jews demand special rights for themselves and that they terrorize the Bonn Government.

With the collaboration of Hungarian fascists and ex-Nazis in America, Africa and Europe, *Free Hungary* repeatedly reiterates the theme of mourning for the executed Nazis, and takes up the refrain made so often in the post-war period that the claims of atrocities committed by Hitler and the Nazis are grossly exaggerated. Again and again it condemns Roosevelt as the man chiefly responsible for the 'world's tragedy', i.e. the Second World War, and warns that men like Averell Harriman and other fellow-travellers will be placed under lock and key on the day of reckoning. In *Free Hungary* Stephen Milotay, the doyen of the Hungarian Nazi press, wrote that the Western powers doomed themselves by 'stabbing Germany in the back'.

Following the flow of refugees from Hungary to the United States in 1956, the inflammatory *Free Hungary* was sent by the truck-load to the principal reception centre for the new arrivals. However, worried about the consequences if these newcomers read this racialist journal, the State Department banned its distribution there.

Despite the zeal of the European-based Hungarian fascist groups operating from their forty-room castle in Teising, near Munich, the United States remains the principal area of Hungarian extreme right-wing activity. The main reason is that there are twenty times more Hungarians and their descendants living in America than are to be found in Germany and Austria combined.

One organization operating in the United States is the Cardinal Mindszenty Foundation which has 3,000 study groups dotted up and down the country. Directed by a council which includes three former archbishops from China and Korea, the movement concentrates on issuing educational and propaganda material on 'atheistic Communism'. Its leaders claim that the 'Reds are making propaganda to end American co-operation with such prominent Catholic statesmen as Adenauer, de Gaulle, Franco and Salazar. Instead, United States aid is directed in the direction of such bitter anti-Catholics as Tito.'

Although the Hungarian exiles in particular are bombarded with fascist propaganda, similar Nazi-style journals printed in different Slavic languages carry the ideas of Hitlerism to the various communities of East European origin. One of these newspapers, a weekly called *Srpska Borba*, is edited by a member of the National Council of the John Birch Society, Slobodan M. Draskovich. A Serbian nationalistic paper, it carries this sort of rhetorical message: 'Are the liberals worried because recent events have filled the American cup of bitter disappointment, humiliation, appeasement, containment, surrender and shame to the brim? Are they alarmed at the USSR launching a man into space before us, at Indo-China, at Cuba, at the visit to the United States of the criminal Khrushchev, at aid to Tito, and at the United States' path from defeat to defeat?'

Another operator in the same field is Alexai Jefimov of New York, a Russian *émigré*, who has written the pamphlet *Under Jewish Rule—USSR*.

The trouble-making potential of these newcomers to the United States has not been overlooked by the native-born extremists. Marschalko's book in the English version is advertised by the Christian and Educational Association in *Common Sense* and in James Madole's *National Renaissance Bulletin*. In the

South the book is recommended by the National States Rights Party.

The *Hungarian Voice of America*, which is printed in New York, has frequent articles written by Somodi, Marschalko, Rattkai and Fay. It follows the usual extremist propaganda line and makes demands that Radio Free Europe operating from Munich should employ only Nazis for its Hungarian department.

Hungarian Fortress, started by the late Father Galambos, prints articles by the same men, and at the time of Dien Bien Phu it declared that the fall of that Indo-Chinese outpost was God's punishment for the West's betrayal of Hitler. *Mindszenty's People* has even presented Marschalko with an award for his outstanding literary activity. Its fellow publications, *Cel* (Aim) of Bavaria, the official organ of the Hungarian Nationalist Party, took up the same theme with even more enthusiasm, demanding that Marschalko be given the Nobel Prize for his writings. Another Hungarian publication, the *Pittsburgh Hungarians*, a weekly edited by a former SS officer, called the American army colonel who was in charge of expelling Hungarian Nazis to Europe a worse criminal than Himmler.

Further south, in Latin America, Hungarian extremists have been as active as in the United States. At least seventy known former prominent fascists from Hungary are busy spreading their ideas and their racialism in the Argentine and other South American countries with even more enthusiasm than the German Nazis who sought refuge there. Two of these Hungarians, who had changed their names to Tolas and Kelemedi, were received by President Frondizi who was unaware of their past. Another Hungarian, Kulksar, who was head of a committee in Hungary during the Nazi régime which classified people in 'Aryan' and 'Semitic' categories, is also living in the Argentine.

These former fascist leaders have formed a Committee for Free Hungarians and have offices in Buenos Aires with branches in the United States and other countries. They have ample funds for their publications, and they work in close harmony 'gingering' up other fascist organizations—both foreign and native—in Latin America.

After the United States, Bavaria has been the most active literary centre of Hungarian Nazi activity in the post-war years. Hundreds of books, brochures and magazines have poured out from the presses there and been sent all round the world. These include the annual year books published by *Hidverok* (Bridge-builders) and other Hungarian Nazi journals; the *Hungarian*; Fuehrer Szalasi's *Way and Goal* (the Hungarian 'Mein Kampf'); *Fighting the Jewish Press* by Michael Kolosvary-Borcsa; *The Wise Men of Zion* by Laszlo Endre, who like Kolosvary-Borcsa was executed for war crimes. There are also dozens more books giving an 'objective' history of the war, as well as scores of racialist novels, poems and plays glorifying the Nazi régime.

So active have been these Hungarians in their propagation of fascist ideals that German newspapers have at various times complained about them and the West German Socialists submitted a memorandum to the Federal and the Bavarian Governments protesting about the activities of the 'Hungarian centre for world-wide Nazi Propaganda'. The chairman of the Hungarian Council in Germany, Imre Patsky, declared that decent Hungarians were ashamed of the activities of three of the Nazi ringleaders: Marschalko, Geza Alfoldi and Geza Ipolyi, who edits a Munich weekly *New Hungarian World Economy News Service*.

Despite the protests, the torrent of 'literature' has not slackened at all, and Hungarian Nazis work as journalists on many magazines financed by other nationalities. The Hungarian desk of Radio Free Europe, the most important anti-communist radio service in the world, and the station which was very largely responsible for misleading the Hungarians into believing that they would be helped from outside during their 1956 revolt, has at one time or another been staffed by Nazis or those holding fascist views.

The 'Hungarist' or 'Arrow Cross' movement in Hitler's day was run by Ferenc Szalasi who was leader of the Hungarian German occupied section of the country from October 1944 to April 1945. He was executed after the war, but his job was taken over by Arpad Henney, a former high official in Szalasi's Government.

It is this movement of war-time Nazis which has worked so hard and with some success to win the allegiance of the young Hungarians who escaped after the 1956 revolt. From their publishing centre at Castle Teising, *Cel* and *Hidverok* are sent out to Hungarians all over the Western world.

The printer of 'Arrow Cross' publications, including some books which appear both in Hungarian and English, is Oliver Ledermuller, a former army officer. He also produces a number of journals published by German refugees and other *émigré* organizations who have their base in Munich.

One such group is the ABN or Anti-Bolshevik Bloc of Nations which describes itself as the 'international organization of the united subjugated peoples' under Soviet rule and in exile. Although chiefly financed by Ukrainian *émigrés*, the military chief of this movement is General Ferenc Farkas who commanded Szalasi's army against the Russians.

Hidverok is edited by Geza Alfoldi, a former deputy Secretary of State in the Szalasi Government. Founded in 1949 it is even more extreme than *Cel* in its outlook. At first the American High Command prohibited the journal, but later they restored its license. Its main theme, reiterated over and over again, is that the 'ablest leaders in Europe (and this includes the death camp commandants) were murdered at Nuremberg by the Allies; that the Jews will be punished for their crimes against humanity, and that the so-called Nazi massacres were all lies.'

'The Jews amply deserved what happened to them in the Second World War and what is coming to them,' says *Hidverok*. 'The lie of the six million Jewish martyrs must be maintained even at the expense of a fraud perpetuated with dead bodies. Corpses are being converted into capital for the benefit of the State of Israel because they are made to serve as the basis for restitution claims.'

Hidverok receives large sums of money from Hungarians and other fascist elements in Canada, the United States, Australia and Bavaria. A brief glance at the list of signed articles in the magazine shows the international links which these Hungarians maintain. They include the former Josef Sueli, editor of *Hidfo* (Bridgehead) in London; Bela Berlinszky, editor of the *Hungarian National Youth* of Regensburg; Eugene Szebedinszky, editor of *Magyarsag*, Pittsburgh; Tibor Barath, editor of *Magyars in the West* of Montreal; Martin Kerecsendi Kiss, editor of *Hungarian Life* of Toronto, and George Olah, editor of *Hungarian Unity* of Sao Paulo.

Nazi ideology is also spread by the Hungarian Institute for Research on Modern History and Society with head offices at

Castle Teising. Its major purpose is to collect and print racialist propaganda from all over the world.

As with Baltic, Ukrainian, and other East European fascists, Hungarian Nazis have changed their names in countries like Canada to enable them to live there and carry out their political activities. One illuminating incident occurred in Montreal where Hungarians claiming to be 'freedom fighters' and shouting 'Hitler is coming' clashed with other Hungarians outside a café. When six of the brawlers were taken to court, the protest was made that, 'These people cannot come here to the peaceful streets of Canada and attack citizens leaving a restaurant threatening them with death and the coming of Nazis and Hitler.' With these fascist immigrants making their influence felt in Montreal, it hardly comes as a surprise to hear that in May 1963 black-booted teenage boys yelling 'Heil Hitler' went strutting through the streets of the city.

A large number of these Hungarians with Nazi sympathies have gone to Australia. They include Ferenz Adorian, a member of the Hungarian Parliament in the Szalasi period; Ferenz Antal, formerly a publisher of a fascist newspaper; Erno Hanvay, a distributor in Australia of German-produced Nazi literature; Bela Kantor, the Australian representative of *Cel* magazine, and prominent former Arrow Cross member in Hungary; Karoly Nesz, a man close to the executed Laszlo Endre and one of the most senior of Hungarian fascists in Australia. Several other Hungarians, who were also closely connected with the Nazis during the war, finally ended up 'down under' after fleeing to Germany at the war's end.

These Hungarians in Australia belong to a number of organizations including the Hungarian Veterans' Association, the Hungarista Mosgalom and the Hungarian Community Centre for Freedom Fighters. Each year members hold functions in honour of their former fascist leader, Szalasi.

As well as the Hungarians, Ukrainian, Czech, Croatian and other Eastern European organizations are a feature of Australian life. Their violent, extremist views were brought to the surface in September 1963 when nine Yugoslavs described as 'terrorists' were arrested by Tito's police and thrown into prison in Belgrade. The men had been recruited in Australia by the Croatian Revolutionary Brotherhood for sabotage and murder in Yugoslavia and were equipped with explosives, pistols, knives and radio, claimed the authorities in Belgrade.

At their trial in April 1964, Josip Oblak, chief of the anti-Tito 'Brotherhood' branch in West Germany, received a fourteen-year sentence. The others were also given long prison sentences.

'They are not terrorists,' said the indignant voice of Father Kasic, the chaplain for Croatian communities in South Australia. 'They are patriots.'

The 'patriots', after returning to Europe from Australia, had taken shelter in Germany where they had received further military training before being sent off on their mission to Yugoslavia.

Their fellow countrymen in Europe had not remained inactive either. For shortly before this incident, the North Rhine Westphalian State Interior Ministry said that another Croatian organization, the Brotherhood of the Cross, was 'the most radical extreme right-wing *émigré* body in West Germany.' The Ministry went on to reveal that twenty-three of the twenty-five Croats arrested after a bomb attack in November 1963 on the Yugolsav trade mission in Bonn had been members of the organization.

In May 1963 a local branch of the German-based Croatian Liberation Movement was formed in Australia with the object of setting up a Separate Autonomous Croatia. Wearing stormtrooper uniforms, the recruits under their Nazi flag, received military training in Sydney and learned terrorist tactics at Wodonga in Victoria.

The group's secretary, a certain Mr Lovokovic, admitted that 'Our Liberation Movement is inspired by Dr Ante Pavelic, the Croat Nazi chief. We are anti-communist and have reported to the Australian security services hundreds of people who have come here whom we believe to be communists.'

Dr Pavelic was the head of the puppet Croatian state set up by Hitler in 1941 and under his rule the 'Ustashas' perpetuated crimes which shocked even the Nazis. The usual concentration camps were set up. But with fanatical religious ferocity, described by Ribbentrop's Foreign Office Intelligence Department as 'a monstrous terror', between one-third and a half of the country's 1,500,000 Greek Orthodox Serbs were exterminated by the devout Roman Catholic 'Poglavnik'—as Pavelic was called.

In 1943 the German commanding-general in the area, Lutters, complained about the regular uprising against the Nazis by the

Chetniks and Tito's partisans. Their popularity and success was due to the revulsion against the 'loathed Ustashas' said the German, and he referred to the '400,000 Greek Orthodox Serbs whom the Ustashas actually boast of having murdered.'

Many local Roman Catholic priests sympathized with the Ustashas because of their proselytizing fervour and a Franciscan friar, Miroslav Filipovic, was at one time the commander of the Jasenovic concentration camp where it is believed that something like 200,000 men, women and children perished.

At the war's end Pavelic and his notoriously cruel Minister of the Interior, Adrija Artukovic, took refuge in Austrian monasteries. In disguise Pavelic reached Rome where he lived in a convent before being given an Argentine passport by a Croat priest.

His colleague Artukovic fled via Ireland to the United States where he now lives in Los Angeles a free man.

Thousands of others like him also escaped justice and it is these men who form the hard core of the 240 Croat extremist organizations which exist all over the West.

Led by Vjekoslav Luburic, who was once Artukovic's right-hand man, the Ustashas have a co-ordinating world-wide movement which operates now from Madrid where Pavelic himself made his way from Latin America. As his war-time leader died in the Spanish capital in 1959, Luburic now sees himself as the next 'fuehrer' of an 'Independent Croatia'.

This new Poglavnik works hand in glove with another *émigré*, Stjepan Hefer, who as president of the International Croat Liberation Movement also found refuge under Franco's benevolent wing.

The most active Croat groups are now to be found in Italy, France, Great Britain, Australia, Germany and the Argentine. In Finland two of the local Ustashas were arrested in June 1964 when President Tito visited the country. It was then revealed that the organization has over 100 active members in Sweden. And in the same month German police launched a nation-wide hunt for Ustasha terrorists who made an attempt to assassinate the deputy Yugoslav consul in Munich by pumping four bullets into his chest.

Like Hungarian Nazis who fled from their native land with the advent of communism, Rumanian fascists also sought refuge in the West after the war. These fanatics, too, have not forgotten their Hitlerian ideals and today they form dozens of extremist groups wherever Rumanian *émigrés* are to be found. One such body is the well-organized Iron Guard.

These fascist movements publish and sell their extremist books, pamphlets and memoirs from Madrid, Rome and Paris. One of these is the *Vatra* (or 'Hearth'). Rumanian *émigré* leaders like Horia Sima also contribute to Nazi journals like *Nation Europa.*

The various Hungarian and other extremist *émigré* publications throughout the West enjoy particularly close relations with each other. This arrangement is of much value to them for it enables their fascist editors to sustain each other in upholding and propagating their undiluted Nazi ideals. In addition the Hungarian fascists in particular make a point of concerning themselves with the politics of the country in which they live. They join the activities of local ultra right-wing groups and often supply them with funds. In France the OAS attracted many of these Hungarians and it has already been recounted that there were Hungarians among the men accused of taking part in assassination attempts on General de Gaulle.

The danger of these Hungarian and other *émigré* Nazis lies not so much in their numbers, for after all they form only a tiny percentage of the population of the countries in which they have found shelter and only a minority are extremist in outlook.

Their real threat lies in the undiluted fanatical adherence to Nazi ideology of the extremist elements among them.

With the powerful financial backing which they seem to enjoy; with their carefully lubricated international links; and with their close co-operation with local fascist organizations, these East European zealots operating behind the smoke-screen of anti-communism are today one of the most dangerous thorns in the flesh of Western democracy.

CHAPTER XII

Spain and Portugal

SPAIN

IN THEIR hundreds of thousands the sun-hungry Europeans from the north cross the Pyrénées by car, train and plane every summer to holiday on the Spanish beaches. Each year the tourist tide grows larger and larger as new resorts open up and prosper.

But the influx into Spain of the 'sixties is not the first the country has known. At the end of the 1939–45 war there was another flood of foreigners across the mountainous northern frontier of the country. But on that occasion the men who came were not seeking idle hours in the sun. The visitors were fleeing for their very lives as the Allied courts sought them out to answer for their crimes during the Nazi occupation of Europe.

In their hundreds the fascists from all over the continent made a bee-line for the Iberian peninsula to escape official justice or private vengeance. Some of these men remained in Spain—men like Leon Degrelle, who had been a top SS official in his native Belgium—while others like Eichmann and Otto Skorzeny, armed with false papers and passports, used the country as a jumping-off ground for escape to Latin America.

But it was not only German Nazis and SS men who found refuge across the Pyrénées. Fascists from other parts of Europe were also made welcome by Franco. For instance, the Rumanian Iron Guard made their headquarters in the country, and the Italian leader, General Gambara, who had fought in Spain during the civil war, also made his way to Madrid. Then there was Ante Pavelic, chief of the Croat terrorist society of the Ustashas and head of the Croatian State during the Nazi occupation, who was responsible for the deaths of many tens of thousands of Serbs. He found a haven in Spain where he lived in tranquillity until his death in December 1959. Later, Peron also became a welcome guest in Madrid.

The Government helped all these groups by organizing colleges and schools, specially tailored for fascist students from Central European countries in order to keep alive a ferment of extremism on the continent. It was to these groups of Balkan fascists, Eastern European Nazis and on-the-run Foreign Legion veterans that the OAS made an appeal in 1962 to set up an International Brigade to fight an underground battle against Bolshevism.

There is little mystery why the fascists in the days following the end of the war as well as their spiritual successors, like the OAS, flocked to the Caudillo for succour. For was it not from Spain that Hitler received much moral and physical support? Did not Franco himself pray for a fascist victory believing that the 'collapse of the Axis powers will mean my own annihilation'?

Repeatedly the Spanish dictator pledged his support for the Nazis. In June 1941 he said: 'The Axis is now a triangle as it includes Germany, Italy and Spain. Democracy and liberalism are old-fashioned in our age. The victory of Nazism is something which is evident for everybody to see. And the stupid war declarations of France and England will reach their logical conclusions, because for the Allies the war is completely lost.'

And Franco assured the German Ambassador in Madrid: 'I am convinced that the victory of Germany will enable our régime to remain in existence. In spite of the irritating declarations that the English and the American Governments send to us from time to time, the victory of the Anglo-Saxons is sure to mean our destruction. Consequently, with all my heart, I pray for the victory of Germany. And I hope that this victory will come as soon as possible.'

Not only in words did Franco support the Nazis. He sent off volunteers in the Blue Division to fight on the Russian front in gratitude for the help received from Hitler and Mussolini when he was waging his own bitter battles during the civil war.

This all happened over twenty years ago, but Franco has not changed his basic sympathies. Nazis and fascists of every calibre still find sanctuary, both officially and unofficially, in Spain. For instance, the Belgian Government makes repeated requests for the extradition of Degrelle, and each request is turned down flat.

Otto Skorzeny, the Nazi paratrooper officer who was sent by Hitler in 1943 to rescue Mussolini from prison, returned from

Latin American exile to make his home in Madrid. It is from his headquarters in Spain that he carries out his fascist activities and issues denials to charges levied on him by the Austrian Government that he helped in the development of a poison pistol tested out in the concentration camps.

Now a prosperous fifty-six-year-old businessman, Skorzeny spent some time helping the Egyptian Government with advice and support. Together with SS man Helmut Cramer, he sets himself up as an example to German youth, and the two men make every effort to white-wash the Nazi régime.

The modern successors to the Nazis, the French army colonels and leaders of the OAS, considered Spain one of their safest bases from which to operate against the legal Government of Paris. That they were not given help more openly by the Spaniards was due to the pressure put on Franco by President de Gaulle. The pressure was backed by threats that the frontier police would turn a blind eye to terrorist incidents provoked by anti-Franco activists living in France. As a result some action was taken by the Spanish authorities and leading figures of the exiled secret underground army who had received assistance from the Madrid police were transferred to the Canary Islands and told to keep out of the way.

Certain other groups of the OAS, for example that of Dr Levre, who were closely connected with the Spanish 'Integrists' and thus with Franco, were actively helped by the authorities. Jacques Soustelle, who is believed to be one of the leading figures in the National Council of Resistance, successor to the OAS, has at various times taken refuge in Spain. Later, when the secret underground army activity had slackened off, and Algeria had been granted independence, a handful of OAS men, including ex-Colonel Jean Gardes and Alin Sarrien, were expelled from Spain to Latin America.

At the time of Eichmann's capture, a rash of articles appeared in Spanish magazines and newspapers praising the Germans and lamenting the fate of the Nazi, while at the same time denouncing the trial as 'nauseating and ridiculous'. Similar articles appeared in extremist journals in other countries, but the special importance of these attacks in Spain lay in the fact that the Government, certainly until the beginning of 1965, had a complete stranglehold on the press and nothing could be said without the approval and perhaps the inspiration of the authorities.

When the Spanish weekly *SP* declared that the war had been won by the wrong side and that the Eichmann trial was a fabrication, it can be reasonably assumed that this was the voice of the Government, if not making an official statement, then at least lending its moral backing and support. In addition press reports of the Eichmann trial were superficial, as though an official effort was being made to prevent the Spanish people reading about the horrors revealed during the proceedings.

'I firmly believe,' wrote the *SP* editor, Rodrigo Royo, 'that the losers were entitled to win, and that the victors deserved to be defeated. The Nazi-fascists were not as bad as the Jews have painted them. If there was some persecution of the Jews under Hitler, then the persecution of the Nazis by the Jews since the war years has been infinitely more ferocious.'

According to Royo, the world finds itself in a sad state today because the 'incompetent victors' of the Second World War harboured 'sentiments of cowardly reprisals against the vanquished. . . . If, after achieving a victory they did not merit, the victors had shown a little generosity, the incurable evils the world is enduring today could have been avoided. But no. The victors had no charity in their hearts, no sense of chivalry, or Christianity. That this is so is demonstrated by the Eichmann trial.'

Royo adds that 'in spite of its defects Spain stands out as an oasis in a world devoid of order, justice, respect for the human person and its lack in the fear of God.'

Royo is a falangist veteran of the Spanish Blue Division and was editor of *Arriba*, the falangist newspaper.

Nostalgia for the old days of Nazism showed up in a lengthy eulogy of Mussolini written for *Arriba* by the paper's specialist on foreign affairs, J. L. Gomez Tello. Like Royo, Tello is a Blue Division veteran, and his article denounced the 'monstrous alliance . . . between capitalism and communism' for the purpose of 'crushing the only ideology worth believing in'.

In February 1965 the Spanish illustrated fortnightly magazine, *Juanperez*, took the death of Sir Winston Churchill as a fine opportunity for indulging in a little pro-Nazi reminiscing. The British leader—referred to as WC—a habit picked up from Nazi publications in other European countries—was described as a 'warmonger' and chiefly responsible for the division of Europe, the world power of Soviet Russia and the decline of the British Empire.

Another three pages of the same issue of the magazine, which is published in Barcelona, was devoted to a eulogy of the memoirs of the 'legendary' Otto Skorzeny.

Juanperez has correspondents in various parts of Europe and Latin America. They include writers who contribute to German Nazi journals, as well as the Swiss fascist leader, Amaudruz. Works by the French fascist, Paul Rassinier, are advertised and *émigré* extremists like the Rumanian fascist chief, Horia Sima, write articles explaining their creed for the benefit of Spanish readers.

There are numerous incidents which demonstrate that the ruling falangist party has not changed its fascist ideological stand. A month before the world-wide outbreak of swastika-scrawling was triggered off by the anti-semitic paintings on the Cologne synagogue, the first swastikas made their appearance in Spain.

These symbols of Nazism were also crudely painted across posters advertising the film *Anne Frank*. Some days later new bills were posted up, but on the 20th of November, the day commemorating the anniversary of the founder of the Falange Party and one of the pioneers of fascism in Spain, Jose Antonio Primo de Rivera, more swastikas appeared, this time with portraits of Hitler and the inscription 'Heil Hitler' scrawled beneath—just in case the point had been missed by less sophisticated citizens. The body of Rivera, who died at the hands of a Republican firing squad, now rests in the Escorial beside former Kings of Spain.

A month later, on the eve of President Eisenhower's visit to Spain, further swastikas and racialist slogans were painted on a number of walls. The Spanish police, although they normally keep very close watch on any opposition, let the swastikas remain —many around and on police stations. And should anyone think that this was solely the work of disgruntled German Nazis who had been living in the country since the war, the mis-spelling of 'Heil Hitler' as 'Hiel Hitler' indicated that the slogan-writing had been carried out by not too well educated Spanish falangists.

Before this, in 1957, a Spanish language broadcast beamed from Radio Madrid to Latin America made a virulent attack on the Jews and criticized the fact that some of them had the temerity to return to live in Germany.

Superficially, Franco's policies have mellowed a little recently to give Spain a more respectable image in the eyes of the West. The benefits of the Common Market are clearly to be seen, and Franco as much as anyone realizes how the economic situation of the country would be helped if her passage into the Common Market could be facilitated. There has been a slight slackening in the tight control exercised over the press, and following top-level talks between the Spanish and French Governments, the position of the OAS leaders who had sought sanctuary in Spain has been made a little more difficult, without going as far as actually expelling or taking vigorous action against more than a handful of them.

This faint liberal trend has not been to the liking of the Falange, the fascist political movement, whose members still give the stiff upper arm salute and wear their traditional blue shirts and jackboots in their club premises and at their meetings.

Considering themselves the real custodians of the Franco régime and its political doctrine, and guarantors of its continuity, they accuse Franco of 'deviationism'—a slightly ironic word to be coming out of Spain in the year 1968. In the journal which acts as the mouthpiece of the Old Guard, Luis Gonzalez Vicen, a former leader of the falangist militia and ex-member of the *élite* corps, Guardia de Franco, accused the state of sacrificing its political doctrines to curry favour with the Western democracies and thus win Spanish admission to the Common Market.

'The foundations on which the structure of the State rests are being eroded day by day,' he says. 'Nobody should be surprised if a disastrous collapse with its attendant tragedy ensues because of failure to correct the deviations now in progress which could transform the State into a Liberal Capitalist régime.'

But the extremists of the Falange movement need not become unduly alarmed. In January 1963 the International Commission of Jurists accused General Franco of perpetuating the 'intolerance and subjugation of all opposition which characterizes a totalitarian system. The State still equates strikes with military rebellion,' it was stated, and to bear out the stricture, in 1963 men were still being tortured and sentenced to long terms of imprisonment for urging strike action in the Asturias mining area of the country.

Because of the immense power of the fascist Falange and the

background of the Gestapo-trained secret police in the country there has been no need for the admirers of Nazism in Spain to start up their own right-wing extremist parties as they have done in other European countries. The Falange, with their eagerness to do battle with the 'evil forces' of bolshevism, their strong streak of arrogant nationalism, and their racial and religious intolerance, make a perfect framework from which the fascist-minded can operate. Franco himself said in 1942 that 'Spain was united with Germany and Italy in a common historical destiny.' And the Iberian dictator's brother-in-law, Ramon Serrano Suner, who was Foreign Minister in the early days of the war, was fanatically pro-fascist.

There is, however, a small movement in Spain which is affiliated to the Malmoe International in Sweden. Delegates from this group as well as falangist leaders attend extremist congresses in Europe and there have been some highly secret meetings of the international fascist movement in Madrid. Because of the strict censorship, details of these conferences are difficult to obtain, but it is known that the Spanish capital has become one of the major centres for maintaining contact between the present-day European fascists and the Nazi leaders who sought refuge in Latin America. Spanish students recently distributed leaflets in Madrid carrying extracts from articles by Konrad Windisch, the Austrian nationalist leader.

Because of the past sympathies of the men who rule Spain today, fascists are assured of a friendly welcome in the country. The welcome is now given discreetly in view of the fact that the country is striving to present itself as a modern land with a moderate face. The discretion is manifested in such ways as discouraging Falange members from openly wearing their uniforms and giving their traditional 'Roman' salute outside party headquarters. But the discretion has never gone to the lengths of modifying the basic dictatorial, anti-democratic and fascist beliefs of the men who are still in power in Spain today.

PORTUGAL

There are striking similarities in the outlook and political thinking of the Iberian neighbours, Spain and Portugal, and the basic creed of fascism is inherent in the philosophy of the rulers of both countries. Both Franco and Salazar are dictators, both of the extreme right-wing and fanatical anti-communist in outlook, while both run their countries by strict police state methods.

The Portuguese régime has been an uncompromising dictatorship since 1930 and the National Union is the sole party allowed to function. The Portuguese Legion, or Greenshirts, formed in 1936 as a para-military organization to protect the state against communism, and the Mocidade Youth Movement were both Nazi in concept. Norre Guedes, the Mocidade's founder, told Baldur von Schirach, the Hitler youth chief, in 1938 that the youth organizations of their respective countries had 'common educational ideals'.

The Gestapo-like secret police (PIDE) have been guilty of torturing political prisoners, hundreds of whom are still at the present time to be found in Salazar's jails. This comes as no surprise as the Portuguese police were trained by the Gestapo as well as the Italian OVRA. Their instructors included Josef Kramer, the Belsen chief.

Salazar's obsession with anti-communism was made clear during the Spanish civil war when he showed his pro-Franco sympathies. Despite being Britain's oldest ally with a friendship treaty of some six hundred years' standing, all official flags in Portugal were flown at half-mast when Hitler died, and a memorial service for the Fuehrer was held to which representatives from other neutral countries were invited by Salazar.

Like Spain, Portugal also attracted fleeing Nazis from different parts of Europe and some were granted asylum. But the men with guilty pasts in Lisbon used more discretion and remained out of the public eye. As in Spain, fascist-minded Portuguese had no need to set up their own specific Nazi movements in the country. They found their spiritual home in official or semi-official Government bodies.

A fanatical 'anti-communist' group called the Centurions has been set up to defend Portugal 'against the vultures and traitors from outside and within'. One of the movement's little habits is to threaten leading opposition members whose houses are marked with a helmet, dagger and the number 100. A French language extremist newspaper, *Découverte*, is published in Lisbon. Also vigorously 'anti-red' this fascist journal talks about 'African nationalists who are nothing but terrorist assassins, paid, armed and directed by the Communist International'.

The French fascists' interest in Portugal was further shown when Spanish police investigating the murder of Humberto Delgado, a bitter opponent of Salazar, announced that they were looking for Jean-Jacques Susini, a former OAS leader. Susini, already under sentence of death for trying to overthrow de Gaulle, is alleged to have hired the gang who killed Delgado. There seems no doubt however that the PIDE had organized the killing aided by the Spanish secret police.

Portugal is today nothing less than a full-blooded fascist state. There is an absence of the rule of law and the press is rigidly censored. The police can arrest and detain without trial, and torture is the accepted means of cowering any opposition. Portugal is the only country in Western Europe which refuses to allow the International Red Cross to visit its prisons.

The various meetings of fascists which have taken place in Europe during the past ten years have attracted their quota of semi-official Portuguese representatives, and Portugal's extreme nationalism has recently outshone that of Spain. The loss of Goa, and the costly colonial war being fought in Angola and Portuguese East Africa, has aroused the anger and patriotic pride of many Portuguese and resulted in an intensification of fascist feeling in Government circles. This may not be of very great significance in itself for, after all, Portugal is one of the smaller countries in Europe.

What is important is that this nationalism and bitterness is bound to become even more intense as Angola and the other Portuguese African possessions in time revolt more effectively against colonial rule. The result is likely to be that the Government finding itself increasingly isolated will turn more and more to its only possible friends—friends like Franco and South Africa's Vorster who stand firmly in the fascist camp of the Western world.

CHAPTER XIII

Latin America

STRETCHING from far north of the Equator to the South Pole, the twenty nations of Latin America, which cover an area greater than the United States and Europe combined, form a region marked by political instability and wide gulfs between rich and poor. With its swamps, its cane fields and high mountain plateaux, its fruitful coastal plains and its pampas, its deserts and its mighty cattle kingdoms, its pine trees and coffee plantations, its mixed and temperamental people emerging into the twentieth century, this continent will surely be the scene of dramatic political dramas during the next few decades. And as events in Cuba have shown, it may well become a major ideological battle-ground between East and West.

Latin America has not as yet experienced the full blast of an industrial revolution. Nor, perhaps with the exception of the Argentine, has it developed a strong middle class. Its wide variety of inhabitants have little in common except the negative quality that none has nurtured any deep heritage of true democratic traditions.

This lack of political stability stemming from weak or non-existent democratic roots is the major factor likely to make the continent the most violently turbulent area in the years ahead. The vulnerable political and economic conditions are enabling groups calling themselves nationalists to exploit the inevitable unrest by means of carefully planned and controlled outbursts of demagogy and by propounding extremist views to achieve their own political ends.

Seething with social differences and ruled by a bewildering variety of military régimes and ruthless dictatorships under the guise of popular democracy, the Latin American continent is fertile ground for mob oratory and political adventurers.

It is hardly surprising that the defeated Nazis from Germany

265

fled to South America at the end of the war, for in the previous decade fascism had made a strong impression on this vibrant continent. The origins of this attraction are to be found in the fact that there are well over a million and a half Germans and their descendants living in Latin America. And even before the Nazis took over in the Fatherland in the 'thirties, German leaders were conscious of the value of these settlers. 'In view of the bitter struggle for South and Central American markets, it is Germany's decisive advantage over both Britain and the USA that she can rely on a strong German element in these countries' was the comment of a statesman in Berlin. The refrain was taken up by Hitler's propagandists who said: 'These German settlers form a bulwark of German culture.'

It was openly admitted that under the Nazi Government every German abroad was considered an agent to be used for the 'greater glory of the Reich'. And before the outbreak of the Second World War the German Minister of Transport commented: 'In the economic field Germany is relying on the German abroad, who, directed by consulates and embassies, will be able to establish valuable contacts so as to secure orders for German industry and provide the export trade with employment and bread.'

As a step in this direction an Ibero-American Institute was set up in Berlin whose aim was to advance the appreciation of German culture and German national aspirations in Latin America. 'South America is dreading the advent of communism, which is trying to expand there in the form of agrarian communism; General Franco's victory has freed the motherland of all Spanish-speaking countries from the yoke of Bolshevism' was the line of propaganda taken by the Institute. The flourishing German private schools in Latin America were to be used for spreading Nazi ideals while German cultural groups became mouth-pieces of fascist propaganda.

German technicians, doctors, teachers and other professional men from the South American continent were invited to Germany before the outbreak of the war to be 'brain-washed' in Nazi ideology. Such a man was the Brazilian, Perry Broad, who became one of the SS guards at Auschwitz concentration camp, eventually to stand trial at Frankfurt in 1964 with twenty-one of his German colleagues for their war crimes.

The largest German colony in Latin America is to be found in Brazil where the Germans and their descendants number well over a million. Uprooted by the Napoleonic wars, these refugees came to South America and settled mainly in the areas of the Rio Grande do Sul, Santa Catharina and Parana. Hard-working and industrious, they did not assimilate easily with the local inhabitants. After 1933 numerous National-Socialist associations sprang up to express their solidarity with the Fatherland.

Not all Germans supported the Nazis, and many were bitterly opposed to the doctrines of Hitler even though the view that 'Latin America is part of Germany's proposed defence line' was an accepted part of Nazi strategy for world conquest. 'I believe in America's German hour,' said the Nazi propagandist, Ross.

Most of the fleeing war criminals, like Eichmann, von Leers and the former SS Colonel Walter Rauff, chose safety in the Argentine under the dictatorship of Peron. But many found shelter in other Latin American countries too.

At first these Nazis stayed underground, but with the growth of nationalism in South America, many of them have come out into the open. Those who decided not to return to Europe or to travel to Egypt now support the more violent and extreme rightist parties on the continent.

This may sound paradoxical, for Latin Americans claim to be ardent lovers of freedom and show a capacity for rebellion against authority. There were ten rebellions in Bolivia alone between 1942 and 1952, but usually such revolts are controlled or manipulated by the military leaders, who are in turn the puppets of the ruling aristocratic classes working behind the scenes. Occasionally the peasant, student or worker succeeds with his own rebellion as was the case in 1946 in Bolivia when the brutal fascist-supporting dictator, Gualberto Villaroel, was lynched by a mob of students and workers on a lamp-post outside his own palace.

Even though they may love liberty, Latin Americans do not realize that real democracy is not simply anarchy and violent revolution. Unlike the United States, which had Britain as tutor, Latin America was colonized by Spain, which believed in blood, wealth, honour, pride, discipline, church, but never the common man. The conquistadores brought no memory of Magna Charta or a Bill of Rights—no new faith of freedom of religion, of expression or of conduct. The priests and the conquerors who came to the new world from Spain came to subdue, not to escape religious persecution.

The Spanish rebel was no hero in the hearts of men. He was a heretic and a national disgrace. Even the great leaders of the revolution against Spain which set the South American countries free, men like Simon Bolivar, San Martin, Moreno, Sucre and Miranda, who were moved by devotion to high ideals and a vision of a democratic society, commented sadly on how little the people of the continent understood the workings and ideals of democracy.

The revolts against Spain did not change the way of life of the ordinary people of Latin American countries. Even today the Indian peasant in the high Andes and other areas is still a serf and virtual slave. The rule of the rich well-born Latin American has taken the place of the rich well-born Spaniard. Poverty and ignorance and disease did not die out. The starvation diet of rice and fish and bananas, the wretched slums, the chronic infection from malaria, intestinal parasites and venereal disease, the lack of educational facilities and medical care, have shown how little the plight of the ordinary peasant or worker has changed.

Very few Government leaders on the continent, except in the heated moment of passionate oratory, believe in the sovereignty of the people. The late President Kennedy realized this only too well when he said: 'Our enemy is not Soviet aid and trade, our enemy is poverty, despair, stagnation and the feeling that only totalitarian methods can lift a poor agrarian society into sustained growth. Our task is to demonstrate in this generation that economic growth and human liberty can evolve hand in hand.'

Despite the backwardness of the vast mass of peasants, the economic face of Latin America is in fact changing. The rural and mining economies which had come down from the Spanish colonial era are being transformed. Small villages are blossoming into big cities. Factories are being built on virgin land. The industrial revolution is beginning to take shape.

One of the principal reasons for today's change in the tempo of development is the catalyst of nationalism which has stirred Latin American countries to free themselves from dependence on world markets and given them the urge to industrialize. Until recently most of these lands were economically dependent upon one or a very small number of agricultural and mineral products.

Chile, for example, was a country of nitrates, then of copper, and Cuba's economy depended on sugar and on tobacco. Costa Rica looked to bananas and coffee; at one time two-thirds of Brazilian exports were coffee. This monoproduct economy gave foreigners an important say in the affairs of these nations which in turn led to resentment by the natives who complained with a certain amount of justification that 'Everything is owned by foreigners and Yanquis.' They cited as an example the copper industry of Chile which was owned by two great American mining combinations, while the chief nitrates interest was owned primarily by British and United States capital.

The United Fruit Company more or less completely dominated the banana industry upon which Honduras, Guatemala and, to a lesser extent, Costa Rica, Panama, Colombia and other Caribbean countries are dependent. The great American sugar combines had complete control over the economic systems of Cuba and Puerto Rico. Railways in South America were largely built by the British, telephones and electric power utilities were in the hands of the Americans and Canadians.

So dependent were these Latin American countries on the world markets that three times in the past generation they have been brought near starvation by events outside their own control. The first blow fell during the 1914–1918 war when many of them were cut off for lengthy periods by the blockade and by the consequences of the war itself.

The second time the continent suffered severely was during the world depression. This was the time of the Brazilian scandal when large quantities of coffee were destroyed to keep up the prices; and it was the same period when the Argentinians used corn and wheat in their railway engines since they could not sell these products abroad. The sugar producing countries also suffered heavily.

During the Second World War the monoproduct South American countries again found themselves facing a crisis, but this time the United States Government guaranteed them a market. As a result they did not have too much difficulty in getting rid of their products—but they did have trouble in getting the manufactured goods they were compelled to import.

Today, as a result of the promptings of nationalism, Latin American countries are going through the first stages of capitalistic development. The sudden flood of prosperity stemming from

the Second World War afforded them the possibility of developing their own industries, freeing themselves largely from their
dependence on imports and paying off their debts to foreign
Governments. It enabled them to become the masters of their
own railways and other utilities, and provided employment in the
urban areas for an increasing number of workers.

The whole continent has huge undeveloped wealth—Brazil has
perhaps the richest iron deposits in the world—and nearly every
mineral except coal is found in abundance.

For all these immense industrialization schemes capital and
technical knowledge is required, but there is a frustrating lack of
skill and money. There is lack, too, of domestic markets. And
forever hovering in the background is the pressing problem that
the vast majority of Latin Americans are living below the bread
line.

To add to the difficulties, the continent is super-sensitive
about its independence and is filled with resentment and suspicion—not without some justification—both against its own land-
owning aristocrats and military cliques. There is resentment, too,
against foreign interests who in the past as well as today have
been guilty of exploiting cheap labour and who have officially
supported repressive régimes in exchange for commercial favours.

It is against this backdrop of turbulent social and economic
change, with unchecked inflation accompanying the first convulsions of industrial revolution, with impoverished masses
struggling for bread and work, that the fascist menace in Latin
America must be viewed.

The military groups of the extreme right, with little popular
support and backed by the ruling classes who are fearful of any
change, are constantly striving to maintain their position in
society by setting up dictatorships.

These fascist-style régimes with a peculiarly Latin American
flavour are supported by former Nazis from Europe who have
never forgotten their racialist ideals and who take full advantage
of the medieval bigotry introduced by the Inquisition which looks
upon Jews as the 'murderers of God'.

It is not only against the Jews that these extremist fanatical
groups operate. In Bolivia, for example, a country which is twice
the size of Spain and the fourth largest state in Latin America,
there is a burning resentment among the illiterate Indians against

all Europeans who have ruthlessly exploited them in the past in working the valuable tin, silver and copper mines. Dr Victor Paz Estenssoro, the president until 1964, was a staunch nationalist and his National Revolutionary Movement or MNR was suspected of maintaining close links with the Nazis even before the war. His opponents accused him of setting up concentration camps.

The MNR appeals to the country's nationalistic pride, but it was under the dictator Villaroel that aggressive fascism made its greatest impact. There has been a strain of demagogic totalitarianism present in Bolivian politics for the past twenty-five years—conditions ideal for exploiting mob violence and building up to eventual complete control by outright fascist groups.

Although there are only a few thousand Jews in Bolivia, Nazi-style anti-semitic propaganda is spread extensively among the downtrodden Indians. The fascist technique of using the Jews or any other convenient racial group to stir up unrest and ferment trouble, so paving the way for the eventual seizure of power, has spread to other Latin American countries from the Argentine, where attacks on Jews, bomb attempts on synagogues and the beating-up of children and students as a means of causing fear and panic, are now almost a daily occurrence.

Even Brazil, often considered tolerant and liberal in its attitude to race and religion, has come under the racialist spell and vandals have desecrated Jewish cemeteries in Curitiba and Porto Alegre. The background to these attacks is clear, for a large percentage of the country's million-odd German population have not forgotten their allegiance to Hitler's racial theories.

These Germans and their descendants have not undergone the horrors of war which their distant relatives experienced in the Fatherland. And so the virus of militarism implanted in them in the days before the war has not suffered the astringent reaction of bitter defeat and disillusionment felt in Europe. As a result many Latin American Germans still harbour their pro-Hitlerian sentiments.

Hundreds of the Nazi fugitives are now believed to be living under false names as respected members of the German-speaking colonies in South America, and they help to keep alive the fascist atmosphere there. They include men like Kurt Wandel who broadcast anti-Brazilian propaganda for the Nazis during the war and who returned to his native land in Latin America where he was eventually arrested.

Another Brazilian of German descent, Maxmiliano Estaud Schmidt, was also jailed for working during the war for the Nazi propaganda ministry. Brazilian Jews stoned the business premises of Herbert Cukurs who they claimed was responsible for the death of 200,000 Jews while he was head of the Gestapo in Lithuania.

As all efforts to bring Cukurs to justice were obstructed by the authorities in Uruguay—whence he had fled—unknown agents kidnapped and murdered the Nazi in March 1965. A few years prior to this incident there was an anti-Jewish demonstration in the Brazilian capital which resulted in the police arresting a former Latvian subject, a notorious chief of the Riga Ghetto who was leading the riot.

A Nazi publication, *Der Brucke*, was published from Brazil after changing its title to the *Germans of the World*. This journal was once described in the British House of Commons as 'anti-British, anti-semitic, and altogether characteristic of the worst features of pre-war Nazism.'

The fascist propaganda was presented from a strong Catholic angle, but this did not stop the editor from mildly criticizing the Pope for failing to support 'Hitler's crusade against Bolshevism'. Critics of the paper were called 'agents of Satan', and among other interesting news items it told its readers that 'Russian Bolshevism and American capitalism were both inspired by the Jews.'

In the days just before the Second World War the Government in Rio de Janeiro took an increasingly anti-German stand. For the Brazilians resented the way Germans resident in the country were being used as an instrument of Hitler's foreign policy. When the country entered the war on the side of the Allies there was an immediate clamp down on all political activity.

Hundreds of German schools were closed and Roman Catholic and evangelical religious teachings in German were barred. German societies were 'de-Germanized' or dissolved and at the end of the war all persons who concerned themselves with German interests were intimidated and frowned upon.

European Nazis and their supporters made sporadic attempts to whip up support for their cause in Brazil by distributing racialist pamphlets and daubing swastikas on synagogues. One of the organizations involved in this work is called the Central Secretariat of Aryan Cavaliers.

The outbreak of fascist activity in the past few years was the first since the liquidation of the pro-Nazi Partido Integralista group in 1944. The refurbished party was defeated in the 1958–9 elections and it seems for the moment unlikely that the under-ground Nazi groups will make much headway in this multi-racial society—the fifth largest political unit in the world.

But should economic uncertainty prevail in the growing giant of Brazil, the largest of the Latin American countries with a population of 75,000,000, these extremist groups, with the green-shirted Integralista at their head, may well try to whip up unrest. For it must not be forgotten that their supporters among the wealthy German community are still numerous and active. Inflation still unchecked in Brazil is the danger sign that the economy of the country is far from stable. The revolt by right-wing elements against President Goulart in March 1964 shows just how sensitive are the men of real power and wealth in the country to any form of social or political progress.

Again in October 1965 right-wing elements in the army and among the ruling classes took action by manipulating their puppet strings and 'supported' Castelo Branco when he seized the reins of power. The reason for this military coup was their growing alarm at the electoral support received by ex-President Kutitschek whom they regard as a dangerous man of the left.

That the escaped Nazis of the Second World War are to be found all over South America was further indicated when in December 1962 it was revealed that the former SS Colonel Walter Rauff, a colleague of Eichmann's, had been working as a salesman in Punta Arenas, on the Straits of Magellan, the southernmost city in the world.

After he was arrested, Rauff was brought to Santiago to face extradition charges brought by the West German Government. The proceedings dragged on and eventually the Chilean Supreme Court rejected the demand from Bonn. As a result this fifty-nine-year-old Nazi still remains in Latin America a free man, but the German Jew who came across Rauff was warned that he would lose his Chilean nationality if he was involved in any incident against him again.

A Nazi underground organization was established at the end

of the war in Chile under the direction of a former SS man, Baron George Mapusch, who landed in the country with forged papers and set himself up in the trucking business.

He was supported by such local Nazis as von Appen, who in 1943 ran a radio station for the Germans near Valparaiso. As a result Rauff was able to find refuge there, as did numbers of other Nazis who had originally fled to the Argentine. These men had decided to quit Buenos Aires after Peron fell in 1955. Santiago has also been friendly to other fascists and their teachings, and the Ku Klux Klan is one of several organizations which has distributed extremist literature from the city.

Prior to this, large sums of money were passed to these fascist groups from Buenos Aires and a regular courier service was maintained with the Argentine Nazis. Mapusch also kept in close touch with Otto Skorzeny who at that time was also operating from Buenos Aires before returning to Europe.

The Germans who settled in Chile during the nineteenth century had become deeply involved in pro-Nazi activities before the outbreak of the Second World War. So strong in fact is the German influence there that there is hardly an important Chilean family which has no German blood in its veins. During the war Hermann G. Schuette, who was born in Latin America, made his way to Germany and became a top member of Hitler's crusade.

It is little wonder that the German radio during the war commented that 'Chile especially is a spring of strength for the German nation'. Later, another prominent Nazi, Egbrecht von Oldershausen, who was arrested by the Allied forces at the end of the war, fled to Chile where he sought refuge.

Extremist activities in the country were greatly helped by the large Arab community who had settled there. They took full advantage of the anti-semitic line of the Nazi propagandists, and the Chilean Arab newspaper *Mondo Araba* served as an organ for the Germans during the war and was blacklisted by the Allies.

At the end of hostilities and with the creation of the state of Israel the Arabs intensified their anti-Jewish attacks in their journals by means of pamphlets and with a carefully organized whispering campaign. At the same time it should be emphasized that the country is one of the most liberal and democratic in Latin America and there is strong opposition to the fascist elements and the propagation of racialist propaganda.

Chile has a long tradition of independence and advanced social thinking, but none the less two important fascist groups still exist in the country. The first is the ACHA (Accion Chilean Anti-Communist). This was at one time a pro-German secret society and was regarded with great hostility by the United States authorities during the war. Like many other fascist groups it now bears a label of respectability by pledging itself to fight 'against a possible communist revolt'. Its views have not changed, however, and its publications are vicious 'hate' sheets.

Secondly, there is the mysterious Movimiento Pro-Chile, a jingoistic group which keeps itself hidden from the public eye. It is believed to be headed by a number of retired military and naval officers.

The pre-war Fascist Party which had close links with Germany and Italy has disappeared, although many of its former members are known to have retained their extremist outlook. Slogans like 'Khrushchev killed more than Eichmann, Why isn't he judged?' made their appearance on the city walls.

In July 1964 a new Nazi party under a certain Franz Pfeiffer claimed that its membership was close on 10,000. Pfeiffer said that he looked upon Hitler as 'more than the founder of our party—he was a genius.'

The arrest of Eichmann also sparked off anti-Jewish demonstrations in Colombia, and Jewish homes, establishments, public buildings and synagogues were daubed with swastikas in the capital of Bogota. This was not the first outbreak of fascist activity of its kind. In 1946 the hand of the Nazis could be traced in the riots in the city which destroyed or damaged nearly all the Jewish shops. In 1950 there were Nazi demonstrations and unhampered dissemination of fascist propaganda in the country. Later the same year, Colombian students in the city of Medellin held a memorial service in honour of executed Nazi war criminals. They wore swastika armbands and listened to German war songs. Pictures of Hitler were distributed and the demonstrations were preceded by special prayers in the city's main church.

Even in distant Quito, the capital of Ecuador, set 9,000 feet up in the Andes, fascist slogans appeared on walls and in October 1961 a bomb was thrown at the house of the Israeli consul.

Mexico, too, considered the most 'reliable' and stable of all Latin American countries, shows clearly just how the trends towards fascism take root. Led to revolution in 1910 with the battle-cry of 'land and liberty', the country is intensely nationalistic, verging at times on almost hysterically narrow chauvinism. Forty-five per cent of the population is still illiterate and, although estates have been broken up, four out of five peasants own less than fifteen acres of land each, while one per cent of all landlords control fifty per cent of the cultivated fields.

In Mexico City there are numerous bookshops where pro-Nazi volumes and 'anti-red' pamphlets are openly on sale. This literature is expensively produced but cheap to buy and is distributed throughout the whole of South America. The country is strongly Catholic, and anti-semitism skilfully exploited by pro-fascist groups like the Sinarquista party has its roots in the Inquisition when Jews were burnt at the stake in the country. Another group is the Anti-Communist University Front, which aims at protecting the country against the red peril and is also racialist in outlook. In this same line of activity is the National Union for Country and Race who urge 'real Mexicans' to boycott Jewish shops and businesses. The Catholic weekly, *Atisbos*, made its own position quite clear when it informed its readers that 'Jews tried to get rid of Hitler in the same way as they tried to get rid of Jesus Christ.'

There is a large German population in Mexico and considerable numbers of Arabs who came to the New World from Syria, Iraq and the Lebanon. Sections of both these communities lend a sympathetic ear to right-wing extremist parties.

Peru was another country given a dose of Nazi ideology when Gestapo experts who sought refuge there helped reorganize and train the Federal Police. It was hardly surprising therefore that there was a sudden revival of fascist sentiment in the country under the military dictatorship of General Odria. Extremist right-wing opinions appeared in *Adelante*, the semi-official Government paper, and were also broadcast from the radio station.

But perhaps the land which has been influenced the most by the growing right-wing extremism originating in the Argentine is Uruguay, which lies on the other side of the Rio de la Plata and where violent anti-Jewish attacks have occurred during the past few years. Among a series of incidents a restaurant was machine-gunned, Molotov cocktails were thrown against a school and in

July 1962 a young Jewish boy had his thighs branded with swastikas.

During one of the terrorist attacks in Montevideo a bomb was thrown against the residence of the Israeli Ambassador which went off prematurely, killing one of the attackers and wounding others. The walls of the city were smeared with inscriptions like 'Juden Raus' and a wide crop of swastikas.

Large crowds attending demonstrations in memory of Adolf Eichmann included men dressed in fascist uniforms giving the Nazi salute. In August 1962 Dr Maximo Handel Blanc had a swastika slashed on his body after he was beaten unconscious in Montevideo. It was the third incident of its kind within a few hours and it was discovered that the attacks in the Uruguayan capital were being carried out by an extremist group which included a number of university students. These youths were inspired and led by the Tacuara organizations across the river in Buenos Aires.

Among fascist publications printed in Uruguay are *La Escoba* (The Broom), which claims a circulation of 16,000, and the strongly racialist *El Debate*.

These various incidents may appear as mere pin-pricks in the tumultuous growth of Latin America, but they are symptomatic of a deep discord in the body politic of the continent. In the decades to come, the rich, the landed aristocracy, the ruling classes, the military leaders and despotic dictators, except for a very few enlightened men, will certainly try to maintain their privileged place in society. They will use every weapon at their command to stave off social and economic change unless they realize the lesson of Cuba before it is too late.

Ready to back them and to take advantage of the political instability and growing tensions are many of the men who fled from Europe at the end of the war. They and their supporters see in the confusion a chance to bring about the type of world which Hitler believed in and so nearly brought about.

Their aims are to sow disorder, create confusion, bring the mobs into the streets and destroy, if they can, established order and any semblances of democracy. Their weapons are classically simple. Exploiting religious bigotry and prejudice they whip up anti-semitic campaigns and beat up Jews in the best early-Nazi style. They pose as defenders of the Western way of life against the communist menace. They exploit anti-American feeling with attacks on 'Yanqui capitalism'. They claim to be champions of the downtrodden peasants and eagerly they encourage native nationalism.

The activities of fascists in Latin America have not gone unnoticed by fellow-thinkers in Europe. In January 1964 an edition of *Jeune Europe*, the Belgian fascist paper, had a special article devoted to a neo-Nazi group called Joven America which is described as 'against Castro, Moscow and Washington'. The journal claims that the movement is particularly strong in the Argentine among university students and Hungarian *émigrés*. In Chile it feels sufficiently strong to nurse ambitious hopes of running a candidate in the next presidential elections. Good prospects are claimed for Colombia, Paraguay and Ecuador. Joven America keeps in close touch with two groups of Cuban exiles, one—the MNC—led by Aldo Rosado and the other by Santiago Gonzalez. Adds *Jeune Europe*: 'One day Latin American divisions will help us to liberate Budapest or Warsaw, just as our community of Europe will help the peoples of Latin America to liberate themselves from the capitalist yoke.'

Latin America has already thrown up one communist state in Cuba. Unless democracy can be helped to triumph in the others, there may well be a straight fight between out-and-out communism and naked fascism. And nowhere are the embryo seeds of this struggle seen more clearly than in that troubled land, the Argentine.

CHAPTER XIV

Argentina

THE CAPTURE of Adolf Eichmann in the Argentine by Israeli secret service agents and his subsequent execution sparked off a violent wave of anti-semitism in this turbulent Latin American country.

Synagogues were blasted by dynamite, Jewish shops, clubs and restaurants were machine-gunned, slogans demanding 'Be a patriot, kill a Jew' were scrawled on walls, students were beaten up and shot at. Nineteen-year-old Graciela Narcisa Sirota was hustled into a car by three young toughs, taken to a lonely field, knocked half-unconscious, stripped, burnt with a cigarette butt and endured the agony of having a swastika carved on her breast with a penknife. In the midst of her tortures, one of the attackers told her: 'This is revenge. You Jews are responsible for Eichmann's death.'

Teenage members of the Tacuara organization—whose identities are known to nearly everyone in Buenos Aires save apparently the police force—roamed the city, as they still do today, insulting not only Jews but also fellow Argentinians and sometimes shooting them up.

So arrogant have the members of this fascist organization become that they do not even bother to wear masks when carrying out their wall-daubing or their bombing and machine-gun raids. During 1962, forty-four important criminals were shot dead and another hundred jailed in the city, but despite the open manner in which the Tacuara terrorists operate, there has been hardly one arrest chalked up by the usually efficient police force under their chief, Captain Horacio Enriques Green.

Even the report of the assault on Graciela Sirota was not released for twenty-four hours; and again, after one attack by thugs on a cultural centre in Buenos Aires, police released several raiders who had been caught by the Jews, explaining that there was 'no evidence against them'. One of the Jewish youths who turned on the attackers was himself arrested and charged with assault.

Police chief Green claims that Tacuara is not a political movement and says that there is no evidence to implicate it—in spite of its black-red Nazi flag and its national socialist creed—in the wave of anti-semitism which has swept the Argentine in the past few years. Green also throws doubts on whether Graciela Sirota and other young Jews really had swastikas slashed on them, despite photographic and other evidence.

The outbreak of anti-semitism has about it too much of a ring of Hitler's Germany of the early 1930's to be dismissed complacently. The physical attacks on individual Jews and the bombing of private houses and public buildings are sufficiently well organized to give one grounds for believing that the Jews are not the real target after all. This anti-semitism is a convenient vehicle for the men behind Tacuara to stir up further trouble in a country already seething with unrest. It is against the background of political and economic crisis existing in the Argentine today that the problem of flourishing anti-semitism must be seen in its correct perspective.

Here we have a country which has known constant turmoil and no real internal peace for the past thirty years. Since the early days of the 1930's the Argentine has passed from crisis to crisis; there have been military revolts, the fascist dictatorship of Peron, rule by Junta, agitation, strikes, and currently the army, navy and air force cliques are divided into struggling factions all jockeying for power—fearful of the advent of communism and the spread of Castro's influence among the largely dissatisfied and inarticulate masses of the country's population.

The Argentine is a staunchly Catholic land and the responsible leaders of the Church have strongly condemned attacks on Jews. Hostility towards Jews is not generally found in the teeming working-class quarters of the city, but exists chiefly as an upper-class activity. Wealthy landowners, high-ranking officers of the armed forces, and powerful industrialists are the chief disseminators of extreme right wing nationalism and racialism.

It is the Argentinian aristocracy which really determines just who should form the Government at any particular time, while pro-Nazi groups have a powerful influence in the police force.

Among these various elements Jews are looked on as communists. They are also depicted as opposing social reform and it is claimed that they rob the innocent native Argentinian of his wealth.

The ruling classes are worried about the influence of Havana and have searched around for some convenient scapegoat to turn the people's minds off the soaring cost of living and the economic and political uncertainties of their lives. They are aware of the changing social climate of the whole of Latin America, and out of short-sighted self interest they wish to deflect the inevitable growth of discontent instead of seeking to remedy the causes. Certain trends in the present situation help them in their aims.

To begin with, the Argentine has a large German population with great influence and wealth. Many of the ancestors of the present settlers arrived in the country as liberal refugees from the time of Bismarck and certainly not all are Nazis, nor do they all harbour fascist ideals.

But a large number of them, as in other Latin American countries, did sympathize with Hitler's aspirations and actively supported his cause. During the Second World War the Argentine was the centre of fascist activities in South America and was notorious as one of Hitler's principal centres of espionage. Influential Nazis, with funds largely supplied by local Germans, sponsored the publication of a number of pro-Hitler periodicals. Juan Peron did not make much effort to keep his pro-German sympathies a secret.

Encouraged by the Argentine dictator's attitude, the country remained the nerve centre of all fascist activity throughout the Western world. Between ten to twelve newspapers in Buenos Aires took a strong pro-Nazi line before and during the war, and as late as 1941, 300,000 pro-Hitler pamphlets were distributed each week from Buenos Aires.

Streets in the German quarters of Argentinian cities were named after Nazi war heroes such as Hanna Reitsch, the ace flyer. Quasi-cultural societies designed to aid war criminals, for example the Kameradenwerk and Scharnhorst, a kind of ex-servicemen's organization, were founded for the purpose of distributing Nazi war literature.

But it was not only the Argentine which had its Nazi network. A Congressional Committee investigating anti-Argentine activities under the Deputy Paul Damone Taborda reached the startling conclusion that 500,000 storm-troopers, consisting of Germans and their native supporters, were organized across Latin America. They had taken the oath to serve Hitler, and to supply the funds needed for such massive military-style activity, German residents were taxed at regular intervals.

The Nazi movements were the best organized and most influential force among the Germans of the Argentine. They published a vast number of books and journals, including the widely read *Der Trommler* which was a replica of Julius Streicher's *Der Sturmer*, and ran a youth movement based on the pattern set by Hitler in Germany.

In 1944 when the Argentine reluctantly entered the war on the side of the Allies, the 60,000-strong Nazi party was disbanded. German schools were closed and the Nazi daily *La Plata Zeitung* was suppressed, but members of the pro-Hitler groups—many of whom were Argentinian nationals of German descent—went underground. They did not have far to dig to escape the attentions of the not very enthusiastic authorities.

When the Third Reich collapsed every high Nazi official, or run-of-the-mill fascist with war crimes on his hands from Germany and other European countries who managed to escape, gravitated naturally to the Argentine, soon to be called the 'last bunker of German Nazism'.

In South America there is a traditional attitude to national sovereignty and the ensuing right to grant political asylum. This attitude has done much to mitigate the cruelty towards the victims of the numerous revolutions which periodically rock the continent. And it may be cited as a reason for the indulgent acceptance of the men who crawled from the hatches of German submarines surfacing off the coast of the Argentine. But it is difficult to explain away the asylum granted to men like Dr Josef Mengele, one of the killers of Auschwitz where he personally performed barbarous experiments on hundreds of human beings and in particular on children; or to Eichmann and his one-time boss, the notorious Obergruppenfuehrer Muller; or to one of the cruellest of all Nazi criminals, Baron von Alwensleben.

Although the authorities in Bonn have tried to extradite these men and punish them for their crimes against humanity, the Argentine Government has steadfastly refused all claims for war criminals to be returned to Germany. The most recent example is Dr Gerhard Bohne, who should have stood trial at Limburg in West Germany in 1964 for his complicity in the Nazi 'mercy-killing' programme which resulted in the deaths of some 200,000 people in Germany. The sixty-one-year-old Bohne fled to Buenos Aires in August 1963, where he was arrested in the fashionable suburb of Belgrano. To escape justice he had first made his way to the Argentine in 1949 and worked for a metallurgical company. Now, although the German Government has demanded that he be handed over, Bohne still remains in Buenos Aires—as far away as ever from the law courts.

The many Germans who came clandestinely to the Argentine were provided with substantial funds from rich German industrialists and were given shelter in Buenos Aires and in Briloche, 1,000 miles south-west of the capital. One of the main centres for the employment of these Nazis was in the Naval Staff College in Cordoba at the foot of the Andes; others were at air force training establishments, in various Government ministries and in particular in the Ministry of Transport where German war criminals were employed as technical experts for the administration of such enterprises as the formerly British-run railways.

Other German 'experts' were invited to join Peron's secret police in the capital city. Dr H. Theiss, formerly of the Gestapo, with three of his colleagues, was soon instructing Peron's henchmen in the methods found most efficacious under Himmler.

The scientists and atomic research men who escaped the Allied net were pressed into service to help the fledgling Argentine atomic centre and the military aircraft industry where Professor Tank, one of Hitler's aircraft designers, was made particularly welcome. Three German Air Force aces, Alolf Galland, Baumach (now dead) and Hans Rudel headed a team of instructors for the Argentine Air Force. And the Navy thought that it could benefit from the help and advice proffered by Admiral Litzmann, formerly chief of the German Black Sea forces, despite his not very distinguished war-time experiences.

At least thirty more of these fleeing Nazis who arrived in 1947 were given jobs with their former colleagues in the Ministry of Transport.

What made these Nazis so dangerous in the Argentine was that they were in constant touch with the German population who had settled there previously. The Government itself was not unsympathetic to these newcomers and among Peron's closest friends and advisers were German Argentinians who had held senior posts in the country's Nazi organizations. Despite his public utterances about not being a racialist, the Argentine dictator showed by his private actions just where his sympathies lay. He had not forgotten his early training as a young officer when he formed an admiration for the ideals of German military nationalism. Before the Second World War, the Argentine army was trained by German military missions.

Until 1949 the head of Peron's personal secretariat was the young German-Argentinian, Rudolph Freude, the son of a wealthy contractor who had been prominent in the Nazi movement and a close personal friend of Peron. Freude senior had been a controlling officer of the Nazi secret service and was one of the most influential Germans in the country. After the war the Freudes founded the Durer Haus, a bookshop and haberdashery firm which became a centre for Nazis who had taken refuge in the Argentine.

Senora Evita Peron, the General's dynamic and highly political wife, had employed a German-Argentinian girl, Elizabeth Ernst, as her confidential secretary. An Argentinian deputy of the Radical Party, Sylvano Santander, who wrote a book about the Nazis in the Argentine, claimed that Peron and his wife had actively worked for the German espionage service.

The Nazi influence in the days following the collapse of Hitler was manifested in various ways, including the awarding of generous public works contracts to struggling German companies which had been linked with the Nazi war effort. But most important of all, this influence in high places was used to open channels for the inflow to the Argentine of thousands of Germans and other Europeans anxious to escape retribution from the Allies or their fellow countrymen. The abduction of Eichmann by Israeli commandos was a direct consequence of the reluctance of the Buenos Aires authorities to act against former Nazis who had taken refuge there.

The request for the extradition of Dr Klingenfuss, another Nazi guilty of war crimes, was one of many such demands turned down by the Argentine Government. So was the request for Jan Durcansky, who as an SS commander led German forces against Czech partisans and through whom 50,000 civilians lost their lives. He arrived in Latin America in 1947 and was given a job in the Argentine Immigration Department. It was during Peron's régime, too, that Nazis transferred to the Argentine from Switzerland and other hiding places an estimated two hundred million pounds worth of cash, gold, stocks, securities and other treasures looted during the war.

Not only did German Nazis make their way to the Argentine, but also fascists from Croatia and Slovakia, with a sprinkling of Hungarians who fled from Budapest in 1956, and who joined other fascists in the country because they were fighting 'communism'. There was also the Dutchman, Willem S. Sluyse, whom Eichmann entrusted with the tape-recording of his confessions published in the magazine *Life*. Sluyse, who was an officer in Hitler's *élite* Guard of the SS and who escaped to the Argentine after being charged with war crimes, wrote for the Buenos Aires German-language newspaper *Der Weg*. This journal, which was set up in 1947 and circulated all over Latin America and in many other parts of the world including Western Germany and Austria, constantly referred to Adenauer as the 'Grand Rabbi Adenauer'. It was so violently fascist in its crudest and most virulent form that even the Argentinian authorities were forced to act—which they did in 1957 by closing it down.

While in existence, however, *Der Weg* was a great success and drew funds from German industrialists and businessmen in Buenos Aires, from rich farmers in the provinces of Misiones and Chaco, and from Germans living in South Africa. Von Leers helped to produce it. A publishing firm called Durer Verlag was also launched and began to turn out works about the war extolling the Nazis, and pseudo-scientific books with titles like *Jewish World Domination*.

Other Nazis to be found in the Argentine in the early 1950's included the gauleiter of the Tyrol, Hans Hofer; leading fascist dignitaries like Carlo Scorza, Ettore Mutti, Francisco Giunta, Dino Grandi, and SS man Otto Skorzeny. From Scandinavia came Johan T. Landmark; Reider Nilsen and Olaf Haavarsholm joined with the former Nazi chief of Estonia, Hans Rothia, and Mario Roatta, one of Mussolini's fascist army chiefs.

Despite the presence of Nazis in the country, Peron said in 1948: 'As long as I am President no anti-semitism will be permitted in the Argentine.' But in the same year he also stated:

'Argentinian efforts to attain economic independence have been obstructed by the great combinations which exploit the world. . . . The Argentine has succeeded in liberating itself from the tutelage of the Jewish banks and foreign trusts.'

In the following year Argentinian Jewish organizations were included on a black list and their leaders accused of treason by the Peronist daily *Democracia* which had a 375,000 circulation.

The tightly organized underground movement of Nazis and their fascist sympathizers in existence in South America was mainly concerned until recently with a co-ordinating campaign among all the groups in different Latin American countries and in Africa and Europe.

For instance, von Leers, who was formerly Peron's adviser on propaganda and who until his death in 1964 worked for President Nasser, continued to collaborate in the production of anti-semitic publications in Buenos Aires. In 1959 a Federation of Argentinian German Associations was openly established. Little wonder that Dr Niemoller who visited South America after the war expressed astonishment at the attitude of the German settlers.

'I find a state of mind,' he said, 'which in Germany would at present be called nationalist if not Nazi.'

The fortnightly magazine *Deutsche Kommentare*, edited by Wilfred von Oven, today keeps alive the torch of German Nazism in the Argentine. A former assistant of Dr Goebbels, von Oven constantly expresses sympathy for Nazis accused of war crimes and also runs a book club which has on offer a vast range of neo-Nazi works.

Great anger was expressed by von Oven in 1965 over the death of Herbert Cukurs, the 'Latvian airman and SS leader murdered in such horrible circumstances by a Jewish gang. Cukurs took a great part in Latvia's struggle of liberation against the Bolsheviks and he was throughout his life a great patriot,' says von Oven's newspaper.

Readers of the journal are also instructed by articles which describe the 'Allied War Crimes' and the cruel fate of Germans in communist Eastern Europe.

The grateful Nazis who were so warmly welcomed in Latin America did not forget their benefactor. They joined the ranks of the ALN (Alianza Libertadora Nacionalista) and supported Peron by provoking riots in 1953 to distract popular discontent caused by rising living costs and food scarcities.

The explosion of violence included the burning down of the Argentine Jockey Club in which a priceless Goya collection was destroyed, while the police stood idly by and the firemen arrived long after the outbreak of the blaze. The members of the ALN showed their feelings only too closely with the use of slogans like 'Mankind kills rats in self-defence and it must do the same to the Jews for the same reason.'

When Juan Peron's corrupt régime was brought to an end in September 1955 many of his Nazi advisers fled the country, but most went underground and bided their time.

Then came the capture of Adolf Eichmann and the growth of the Tacuara and similar organizations like the Mazorea. Although anti-semitism has not yet bitten deeply into the bulk of the civil population of Buenos Aires, where eighty per cent of the country's Jews live, a sudden wave of terrorism was unleashed against the Jewish community in the city.

This racial gangsterism is led by the Tacuara youth movement, the vast majority of whose members are the sons of wealthy aristocratic families, landowners and high-ranking officers of the armed forces. Founded in 1930 by Juan Queralta, a high school student, Tacuara was evolved into a Government and Peronist organization and went underground when Peron was overthrown.

Tacuara itself—an Indian word meaning spear—is an old South American term used to refer to nineteenth-century gauchos who served the harsh dictator Juan Manuel de Rosas. Its members are now trained in military combat and indoctrinated with racialist ideology by former SS men and other Nazis on the estates of the wealthy landlords in Buenos Aires province.

In December 1962 the police forces, which are heavily infiltrated by former Nazis and their supporters, were forced to investigate an Argentinian National Socialist Movement whose leaders were punishing defaulting members and opponents by the traditional fascist method of making them take strong doses of castor oil.

Since 1960 leading figures in Tacuara have been young men like Jose Baxter and twenty-five-year-old Alberto Ezcurra Uriburu, whose father, Jose Felix Uriburu, held power in the Argentine for two years in the early 1930's. With 'Heil Tacuara' as its imitative Nazi-type salute, and its 'Patriotism yes—Jews no' slogans, the movement has nearly 7,000 active members in Buenos Aires and also supporters in other parts of the country.

Its influence has spread to other Latin American countries and to South Africa, and it claims that its membership is growing rapidly. New converts go through an elaborate initiation cere-mony in the best secret society tradition and Uriburu admits candidly that the movement's keystone is anti-semitism.

'We fight against capitalism and Zionism with one hand,' he proclaims, 'and with the other hand against communism.'

Because of their connection with well known and highly influential Argentine families, the members of Tacuara know that the police will not dare to take action against them, even if they had the inclination to do so. They are encouraged by certain fanatical sections of the Roman Catholic Church which Uriburu says is Tacuara's spiritual benefactor. He is in fact referring to the Jesuit priest, Julio Meinvielle, whose anti-semitic diatribes are known throughout the country. This dedicated father has written at length on the subject of anti-semitism and phrases like 'The Jews are the cursed race' and 'they are agents and sons of the Devil' appear in a book which he has written entitled *The Jew—a Historical Tragedy*.

'It is necessary to adopt the tactic of the sword,' Father Mein-vielle warns, and he goes on to lambast the Jews as the biggest capitalists and the progenitors of communism. 'Jews,' he says, 'started all the trouble in the Argentine and provoked the attacks on themselves. . . . Jews are striving to take over the riches of all people, to corrupt them, to reduce them to the state of slaves.'

Meinvielle was perhaps over-stepping the mark a little in his appointed task of guarding the spiritual welfare of his parishioners by delving so deeply into the murkier ends of political life. The Archbishop of Buenos Aires suspended him for three months as editor of the magazine *Presencia* for having hinted that the former President Frondizi was a communist agent.

Shortly before the Ecumenical Council met in Rome in 1962, Dr Carlos Cucchetti, a leading Roman Catholic cleric, denounced another priest, Father Virgilio Filippo, of the Church of the Immaculate Conception in Belgrano, for using his pulpit to preach racialism. Meinvielle was later ordered by an Ecclesiastical Court to apologize to army officers whom he accused of serving international communism.

Under the influence of the Iglesia Catolica Espanola, a number of private Catholic schools and universities have become hotbeds of fascist activity and racialism. It came as no surprise, therefore, when it was discovered that Juan Repetto Garrido, a nineteen-year-old hoodlum who shot and gravely wounded a fifteen-year-old Jewish boy, Manuel Trilnick, came from the Catholic college of El Salvador, notorious for its anti-semitism.

The Tacuara takes full advantage of the fact that according to Argentine law teenagers are immune from arrest for petty offences. Although its members might be the spoilt sons of wealthy men, the leaders in their middle twenties and the Nazi army officers who train them very carefully plan all their terrorist activities.

This is evident by the well organized and efficiently executed acts of bomb-throwing and machine-gun attacks carried out in the streets of Buenos Aires and other Argentinian cities from high-powered American cars. The members of the movement are made the more confident in their raids and attacks by the knowledge that they stand little danger of being arrested and brought to trial.

The Uriburu-led Tacuara, however, does not have a monopoly of all the hooligans and bully boys in the city. Jose Baxter broke away to form his own Movimiento Nacionalisto Revolucionario Tacuara and set up guerrilla groups outside Buenos Aires. In addition there are dozens of other groups all advocating—and exercising—the use of force to further their anti-democratic aims. Among them is the UCN (Union Civica Nacionalista) claiming a membership of 15,000. This movement holds the view that Jews stand in the way of national redemption and are the corrupters of Christian virtue.

Then the GNR (Guardia Restauradora Nacionalista) is particularly powerful having the support of many of the 'old and wealthy families'. Its activities are carried out in great secrecy under the leadership of Meinvielle and other extremists like Augusto Moscoso.

Some of the most violent forms of racialism are found in organizations on the fringe of the educational system such as the

Union Nacionalista de Estudiantes Secundarios (UNES) and on the University level the Sindicatito Universitatio Argentino (SUA).

These two movements aim at combating the secularization of Argentine education of which the Jews are said to be advocates. They claim that the division between the world of learning and world of theology is a 'Jewish plot to destroy the integrity of the Argentine'.

As a result of their propaganda, large numbers of incidents involving discrimination against the Jews have developed in the world of education. To give but one example: at the Villacresca Girls' High School all 750 pupils went on strike because the headmistress ordered Jewish girls to sit apart from their class mates after she had branded them as 'communist agitators'.

Before the Second World War attempts were made to blow up synagogues but it was not until 1950 that anti-semitic incidents in the streets of Buenos Aires were again carried out openly. Today anti-semitic literature from Sweden, written in Spanish, is distributed in the capital and other Argentinian cities. Racist advertisements are also placed in newspapers paid for by a 'Syrian Cultural Association'.

This body is but one of a number of extremist groups aided financially by Argentinians of Arab descent, who number many tens of thousands. Most of these Arabs are engaged in business and are chiefly of Lebanese and Syrian extraction although the majority have since been converted to Catholicism. Until the establishment of the State of Israel they were on friendly terms with the Jews of the country, but in recent years they have turned to support the growing fascist movements.

The Arab League's agent in the Argentine, Hussein Triki, admitted that he had made contacts with the terrorist groups in the country. Boasting of his heroic deeds as a fascist, Triki claimed that he had a distinguished record in the service of the Nazis during the Second World War.

In 1964 the indiscreet Triki was replaced by the Arab League after his statements were quoted in the international fascist journal *Nation Europa*.

Today the methods of the fascist groups in the Argentine grow ever more violent. The shooting of a young boy in front of the Sarmiento High School in a fashionable suburb of Buenos Aires was but one of a series of such terrorist attacks.

Molotov cocktails were thrown at a synagogue during a religious service, and a tear gas raid was made on a Jewish co-operative institute. Tear gas and home-made bombs were thrown at another house of worship during a wedding ceremony and there were numerous stabbings of young Jewish students. A bus carrying children was attacked and partially destroyed, and the wreckage daubed with the words 'Death to the Jews'.

After Eichmann's execution, a former Jewish congressman in Tucuman, Senor Abraham Rosenberg, was charged with being involved in removing from police headquarters the private dossier of a Ricardo Clement, the name by which Eichmann was known in the Argentine.

Jewish restaurants and an Israeli travel agency office in the heart of Buenos Aires was machine-gunned from fast-moving cars and eighteen-year-old Ricardo D'Alessandro was seized and branded with a swastika. Scores of incidents were reported from the Argentine capital, and from Cordoba, Mar del Plata, San Juan, Sante Fe, Lanus and Bahia Blanca.

There was a public outcry and vigorous protests from large numbers of trade unionists and Catholic leaders as well as the ordinary people of Buenos Aires. 'The renewal of incidents provoked by neo-Nazi elements,' said one leading citizen, 'may take the form of anti-semitism, but the aim is the destruction of Argentine democracy.'

The DAIA—the central Jewish representative body—was assured by the Interior Minister that the Government would take firm action, but the Minister resigned three weeks later in despair. Because the Government refused to do anything, on 28th of June 1962 the Jews of the Argentine throughout the country closed all their businesses, factories, schools, banks and other institutions as a measure of protest. Many non-Jews risked the wrath of young Tacuara hooligans by shutting their shops in sympathy.

Labour leaders, political groups, intellectual centres and Catholic organizations expressed their sympathy, and leading universities joined in protest demonstrations against the Nazi aggressors. The Dean of the School of Economics in Buenos Aires University ordered the fixing of posters denouncing the anti-semitic attacks and the swastika-slashing of the young girl, Graciela Sirota.

Argentine businessmen were approached by leaders of the protest shut-down and they agreed not to dock the pay of the workers who joined the strike. Teachers cancelled classes. Newspapers condemned the anti-semitic violence.

During the strike, Police Chief Green sent his steel-helmeted men into the streets to 'keep order' after accusing the Jews of taking the law into their own hands. No action was taken against any of the young Tacuara members who toured the city in cars showering provocative leaflets on to pavements, but four students who were persuading fellow classmates to join the strike were arrested. Jewish youths mounted guard at certain synagogues and at one of them fought a pitched gun battle with plain-clothes police, each side suffering casualties.

The situation resembles the atmosphere in Germany in the early days of Hitler. Life for the Jews has become almost unbearable; so serious a pitch has the hooliganism reached that the Minister of the Interior, Dr Adrogue, decided to make a nation-wide TV and radio broadcast bluntly condemning the wave of anti-semitism.

'The country is suffering from the uprising of anti-democratic groups who are heirs to the Nazis,' he said. 'And this coincides with the sad situation of the country's economy and the dramatic times the Argentine has gone through.'

'Attacks upon Jews, their synagogues, institutions and homes are a disgrace to Argentinians. Such deeds occurring in a Catholic country are a denial of Papal injunction. I want it to be known that the Government is determined to stamp out such shameful activities and will prosecute the offenders energetically and with all the means at its disposal.'

Adrogue further said that anti-Jewish organizations were to be disbanded and their offices closed. The 'evidence of barbarism and violence' was sternly denounced in the two great Argentinian daily papers, *La Frensa* and *La Naciono*.

But the fascist elements have the situation under such firm control that the worthy and, no doubt, sincere intentions of Adrogue and other Argentinian leaders had no effect whatsoever. Only twenty-four hours before the Minister's nation-wide broadcast, the former secret police chief, Raul Angelini, in another television programme, asserted that the Jewish community faked the attack on the young girl, Graciela Sirota, in order to conceal a number of economic offences. The Jewish leadership, he added, was acting in concert with the communists and was in fact a 'tool in the hands of the Reds.'

'All this agitation about anti-semitism is merely a communist fabrication to divert attention from the various financial scandals which Jewish bankers have been involved in during the presidency of Arturo Frondizi,' said Angelini. This reference was to a scandal in 1959 which involved the Jewish People's Bank as well as some high Argentine Government officials.

Although there have been scores of serious racialist incidents reported, police chief Green asserted that 'anti-semitism has been exaggerated and is exploited by the communists.'

Assurances and stern warnings by the authorities are no doubt sincere but the hard facts show who is in real command of the situation in the Argentine. Despite ample evidence of identification of the men who are guilty of committing the acts of violence, police officials themselves, harbouring fascist sympathies and fearful of the consequences of arresting the sons of influential men, do absolutely nothing.

Green even went further and warned the President that there was a danger that the manner in which Jewish organizations were taking the law into their own hands would provoke a clash with racist groups to the detriment of 'law and order'.

Liberal politicians in the country have also accused the Intelligence Department of the Government (SIDE) of encouraging the various fascist organizations like the Tacuara as part of their 'anti-communist' campaign. A number of military men, including the usual clutch of retired colonels, have also expressed their extreme right wing anti-communist views by either forming new fascist groups or joining existing movements. For instance, Commodore Agustin de Vega set up the violently racialist Legion Nacionalista Contrarevolucionaria which includes a number of former Peron men. The philosophy of this Legion is that the 'Jews are responsible for all the ills that beset the Argentine and for that matter the rest of the world as well.'

Recently a fresh wave of anti-semitism started up, and among the many shooting incidents a theatre where a Jewish play was being presented was machine-gunned. In March 1964 two home-made bombs were hurled through the ground floor display window of the British Overseas Airways Corporation offices in

Buenos Aires—an indication that the Jews were not the only target of the Tacuara organization.

Several bombs exploded at other points in the city's northern residential district which broke windows and damaged doors. Leaflets signed 'Tacuara National Revolutionary Movement', indicating the handiwork of Jose Baxter, littered the pavements of Santa Fe Avenue, scene of the explosions.

The previous month four men were killed and twelve others wounded when trade union officials exchanged fire with a group of armed Tacuara terrorists who broke into a General Confederation of Labour (CGT) conference in Rosario City. Three CGT officials who went to the police station to formally denounce the attack were themselves detained and held incommunicado.

In 1964 the latest Minister of the Interior, Jual Palmero, under President Arturo Ilia, announced that prominent Jews in the Argentine were to be given special protection following further bomb-throwing and threats to their lives. In all, there have been hundreds of such attacks on Jewish property, synagogues, businesses, private homes, newspaper offices and schools during the past few years.

In January 1965, following a gun battle between terrorists and police on the outskirts of Buenos Aires, an arsenal of molotov bombs, hand grenades and other high explosives was unearthed. Lists of Jews whom the extremists planned to attack and maps showing where their homes were located were also confiscated.

Earlier the United States Government felt sufficiently alarmed to 'advise' the Argentine authorities that these Nazi-style activities were giving the country a bad name and were causing unfavourable comment in North America. The 'advice' was tempered by saying that it was made only as a friendly gesture and did not carry any criticism of the Argentine authorities.

But nothing changes. National and local newspapers play up Jewish-sounding names involved in 'economic' trials. The general public is led to believe that Jews are responsible for the desperate situation in which the country finds itself; that most of those charged with fraud and smuggling are not Jewish is glossed over. An attempt is being made to create a psychological atmosphere in which the Jews could be held responsible for the evils and calamities which the Argentine is at present experiencing.

As one leading civic dignitary stated in Buenos Aires: 'The

problem is of the reawakening of Nazism in a milieu of social unrest for which the Jews are a target for diverting the attention of the masses from the real problem at issue. In this atmosphere of social evolution and instability, incitement against Jews is a cheap fuel to create greater confusion and thereby attract greater support.'

And so the Jews are attacked on two grounds. First, they are bloated capitalists and are sucking the blood of the country, and secondly, that they are communists and behind the underground 'red' threat in the Argentine. They are also accused of being allies of Castro—although the Jews are just as fearful of the advent of a Castro-type régime as their accusers.

The panic wave of anti-Castro sentiment felt by rich Argentinians has given Nazi groups the chance they were looking for to launch an 'anti-communist' and anti-semitic drive. What they are after is power, and their real object is to stir up further trouble and unrest.

They are playing for higher stakes than the smashing of a few windows or the gratification of the sadistic urges of upper-class university students. This was clearly shown in March 1964 when an ultra-nationalist military coup backed by the Tacuara and Peronist elements in Cordoba and Mendoza provinces was uncovered, and thirty officers of the Seventh Air Brigade were arrested. All leave for the marines and infantry was cancelled and federal units posted guards at radio and television stations in the capital. Some of the arrested officers were linked with another abortive right wing army revolt in Cordoba province in 1963.

Early in October 1966 an offshoot of the Tacuara calling itself the El Movimiento Nueva Argentina hijacked a plane and 'invaded' the British owned Falkland Islands during the Duke of Edinburgh's visit to Buenos Aires. The aim of this 'spontaneous' nationalist gesture was to win popular support for the Government and hide the country's serious economic plight.

It is true to say that the ills of the Argentine are the ills of the Latin American continent; in Buenos Aires they are magnified and so show up in sharp relief the political extremism simmering beneath the surface.

CHAPTER XV

South Africa

WHEN Graciela Sirota, the young student, was beaten and a swastika carved on her body with a knife in Buenos Aires by members of the Tacuara fascist movement, the news was reported throughout the world. It aroused reactions ranging from indignation to mild curiosity, but generally it was dismissed as 'an isolated incident' or a 'local distasteful phenomenon'.

In South Africa the attack aroused more than usual interest. A police detective, Aubrey Marais, who had been investigating an explosion which damaged the Great Synagogue in Johannesburg in January 1961 discovered that the tentacles of the Tacuara had spanned the two continents. This highly secret organization trained by former Nazis and their followers in the Argentine was building up support in Johannesburg and other South African cities.

Marais also discovered that a number of Hungarian businessmen who had settled in South Africa after the collapse of the Reich, and who had prospered in Johannesburg, were backing the movement with money and moral support.

Large quantities of documents and pamphlets from South America giving instructions on how to make and use explosives, as well as leaflets filled with racialist propaganda, were found. The inquiries by the police revealed that other explosions which had taken place in South Africa outside synagogues and on the premises of Jewish shops and buildings, as well as the daubing of swastikas on walls and an outbreak of anti-semitic slogan-painting in many cities, were at least partially the responsibility of this fascist organization.

The pamphlets had been printed in Buenos Aires and had been smuggled into South Africa in large batches at monthly intervals. A secret 'shrine' was unearthed in a Johannesburg flat decorated with a huge picture of Hitler, a large swastika flag, copies of *Mein Kampf* and other Nazi emblems.

Johannesburg was not the only city affected. Mr Lawrence Miller, national chairman of the Federation of South African Students Jewish Association, said that 'a fascist society has reared its head at the University of Natal in Durban and posters proclaiming its existence have appeared there.' In May 1963 large black swastikas and slogans saying 'Juden Raus' (Jews get out) were painted on Natal University buildings, prompting the principal, Dr E. G. Malherbe, to comment: 'It is an extremely dirty thing to do.' This was the second anti-semitic outbreak to occur in South Africa within a fortnight, for at a Warsaw Ghetto exhibition at the Witwatersrand University in Johannesburg, the walls were defaced with swastikas.

This type of activity was repeated at other South African centres of learning where Jewish students received a spate of threatening letters saying: 'Get out Jews. Go back to Palestine or you will wear yellow armbands in a kaffir ghetto.' In July 1962 there were complaints that attempts were also being made in Cape Town to recruit members for a fascist society.

These manifestations of open racialism are but minor facets of the wider atmosphere of extremism which has gripped South Africa since 1948 and which has turned it into the country resembling more closely than any other the fascist régime in Nazi Germany in the period before the Second World War.

In South Africa the present Government is run by men who quite openly supported Hitler during hostilities and is backed by powerful groups who admire the ideals of national socialism. Indeed, it was only by a narrow majority that in 1939 the South African Parliament under General Smuts voted to enter the war against Germany. The vast majority of the Afrikaner (people of Boer descent) leaders were violently opposed to fighting against Hitler and there were numerous acts of sabotage during the war as well as vicious attacks on soldiers who had signed on to fight against the fascist armies.

The pro-German sentiments and Nazi sympathies held by so many Afrikaners who form nearly 60 per cent of the white population of South Africa can be traced back to the turn of the century when the Dutch settlers under Kruger fought the British. During this violent struggle the Boers alleged repeatedly that

British troops tortured and caused the deaths of many thousands of men, women and children who were rounded up and kept in primitive concentration camps.

Many of these reports were grossly exaggerated, but there was some basis for them as the war was a violent one and the Boers fought a skilful unconventional guerrilla campaign against their enemies. In the end the Boers were crushed. But it was hoped that the memories of this fight would wither away when the four provinces which make up South Africa came together in 1910 to form a Union. Under the banner of 'Unity is Strength' the idea was that the English and the Afrikaans sections of the community should forget the past and build a new country based on compromise and co-operation.

But the Afrikaner politicians have gone on whipping up the atrocity stories against the 'rooineks' (red-necks'—the nickname for the British) and pointing out that the German Kaiser expressed strong sympathies for the Boers in their struggle against the British.

This anti-British sentiment was kept alive to help the Afrikaner politicians' aim of setting up an Afrikaner Republic divorced from Britain and the Commonwealth. The sympathies which the Boers had for Germany during both world wars were, therefore, as much due to anti-British feeling as anything else. Further, the neighbouring German colony of South West Africa with its capital at Windhoek was absorbed by Dr Verwoerd's Government. Many Germans live there and shortly before the outbreak of the Second World War a number of 'tourists' arrived in the country from the Fatherland with the intention of preventing South Africa entering the war against Germany and if possible forming a pro-Nazi guerrilla movement.

The influence of the Germans in South West Africa was strong and Hitler found sympathizers there as well as in South Africa where a powerful fascist 'Greyshirt' movement sprang up before the war. Dr Verwoerd himself was part of a delegation of professors to the Government who protested at the admission of Jewish refugees from Germany into South Africa because they 'would dilute Afrikaner stock'.

At the outbreak of the First World War Verwoerd had been a pupil in a British school in Bulawayo, Rhodesia. Already the boy's feelings towards the 'rooineks' were influenced by the insidious propaganda of the Afrikaner politicians and he told his headmaster that he wanted to return to the Union to join in the 'rebellion' against South Africa's entry into the war. Young Verwoerd was kicked down the corridor by the irate master and this incident had an incalculable influence on the future course of his life. His bitter feelings towards the English changed very little since those early formative years, and as a young man the brilliant Hendrik Frensch Verwoerd turned down a generous scholarship to study at Oxford University. Instead he chose to travel to Germany where he spent some time at the Universities of Leipzig, Hamburg and Berlin before returning to South Africa to become a professor of psychology at Stellenbosch University.

But the professor had strong political ambitions and he gave up his scholastic career to move to the gold-mining city of Johannesburg where he started up a dreary propagandist newspaper of the Nationalist Party called the *Transvaler*. Demonstrating clearly his anti-British sentiments, Verwoerd's journal was a vehicle for Nazi propaganda during the war. In June 1943 in the Supreme Court, the highest judicial seat in the country, Dr Verwoerd, as editor of the *Transvaler*, unsuccessfully sued the English evening newspaper *The Star* which had accused him of falsifying news to support the German enemy. At the trial the Judge said of Dr Verwoerd: 'He did support Nazi propaganda, he did make his paper a tool of the Nazis in South Africa, and he knew it.'

During the 1939-45 war, Dr Verwoerd was also closely associated with a group of Afrikaners who drew up a 'Draft Constitution' for a Republic which was a straight Nazi blue print for South Africa. This document, which called for an authoritarian system of government which would show 'respect only to God' and which would 'vigorously control all unnatural elements', first appeared in the *Transvaler*.

Nor did the newspaper hide its anti-semitism. The editor complained: 'The commercial and industrial undertakings in South Africa are mostly in foreign hands, latterly mostly Jews.'

Afrikaner leaders like Dr Verwoerd, who boasted of being an extremist, and movements like the Greyshirts, were imbued with the spirit of fascism. But of equal importance at the time was the birth of the Ossewa Brandwag (Ox-wagon Sentinel). This movement attracted tremendous emotional support from people of Boer descent for it reminded them of the year 1836, a date drummed into every South African schoolboy.

The significance of the early nineteenth century lies in the fact that the Dutch settlers at the Cape came under the rule of the British who took over the country from the immensely rich Dutch East India Company. The British had comparatively liberal ideas about how the indigenous black population should be treated, and the Dutch settlers—the original Boers—resented the way the newcomers tried to stop them from keeping slaves and exploiting the blacks as was their custom.

Angry and frustrated, the Boers finally packed their belongings into covered wagons pulled by teams of oxen and trekked off from the Cape into the unexplored interior of the country. They hoped to move away from the influence and the authority of the English with their outlandish progressive views and at the same time avoid paying the taxes imposed by their new rulers.

They survived immense hardships both from the rugged terrain and from the hostile black tribes they encountered. Ever since that epoch these pioneers called Voortrekkers, who started their great trek in 1836, have played a heroic role in Afrikaner mythology and folklore.

As a result of this emotive symbolism the Ossewa-Brandwag attracted sympathetic support from a large number of Afrikaners. Originally intended to be a cultural organization, it became a secret, semi-military movement and during the Second World War went underground. Its leader during this period was the German-educated Dr Van Rensburg.

The object of this movement was to set up a Christian National Republic on Nazi lines. During the war its Generals were interned by the Smuts Government after Nazi uniforms were found on its premises, complete with swastika armbands, guns and ammunition. And at the movement's rallies echoed the familiar chant of 'One God—One Faith—One People'.

Numerous acts of sabotage were carried out by the storm-troopers wing of the Ossewa-Brandwag known as the stormjaers, who drilled at night from barracks with names like 'Munchen' and 'Nuremberg'. They attacked soldiers who had volunteered to fight in North Africa and Europe against the Nazis and even threatened the Prime Minister's life.

The man who succeeded the assassinated Verwoerd, Balthazar

Johannas Vorster, was the General of the Port Elizabeth branch of the Ossewa-Brandwag. Vorster was interned for eighteen months during the war for his pro-Nazi activities but was allowed out on parole in 1944 and kept under house arrest.

This prominent member of the Ossewa-Brandwag, who envisaged victory of Afrikaner nationalism through an alliance with Hitler, defined his position in this way: 'We stand for Christian Nationalism which is an ally of National Socialism. You can call the anti-democratic principle fascism; in Germany it is German National Socialism and in South Africa Christian Nationalism.'

The extremist Greyshirt movement received funds from Hitler and was a full-scale Nazi organization, but it gradually faded away in 1939, its members joining other groups which today form part of the ruling Nationalist Party.

In 1941 General Hertzog, a former South African Prime Minister, openly advocated a nationalist socialist government for the country and plots to seize power and military bases by a storm-trooper division of pro-Nazi elements were crushed in 1942. Nazi agents working from the neighbouring Portuguese East Africa infiltrated into the country, while units of the South African Army were fighting against Rommel's forces in North Africa.

One of the most colourful of South African sporting figures, Johannes van der Walt, a champion wrestler, was shot by the police after he escaped from prison where he had been interned after it was discovered that he had become one of the Ossewa-Brandwag generals.

The end of the war naturally dealt a blow to fascist ambitions in South Africa, but the right-wing anti-democratic forces were soon on the march again. The Reddingsdaadbond, a pseudo-welfare organization following the lines of Hitler's 'Winter Help' was formed. But of far greater significance was the growth of the Broederbond (League of Brothers) which is a secret society aiming at infiltrating all sections of the community.

This group has become so powerful that today its members are found in the police force, among teachers, in the army, in the civil service and in key positions in Government departments. The Broederbond believes in the policy of white supremacy and according to Professor Leo Kuper of Durban University in

Natal, 'its creed of apartheid is a direct descendant of Hitler's theories of a master race. The chief upholder of these theories of white supremacy is the Afrikaner Broederbond. It permeates the entire Afrikaner-speaking community and its cells are organized to exert influence throughout the whole country.'

Dr Verwoerd was one of the leading lights in the Broederbond and so widespread became the insidious activities of this extremist underground group that in April 1964 the leader of the opposition party in the South African Parliament demanded that an inquiry be held into the movement and its methods.

There were riots and demonstrations in South Africa, especially in Johannesburg, after the war when the fascist groups tried to hold meetings which eventually had to be banned. Anti-semitism which had played a big part in Afrikaner politics curiously sub-sided for a while when the Jews in Palestine were fighting against the British—the Afrikaner's traditional enemy.

In 1948 the Nationalist Party, popularly known as the 'Nats', came to power. At last the decades-old dream of a South African Republic completely divorced from the British could be realized. Knowing the pro-Nazi and fascist backgrounds of so many of the leading figures of the new Malan Government, people with demo-cratic or liberal ideas were understandably dismayed.

One of the first acts carried out by the Nationalist Party—which rules today under Vorster—was to release men like Erich Holm and Robey Leibbrand, who had been convicted as traitors during the war. And the notorious L. T. Weichardt, who led the Nazi Greyshirts before the war and who was known as South Africa's 'Jew Baiter Number One', is now a Nationalist Party member of the upper house of Parliament—the Senate. Another leading Government M.P. is J. S. von Moltke, who was one of Weichardt's right-hand men in 1939.

Dr Erich Holm was born on a Cape farm in 1907, the grandson of a rabbi and the nephew of a famous German surgeon. He was educated locally, but at the age of sixteen went to Germany to study. There he had to borrow money from the South African Government to return home to take up a teaching appointment.

Just before the outbreak of the Second World War, Holm returned to the Reich where he broadcast Nazi propaganda to South Africa from Zeesen Radio. More effective than Lord Haw-Haw, Holm received further publicity in his own country when his programmes were published in the Malan Nationalist Press.

In 1947 he was sentenced to ten years' imprisonment for high treason but was freed eighteen months later when the 'Nats' won decisively at the general election. This unrepentant Nazi has never deviated from his fascist ideas and still calls Hitler 'one of the great figures in world history' whose 'titanic heroism would one day be found to be justified'. In 1950 Holm, speaking at a Committee for Aid to Germany in the town of Britz, urged the release of Nazis serving prison sentences for war crimes.

Holm holds a senior post in the National Bureau of Education and Social Research, a sub-section of the Government Department of Education, Arts and Science, where he is compiling a bibliography on the entire field of African studies. This former Nazi propagandist still shows his out-and-out pro-Hitler feelings in his books, but that does not preclude him from drawing a state salary. He attacked Churchill as a 'desperado' and an 'ostentatious adventurer', and he calls Jews 'sinister agents of the East who, with satanic efficiency, have usurped control of the West'. South Africa, he adds, has to contend with 'dangerous ideas of a purely Jewish origin such as the principles of human rights, freedom of belief and speech, and the equality of man.'

An opposition member of the South African Parliament from the United Party attacked the 'filthy, ugly and disgusting book by this unexpiated traitor', and demanded that he should be dismissed from his post.

The reply of Dr Verwoerd's Deputy Minister of Education was that 'so much dust had been kicked up'. The Minister claimed that Holm was not a Government official and that no disciplinary action could be taken against him. In fact, the National Bureau of Education and Social Research is subsidized by the Government and alone is responsible for employing the former traitor and Nazi broadcaster. Holm himself says: 'I do not feel guilty about what I did.'

Another Nazi who was grateful for the electoral victory of the Nationalist Party was Robey Leibbrand, a former South African boxing champion and a Nazi paratrooper in the early days of the Second World War. Later he was landed by submarine off the coast of South Africa to organize sabotage, but he was caught and sentenced to death for high treason in 1943, only to be released from prison by the Nationalists in 1948. Still active today, Leibbrand claims that he has organized a secret army on South African soil to 'oppose communism'.

Although in a newspaper interview in June 1962 Leibbrand denied that he was a racialist, he added: 'I followed Nazi Germany and was proud of it.' 'I am a national socialist,' he said, and spoke about 'several good men who are following me'. Leibbrand announced the setting up of an Anti-Communist Protection Front, and complaints about his private army which were aired in Parliament at Cape Town received scant attention.

Another well-known fascist organization in South Africa is the Boerenasie (Boer Nation) which claims a membership of 40,000 and is controlled by a Natal farmer, 'Commandant General' R. K. Rudman. This extremist started his career as a fascist agitator in the early 1930's and linked up his Boerenasie with the European right wing organizations after the downfall of Hitler.

Rudman claims that the aim of the Boerenasie is to seize power in the country, and he hopes to solve the colour problem by Third Reich methods. Based on Hitlerian ideals, the movement is violently 'anti-Catholic, anti-Indian, anti-Liberal, anti-Jew, and anti-Communist'.

Rudman says: 'The utterances of all prominent Jews and Communists are being filed for reference. We stand for the blood question. Blood is everything, and the biggest crime of those who are our members is to mix their blood.'

The movement's operations are partially carried out in secret and it is believed to have a para-military wing. The Boerenasie advocates that all Indians should be sent back to India, all Jews to Israel, and there should be no more state education for kaffirs (Negroes).

'Philosophically we strive for a state as described by Hegel,' says Rudman, and goes on to explain: 'We have borrowed much from National Socialism as proclaimed by Adolf Hitler in the Third Reich and have adapted it to South African conditions. . . . Above all it is our aim to free our Fatherland—which we love fanatically—from forces which undermine our state and people. These include international capitalism, Roman Catholicism, the Jews, and other secret movements which aim at forming a state within a state.'

The Boerenasie was founded in 1940 by General Manie Maritz

as a National-Socialist Movement and its deputy was D. A. J. de Flamingh who was interned for pro-Nazi activities in 1941. Now under the leadership of Rudman, the fascist ideals of the movement have not lost any force. Members salute each other with the symbol '88'—which means 'Heil Hitler' ('H' being the eighth letter of the alphabet). In August 1962 Boerenasie sent a representative to attend international fascist conferences in Europe.

A branch of the Boerenasie organization is the South African Anglo-Nordic Union which has links with similar movements in Scandinavia, and which aims at the 'protection of our Protestant heritage'.

'We are a Nordic organization,' explains Rudman. 'We want English, Afrikaners, Norwegians, Germans and other fair races in our ranks.'

The duplication of the Natal farmer's efforts in two separate movements with exactly the same aims is an interesting reflection on the vexed racial question in the country. Boerenasie caters for Afrikaans-speaking fascists, and the Nordic Union serves English-speaking fascists. The two communities have never really hit it off in South Africa, and even when there are such great links as a common admiration for Adolf Hitler and a united belief in national-socialism, his followers still decline to show brotherly love and insist on serving under two separate flags.

There is also a branch of the Ku Klux Klan in South Africa which distributes leaflets and membership forms from its Pietermaritzburg headquarters, and in September 1962 a new party was created called Die Suid Afrikanse Blanke Werkersbond (The South African White Workers' League). This movement is extremely racialist and behind the scenes appears the hand of Rudman who must have little time to spare for his farming activities.

The White Workers' League aims at the 'Nationalization of all mineral wealth; the abolition of the treacherous Marxist foreign income tax system; the repatriation of all foreigners to their own countries; no more education for kaffirs;' and finally, as a bait for the less subtle of his followers, the White Workers' League wants 'free holiday train tickets every year for each European family'.

So impressed were the Argentinian leaders of the Tacuara Organization by Rudman's unswerving fascist views that he

received an invitation from Buenos Aires to become the movement's Honorary General in South Africa. In September 1962
Rudman claimed that there were 'many prominent men in the
Government today who have said that I am a very staunch
patriot. They know my past and they know what I stand for.'

Rudman was a General in the Ossewa-Brandwag during the
war, and the leader of the Greyshirt movement. He was disappointed with the policies of Dr Verwoerd whom he considered to be far too liberal-minded. For example, Rudman
believes that the policy of giving Negroes certain areas of the
country like the Transkei where they can form their own states is
a betrayal of the white man's heritage.

'The kaffirs should be given nothing,' he says.

In June 1965 it was disclosed that Rudman had been in contact
with former Nazis living in Egypt in a bid to try and get arms for
his movement from North Africa. In a letter to Cairo stamped
with a swastika he said: 'Forward National Socialism. Heil
Hitler.' Rudman is not the only man in South Africa who thinks
that Dr Verwoerd was too 'liberal'. In 1966 the Republican Party
led by Professor C. F. van der Merwe proclaimed a racialist
policy even more extreme than that of apartheid. Wanting to
insult Harold Wilson, Mr van der Merwe pondered a while
and came up with: 'He is nothing more than a cheeky white
kaffir.'

Johan Schoeman of Broederstroom is another vocal fascist
supporter. He offered to contribute funds for Eichmann's defence
when the Nazi was brought for trial and he appealed to others to
be as generous and make similar donations. In a booklet Schoeman
praises Eichmann for the work he did in trying to rid Germany of
the Jews. Other fascist publications he has written are *Eichmann
Is Not Guilty* and *Whose is the Hidden Hand?* In Durban another
pro-Nazi group was started in 1962 with the avowed aim of
'fighting communist penetration and preventing the West from
sliding into the morass of decadence.'

The pro-Nazi sympathies of Schoeman and his like in South
Africa do not find expression only in the printed word. Some of
them believe in action as well and this was demonstrated when the
front door of the Pretoria synagogue was damaged by an explosion
in 1961. In June 1962 there was a dynamite explosion at the
Jewish Martyrs' Monument in Johannesburg West Park cemetery

and another synagogue—in Cape Town—also attracted the attention of bomb throwers.

In 1964 there was a further spurt of swastika daubings and a cemetery was desecrated in Pretoria.

Jews are not the only target of the fascist extremists behind these manifestations of violence. In November 1965 the graves of British soldiers who died in the Boer War and who were buried at Nooitgeducht in the Transvaal were defaced and smashed.

Dr Teddy Schneider, chairman of the Jewish Board of Deputies, said in September 1962: 'there are individuals and organizations whose avowed purpose is to propagate the hateful doctrine of Nazism. These activities cannot be viewed out of context of the revival of similar organizations in other countries.'

The point was illustrated in 1965 when *Afrika Spiegel*, published by Helmut von Lichtenfeld in Pretoria, applauded the Government's action in barring so-called 'communist' lawyers and university teachers from working at their professions. 'When will the rest of the Christian Western world act upon this command of common sense?' he asked. Copies of this journal were widely distributed to extremist groups all over Europe.

The friendship which Dr Verwoerd felt for Sir Oswald Mosley, who shared many of his views, was shown when the leader of the British Union Movement on one of his frequent visits to South Africa was allowed to speak on the Government-controlled radio where he was introduced by the announcer as a 'leading statesman'. A branch of Mosley's organization called the Europe-Africa Association was established in Johannesburg where it publishes a fortnightly magazine *Action* on sale at state-owned bookshops.

In 1959 an off-shoot of the international European National Movement was formed in the country under the control of Mosley's chief South African lieutenant Derrick Alexander. Addressing a branch meeting of Dr Verwoerd's Nationalist Party at Thabazimbi, Alexander said that he was giving up his work as a teacher to concentrate on a nation-wide campaign on behalf of his fascist movement. Three years later—in 1962—a former professional boxer, William Webster, came to South Africa to raise funds to help Mosley's Union Movement with its campaign in Britain.

In a successful tour of the country Webster claimed that he

collected £100,000 and boasted that he could have raised much more.

He even approached Dr Verwoerd's Government for a contribution and was sent along to the Nationalist Party headquarters for a donation. Mosley again visited South Africa in 1965 when he praised the 'latent power' of the Verwoerd Government.

Mosley is not the only English politician to take an interest in the South African scene. In January 1965 the Candour League of South Africa launched by the British Empire Loyalists offered its members publications from a lending library.

The works included *The Politician* by Robert Welch, head of the John Birch Society of the United States; *The World Conquerors* by Louis Marschalko, the Hungarian Nazi; *Fraudulent Conversion* by Colin Jordan, the British Nazi, and Victor Marsden's edition of the Protocols of Zion under the title *World Conquest through World Government*.

The Candour League was quick off the mark to support Ian Smith's breakaway extremist white régime in Rhodesia. An 'emergency fund' for Rhodesian purchases was established, and across the Indian Ocean in Australia Eric Butler suggested that the Government call off the economic boycott of Rhodesia because 'this can only benefit the forces of international communism'.

Fascists throughout the West welcomed the white Rhodesian Government.

In the United States the National Coordinating Committee for Friends of Rhodesian Independence composed of extreme right-wingers including supporters of the John Birch Society took full page advertisements in American papers appealing for financial aid for Mr Smith. President of the committee is novelist Taylor Caldwell whose previous causes were 'Aid for Katanga Freedom Fighters' and the 'Federation of Conservatives' which was set up to save America from 'socialism'.

Smith's choice for a 'Chief Censor' to muzzle the press was true to form, for the man given the job, Ivor Benson, has written articles for Nazi journals like *Nation Europa* and praised Oswald Mosley on one of his visits to South Africa.

The European fascist *Nation Europa* also turned its attention to South Africa when in August 1964 an article written by a certain Myron Kok denounced the 'more than 100 years old aggression by influential financial pirates in the City of London against the deeply-rooted peasantry of our country.'

The author, himself a South African, continued: 'Though the Boers by the proclamation of their independence in 1962 had won an impressive victory over the "alien financiers", the "pirates" were continuing the struggle, which was dangerous, because the entire world press is being systematically filled with tendentious British information.'

'The inglorious tradition of Britain's policy of race treason meant the death of tens of thousands of peace-loving white settlers. British propaganda is and remains brutal, stupid and barren of ideas. We have seen this in two World Wars, and it is being revealed again by the unceasing shameless incitement carried on against our Government who cannot apparently be forgiven having found a practical approach to a settlement between black and white while London only knows that "one African policy"—race treason—the shameless surrender of the best English blood to black despots who brought home from London, Oxford and Cambridge nothing but luxurious living, greed for power and the arts of lying practised by the pirates.'

The activities of men like Rudman, Alexander and others are but details in the broader canvas of full-scale fascism which is the only way to describe the policy of the police state Government reigning in South Africa today.

The International Commission of Jurists from Geneva in May 1963 describing South Africa said: 'Liberty has gone. Justice is blinded and maimed despite the efforts of the Bench and the Bar to save such remnants as still remain in that unfortunate country.'

Analysing the General Law Amendment Act passed in South Africa in 1963 the Commission, which is backed by more than 40,000 lawyers, judges and teachers of law, and which has consultative status with the United Nations said: 'The present measures introduced by the South African Government, as did those that preceded them, call for strong condemnation by all the civilized world. . . . They cause grave concern to all who love liberty, fair play and justice. . . . They border on tyranny.'

In March 1964 Mrs Helen Suzman, the lone Progressive Party member of Parliament, said that this legislation was being used to smash the non-white trade unions. Dozens of coloured trade unionists have been arrested without trial, she added. Mrs

Suzman put down a motion calling for the repeal of all laws and regulations under which people can be deprived of their liberty without recourse to the courts, but not a single voice in the House supported her.

The particular law under criticism is known as the No-trial Act, which gives the police power to hold suspects for repeated periods of ninety days without trial, and is the latest in the series of cruel and repressive legislative rules introduced by the Nationalist Government since coming to power in 1948.

Mr Strydom, the Prime Minister who preceded Dr Verwoerd, declared: 'The European is the master of South Africa. Quite apart from his economic hold on the country, and quite apart from his culture and civilization, because he is ruler of the country. . . . The entire position of the European is based on discriminatory legislation in so far as the races in South Africa are concerned.'

During the ten years 1951–1961 three and a half million Africans out of a total of 10,000,000 who live in South Africa have been convicted of pass offences—a pass being a type of identification document which is a dossier of an African's working and living activities and which he is compelled to carry on him every moment of his life. Today one out of every 236 inhabitants in the country is in prison either serving sentences or awaiting trial.

Even *Die Burgher*, a newspaper which normally supported Dr Verwoerd, protested: 'Severe—even frightening administrative powers have been sought and such powers lend themselves to serious abuses.'

The point was driven home when it was revealed in 1964 and again in 1965 that police throughout the country were in the habit of beating, torturing and murdering prisoners who were undergoing questioning for even routine crimes.

In May 1965 a United States official in Washington likened South Africa's racial policies to those of Nazi Germany.

It is not only Africans, Indians and coloureds of all descriptions whom Dr Verwoerd despised. His anti-semitic and anti-British outlook which he nursed ever since his early days at Stellenbosch University never changed. Both he and his ministers rebuked Jews in the country who voted in large numbers for the liberally-minded Progressive Party.

The Nationalist Government has been angered by the way

Israel has supported African-Asian anti-apartheid resolutions in the United Nations and in other international bodies. Strong hints have been made that South African Jews would be 'affected' by Israel's hostile attitude at the United Nations. The Labour newspaper *Davar* in Tel Aviv retorted angrily: 'Dr Verwoerd's statement implied that South African Jews are considered hostages. This is a threat and Verwoerd made no attempt to conceal it.'

In the spring of 1965 a party of twenty-five Germans organized by the neo-Nazi weekly *Deutsche Wochen-Zeitung* visited South Africa where they were given a warm welcome by Government officials. Invited to appear at various German clubs, the visitors spoke glowingly of South Africa's apartheid policies—so close to Hitler's own racial theories. An unwitting visitor at one of these meetings was a special adviser to the Bonn Press and Information Office who happened to be in South Africa at the same time.

Incensed by what he heard, the man from Bonn walked out saying that he did not want to listen to the speakers 'putting across the well-known Nazi line.' On his return to Germany the official commented that the neo-Nazi groups visiting South Africa 'were preaching racialism and white supremacy'.

Little wonder then that cries of 'Go to Israel' and 'There go the Jews again' were heard in Parliament as a bitter row broke over complaints by opposition members about racialism.

Another German visitor to South Africa in April 1965 was Otto Skorzeny who had come to exhibit Spanish Industrial Machinery at the Rand Easter Show. The guest of Senator L. T. Weichardt, the South African pre-war Nazi leader, during a visit to Cape Town, Skorzeny boasted: 'If I had my life over again I would fight for Germany just as I did in the last war.'

Dr Verwoerd intimidated or imprisoned most of his effective opponents in the country. The South African Broadcasting Corporation is now a completely controlled Government propaganda machine, so much so that a magistrate in Johannesburg in 1963 had to protest about the radio's biased report of a court case involving the arrest of some journalists. In addition Verwoerd extended his newspaper empire and controlled virtually all the Afrikaner press in the country before his death in 1966.

Warnings have been issued to the opposition English newspapers 'that they had better get together to organize themselves into some form of self-control or the Government would have to take action.' The smearing of English-speaking journalists by calling them 'unpatriotic', the campaign of vilification against the courageous Johannesburg newspaper, *The Rand Daily Mail*, and the constant threat of imprisonment and censorship is all part of the policy of ruling by force and inspiring fear in anyone opposed to the present rulers.

In 1964 Verwoerd warned the English press: 'You are close to the brink of treason.'

The infiltration of the army, too, has not been neglected. In June 1965 officers and men of the armed forces were angered by the appointment of Lt-General Rudolph Hiemstra as Commandant-General of the South African Defence Force. Hiemstra, once described as a 'nondescript adviser' by Field Marshal Smuts, had refused to fight for his country in the 1939–1945 war.

Attacking the decision, the chief defence spokesman of the opposition United Party said in the South African Parliament: 'It is a sad day when the country chooses an officer who from his own choice took off his uniform and elected not to serve with his military comrades in defence of South Africa against Nazi and fascist domination.'

Nothing has been left to chance. By rearranging constituencies in their favour, the Nationalist Government leaders have ensured that they can never be beaten at the polls, while the normal right wing extremist bogey of the 'communist menace' is perpetually exploited by Vorster and his men.

'Communist' in South Africa can mean anyone whom the Government chooses to label as such, and in the same category— perhaps even worse—are all those who are branded as 'liberals'.

In June 1965 the Government under its anti-communist crusade sought new and far-reaching powers which were really aimed at crushing the last few shreds of democracy left in the country. Despite threats and warnings aimed at silencing them, English language newspapers described the fresh proposals as 'fantastic, incredible, unbelievable and containing the sinister elements of Nazism.'

Among other proposed measures, authority was sought to arrest and detain for up to six months before a trial any state witness who might be open to intimidation or considered likely to abscond.

Dr Donald Molteno, senior lecturer in constitutional law at Cape Town University, described the proposals as 'uncivilized and a gross interference with individual liberty.'

Even more outspoken were the words of an Afrikaner, the Reverend C. F. Beyers Naude, Director of the Christian Institute of South Africa, in the summer of 1965. Mr Naude stated: 'It must be obvious to anyone who experienced or studied the development of the religious situation in the Third German Reich that more and more parallels exist between the situation in Nazi Germany and South Africa. These parallels are not only found in methods adopted in South Africa, but also in the general reaction of fear among an increasing number of Christians, both ministers and members, both on the Afrikaans- and English-speaking sides. This fear leads to untenable compromises or unbearable silence.'

Taking up the theme, the *Rand Daily Mail* commented: 'It must have come as a shock to many people to find a South African clergyman calling on our churches to resist authoritarianism and un-Christian elements in race policy as the German churches resisted the Nazis thirty years ago. . . . It is an ugly thought that it should be necessary to go back to Hitler's Germany to find a parallel of what is happening in South Africa today. But who, after studying the evidence, would care to say that Mr Naude is exaggerating the situation? Surely, in any case, it is better to see Nazism coming and to forestall it rather than to wait until it is too late.'

The brooding sense of violence and extremism generated by the racialist laws introduced by Dr Verwoerd was an important background factor in the mind of the man who stabbed him to death in Cape Town in September 1966. Verwoerd's successor, Balthazar Vorster, promises to be even more extreme in tightening the grip of fascism in South Africa.

The grim prophetic warning given two years previously by Dr Jan Steytler, leader of the Progressive Party, seems to be borne out more and more by events. He said: 'The parallel between Germany under Hitler and South Africa is now complete. What we are witnessing today is not the domination of one group by another, but the utter decay of civilization that has been built up over a thousand years.'

CHAPTER XVI

Egypt

IF THE ideology of Nazi Germany pervades the thinking of the rulers at the Cape, then the authorities at the other end of the African continent in Cairo might well claim to have gone one better. For large numbers of top-ranking Nazis who fled from Germany at the end of the war to Spain, Portugal and to Latin America are now happily at work for their new masters—the Egyptians.

These fugitives have been living on the banks of the Nile for the past ten years, but only recently has attention been focused on their activities following the arrest in Switzerland of two Israeli secret service agents who were trying to intimidate Germans working for Nasser's Government.

One of the men, an Austrian, Otto Joklik, claimed that he had formerly worked in Egypt but gave up his post when he realized that deliveries of strontium and radio-active cobalt were to be used for 'the extermination of the Jews'. Joklik said that Doctor Wolfgang Pilz, a former Nazi and head of the team of German scientists engaged by the United Arab Republic, planned to provide the rockets being built in Egypt with capsules containing radio-active material. Among other Germans working on the project of 'developing rockets with atomic, chemical and biological war-heads, intended for the destruction of Israel' were Professor Paul Goercke and Dr Hans Kleinwaechter, an ex-Gestapo man who has his own personal bodyguard in Egypt.

During the trial of the two secret service agents evidence was given that Professor Pilz had ordered the transfer of money to a Swiss bank for the purchase of laboratory equipment and material for the construction of 900 rockets at a factory under the direction of Hassan Kamil near Cairo. Some of the revelations of the activities of former Nazis in Egypt were so startling that the Public Prosecutor, Dr Hans Wieland, asked for conditional sentences to be passed on the two Israelis, commenting that 'the activities of German scientists in Egypt have quite understandably created the gravest concern to the whole world.'

It has now been established that at least fifty German experts who worked during World War Two at Peenemunde, Hitler's rocket base against Britain, are on Nasser's payroll doing exactly the same sort of research. There are also dozens more Germans who are employed by MECO, the joint Swiss-Spanish-West German firm headed by Hassan Kamil which has its headquarters in Zurich and which purchases and assembles aircraft for Nasser.

The rapid progress made by these Germans, backed with Egyptian money, at their secret military '333' rocket factory near Cairo at Heliopolis, has greatly alarmed the Israelis and brought about a number of acts of terrorism. An attempt was made on the life of Dr Hans Kleinwaechter at Loerrach and there is a mystery surrounding the plane crash in Westphalia which killed Hassan Kamil's wife. Bombs packed in parcels and addressed to Dr Pilz in Egypt are known to have killed at least five people and seriously injured others including his wife Hannelora.

Dr Heinz Krug, once personnel officer at Peenemunde, was kidnapped after it became known that he was head of the Research Institute for Physics and Jet Engines, which was closely associated with Egypt's armaments industry. His company, Intra, was set up on Nasser's behalf to purchase, through heavily camouflaged Swiss subsidiaries, the complex systems used in rocket engines.

Another German, Dr Eugen Saenger of V-2 fame, who in 1935 formed one of the first rocket research units in the world on Luneburg Heath for the Nazis, was persuaded to go to Egypt with his scientist wife Irene to work for Nasser. Later he was induced by the Bonn Government to give up these activities.

The efforts of the German scientists in Egypt were warmly praised by Dr Gerhard Frey, editor of the extreme right wing weekly *Deutsche National Zeitung* after a visit to Cairo. 'They work for the peace and progress of mankind,' he said. 'Any action against them by the Bonn Government would be the heaviest blow in the face of the world and of freedom. It would be the most serious obstacle in the process of civilization.'

Many former Nazis are also engaged in the aircraft industry. One of the top men concerned in this work at Helwan, fifteen miles south of Cairo, is a former Nazi paratrooper, Professor Ferdinand Brander, who spent ten years in Russia after the war but who now finds Cairo more congenial. He heads five hundred specialists employed in building top secret jet aircraft.

Living with their families in the wealthy Cairo suburb of Meadi, these Germans are engaged at two State factories, No. 36 and No. 135. Here are produced the engines and the fuselage of two Messerschmitt-type planes which were laid down in the Hispano-Suissa factory in Spain—the HA 200, a two-seater jet, and the HA 300, a single-seater supersonic fighter and reconnaissance aircraft. Directing operations is the brilliant German designer Willy Messerschmitt, and another expert at the factory is Fritz Hense who played an important role in the development of the original Messerschmitt plane.

German aircraft specialists and builders in Egypt have been co-operating with former Nazis like Professor Kurt Tank, who designed the long distance German Condor plane and the Focke Wulff 190, and who fled to the Argentine after the war where he helped Peron's aircraft industry before he moved on to India.

The Israeli Foreign Minister, Mrs Golda Meir, in 1963 charged that German scientists were deeply involved in Egyptian rocketry programmes, in the aircraft industry and in the field of chemical and bacteriological warfare. It was revealed, too, that a former Nazi colonel who conducted nerve gas experiments on prisoners at Dachau and Ravensbruck concentration camps was in charge of Egyptian chemical warfare research. And heading a 120,000-kilowatt reactor project in Egypt is the German nuclear scientist Professor Hahn.

Like ghosts from the past the names of former Nazis or those who worked for Hitler's war machine keep turning up in Egypt. Many are recruited from abroad for specialist work, but many fled there purely out of instincts of self-preservation. They are given asylum and put to work in one or another of Nasser's Ministries.

These Nazis are highly useful to Nasser in building up his armed forces and manufacturing the most modern equipment. Whether Nasser agrees with the doctrine of national socialism with which these men are imbued is another matter. Certainly that veteran French fascist, Maurice Bardèche, rates the Egyptian dictator as one of the best examples of the modern fascist breed.

Nasser sees the Israelis as his major enemy in the Middle East and it is perhaps understandable that he should turn to the men who ruled in Hitler's Germany for allies. He relies heavily on these men and so there can be little doubt that he is to some extent influenced by their extremist views, not only with regard to the Jews but also with their anti-communist and anti-West sentiments. This, of course, does not preclude Nasser from obtaining what economic and military aid he can lay his hands on, either from the East or West. However, the Egyptian dictator has no intention of allowing the philosophy of Marxism to make any headway in Cairo.

Excluding the scientists mentioned above, the Nazi fugitives from justice who now live in Egypt number several thousands. In the dramatic days in 1960 following the kidnapping of Eichmann, Leon Degrelle, the former fascist leader in Belgium who had sought refuge in Spain after the war, thought that even Franco could not afford him sufficient protection. Complaining indignantly that the Israelis were plotting to seize him as well, he hurriedly left for Cairo with Herr Ers, a former Goebbels collaborator, to take part in discussions about the 'dangers facing Nazis in hiding'.

Only after the air had cleared sufficiently for it to become apparent that Israeli commandos were not after his head as well did Degrelle make his way back to Madrid.

Before his recent death, one of the leading figures among the ranks of top Nazis serving Nasser was Professor Dr Johannas von Leers, who was highly active as a professional anti-semite and propaganda expert.

Von Leers, who preferred the name of Omar Amin von Leers which he adopted following his conversion to Islam, was known to have helped draft passages of many of Nasser's speeches. He was a leading Nazi Party member since 1929 and made a rapid rise to prominence after his talents were spotted by Dr Rosenberg, the master racialist of Nazi Germany. The right-hand man of Dr Goebbels when the Nazis were riding high, von Leers churned out books, pamphlets and brochures by the score. Among his earlier works were *History on a Racial Basis* and *The Jews have their Eye on You*.

Between 1933 and 1941 he produced a total of twenty-seven known volumes mainly dealing with Nazi ideology, race theory and why it was necessary to exterminate the Jews. His *Juden Sehen Dich An*, a virulently anti-Jewish publication, became required reading in all German schools and during the war he saw his theories and plans for mass murder carried out in practice. Articles written by von Leers frequently appeared in *Der Angriff*, Goebbels' evening paper.

At the end of the war von Leers, fearful of facing trial, and like many another Nazi leader with something on his conscience, made his way post haste to the Argentine. Perhaps he was not quite fast enough, for he first spent eighteen months in an American prisoner-of-war camp. This he once described, when safely ensconced in the Ministry for National Guidance in Cairo, as an 'American concentration camp run by Jews'.

After the fall of Peron, von Leers, who if nothing else knew how to make himself scarce, disappeared, only to turn up hard at work in Colonel Nasser's official propaganda department.

Von Leers had a pathological, life-long hatred for Jews and the British, and he helped pour out the anti-Israel and anti-Western propaganda broadcast daily from Cairo Radio. He maintained contact with former cronies, signing his letters 'Heil Hitler'. Dispatching scores of his articles to fascist magazines and newspapers, von Leers wrote to journals like *Der Spiegel*, in which he once complained bitterly about the reparations the Bonn Government was making to Israel and to the victims of Nazi terror.

'The scandalous waste of the results of German work through the so-called "restitution" to the Jews is devaluing the money. Because of it, millions of lazy and racketeering Jews are being stuffed with rewards,' wrote von Leers.

Knowing the full value of flattery, von Leers paid Nasser the doubtful compliment of saying that he was 'better than Hitler, because Hitler wanted to do everything at once, while Nasser is prepared to take his time.' His feelings about Christianity were as hostile as those concerning the Jews, and before the war von Leers said: 'Hundreds of thousands of nationally-minded Germans have long ago turned away from Christianity. They feel repelled by Christianity on account of its Jew foundation (the Old Testament, Paul, etc.).'

The Nazi influence on Nasser of men like von Leers was illustrated by the campaign of terror opened up against the Jews living in Egypt. Yellow identity cards were introduced which had to be carried by all Jews—a custom which originated in the Middle Ages and which was revived with grim Germanic thoroughness by the Nazis.

During this period Jews living in Cairo were expelled and their property and possessions confiscated before they left the country. A hate campaign reminiscent in detail and style of Nazi Germany was launched and individuals were abused and beaten up. Subterfuge and blackmail were used by Government officials and army and police officers to gain possession of Jewish property which they then shared out among themselves.

In 1965 an Egyptian Government sponsored pamphlet, *Israel —The Enemy of Africa*, stated: 'Before we examine in detail the racial and religious discrimination practised by Israel which also sucks the blood of the countries struggling to attain freedom, let us look at what the Talmud says.' There followed numerous quotations straight from Nazi propaganda handbooks such as 'the Jews condone the murder of non-Jews'.

The same pamphlet also quotes from the notorious forgery 'The Protocols of Zion' such statements as 'It is laid down in the 14th Protocol of Zion which says "When rule is concentrated in our hands, any religion other than Judaism would have to be destroyed".'

Anti-communism is another theme exploited by Nazis working for Nasser. This is evident in the type of crude propaganda which comes pouring out over Cairo Radio. 'Soviet aid to Zionism, arms and diplomatic support and early recognition of Israel' is explained by the fact that 'Stalin, Molotov and Voroshilov were married to Jewesses and that many Soviet leaders including Kaganovich and Beria were Jews.' Jewish influence in other communist countries is further 'proved' by making references to Jacob Berman, Anna Pauker, Rudolf Slansky and Mattias Rakosi. Cairo radio voices the complaint: 'By contrast there are no Arabs in the Supreme Soviet.'

The colony of Nazis in Cairo make every effort to help their former colleagues who from time to time turn up in Egypt. One such man was Ludwig Zind, who was arrested in Naples as he was boarding a ship for Libya where he taught at an Arab University. In 1958 this fifty-five-year-old schoolmaster was sentenced to twelve months' imprisonment by the Bonn Government for his extremist activities, but he jumped bail and fled to

Egypt through Italy where with local Nazis' help he settled down to work for the Arab cause under the name of Mahmoud Salah. In 1960 he returned secretly to Germany and before leaving again sent a plea for pardon to the German President. When captured in Italy, Zind had an Egyptian passport in his pocket.

Perhaps one of the highest ranking Nazis who was believed to have found his way to Egypt was Heinrich Mueller, the Gestapo General who acted as Eichmann's commanding officer. After escaping from Germany via Austria, Mueller sought refuge with Yugoslav Roman Catholic priests in Rome before making his way to Spain. In 1949 he travelled to Egypt where he worked with von Leers in the Propaganda Ministry. Once his identity was disclosed Mueller again disappeared and is now believed to be in Latin America.

Another leading Nazi who found sanctuary in Egypt was a former SS doctor, Hans Eisele, who was responsible for experiments on prisoners at Buchenwald concentration camp. After 1945 Eisele set himself up in a private practice in Munich without even bothering to change his name, but late in 1958 he was denounced by Joseph Ackermann, then a press officer in Munich and a man who had tasted concentration camp life from the inside.

Before Eisele could be brought to justice for his crimes he fled to Cairo where, helped by von Leers, he was given a villa. Soon Eisele, whose speciality had been to kill hundreds of people with poison injections, was back at work as a private doctor in a Cairo suburb, and requests by the Bonn Government for his extradition were turned down flat.

SS Major Alois Brunner, a man closely connected with Eichmann as one of his chief aides, is another Nazi who has made use of Cairo hospitality. During the war Brunner organized the deportation and murder of several tens of thousands of Jews from Austria, Slovakia, France and Greece, but was able to live in West Germany undetected until 1952 when he sought refuge in Egypt. With a new identity and passport he made his way to Damascus where he worked until 1960 for an American soft drinks firm before getting a job with a Syrian export company under the name of Dr Georg Fisher. In his bid for freedom, Brunner used one of several Nazi escape and welfare organizations which are still in existence today.

These groups arrange a carefully concealed journey to Rome or

Bari where for various fees ranging from £175 to £535 a head, with special rates for hardship cases, on-the-run Nazis are flown either to Spain, Portugal or South America. For quick getaways, however, the Middle East is the most favoured route. Air passages are booked by these organizations which maintain links with HIAG, the highly active German aid association for former SS men.

Another leader of the Cairo Nazis is Leopold Gleim, formerly Gestapo chief in Warsaw. Now serving in Nasser's army as Lt-Colonel A. L. Nacher, Gleim was sentenced to death in his absence by the Poles at the end of the war. Hans Appler, a former assistant of Julius Streicher, arrived in Egypt from Spain in 1955 and now works as a psychological warfare expert against Israel.

A separate group of Nazi refugees in Egypt consists of former SS officers employed by Colonel Nasser's security network. They have a different function from the Germans in the propaganda department but are closely linked with them. In the group is Joachim Daemling, a former SS major and Gestapo chief in Dusseldorf. Daemling now works as an adviser to the Egyptian security services on People's Tribunals and internment camps, and he also helped reorganize the country's police force. Heinrich Sellmann, who was a Gestapo official in Ulm, is working with Daemling under the Islamic name of Mohammed Salaiman.

The normally sombre account of Nazi war criminals finding refuge in Egypt was given a slightly comic touch by the story of SS man Hans Walter Zech-Nenntwich in 1964. Found guilty in a German court of committing war crimes, Zech-Nenntwich was sent to prison for four years but escaped from Brunswick jail shortly after conviction. Fully expecting a warm welcome from von Leers and the other criminals in hiding in Cairo, Nenntwich made his way to the Egyptian capital. But to his dismay, this former SS lieutenant was not only cold-shouldered but forced to flee to South Africa.

Nenntwich had forgotten that he had committed the sin of changing sides in the war and assisting Allied propaganda from Britain. Considered a traitor by the other Nazis in Cairo, he was eventually forced to give himself up to the Bonn authorities.

Franz Rademacher is yet another war criminal who fled from Western Germany with the charges of murdering 1,300 Jews still hanging over his head. Rademacher was tried by a German court in 1952 but escaped before final sentence had been passed and at first went to the Argentine before making his way to Egypt.

Other high-ranking SS and SA men like Major Bernard Bender, Moser, Willermann and Group-leader Bubls have also found haven in Cairo.

In 1962 the United Nations was told that Gleim and Bender were counted among the officials in control of Nasser's secret police. The United Nations was also informed that Ahmed Shukairy, chief Saudi Arabian delegate, had publicly identified himself with Nazi groups in the Argentine.

A prominent member of the German colony in Cairo is Louis Heiden, an ex-Nazi journalist from Berlin who translated *Mein Kampf* into Arabic. The first few thousand copies of this work were sold out within a few days—which gives an indication that the interest in Nazism is not confined solely to the new Germanic converts to Islam.

The man who was Egyptian Minister of Propaganda in 1956, Fathi Ridwan, was a former leader of Young Egypt, the country's fascist party. Colonel Anwar Sadat, a member of the original junta and the director of the largest publishing house in Cairo, Dar al Hilal, gave his opinion that 'Hitler was a great German patriot who had many outstanding merits and from whom we learn much, though he was not fully appreciated by his own people.'

Another official spokesman of the Nasser régime, Sami Daoud, said that 'Every Egyptian is proud to be like Goebbels'.

Out-of-work Nazi military men have been employed by successive Egyptian régimes ever since the late 1940's. Following the withdrawal of the British military mission from Cairo, Germans were given important advisory and training posts in the army, air force and navy.

These German advisers were at one time headed by General Wilhelm Fahrmbacher, who served with Rommel's Afrika Korps in the desert and whose deputy was a former SS man, Tiefenbacher. Fahrmbacher has also seen service in Russia and fought against the British and the Americans after the Allied invasion of France. He later returned to Germany where he is now living in retirement in Upper Bavaria.

Also helping to train the Egyptian army was Major-General Oscar Munzel, a Panzer officer and tank expert, and Major

Gerhard Mertens who instructed Egyptian paratroopers. In 1954
Lord Reading said in the House of Lords that there were about
eighty Germans employed at that time in the Egyptian Ministry
of War and Marine. Wilhelm Voss, the former SS officer and
deputy director of the Skoda arms works in occupied Czechoslovakia during the war, was at one time head of the German
military mission known as the Cairo Central Planning Board. His
chief job was to train Egyptians for war, but he also recruited
other ex-Nazis to come to Cairo. Otto Skorzeny also spent some
time in Egypt advising the Government on commando tactics.
Professor Heinkel, one of Germany's leading aircraft designers,
and Major-General Otto Remer, a post-war neo-Nazi chief in
Germany, have both been called upon by Egyptian Government
officials to help them with their military effort.

Remer and one of his officials in the banned Reich Party, a man
called Springer, also spent some time in Damascus.

The names of the men who have found refuge in Egypt read
like a Nazi *Who's Who*. There is Baron von Mildenstein, an ex-
chief of the Near East Bureau in Goebbels' Propaganda Ministry,
and Baron von Harder, an administrative expert in the same
department. There is also D. Werner Wietschekle, and another
Baron, Friedrich von Bechtolsheim, who was a top Nazi frogman
and who became one of Nasser's chief naval advisers. Bechtolsheim maintains business contacts in Portugal and Sweden. And in
1952 Major-General Julius Braun was to be found in the land of
the Pharaohs, together with Kurt Fuellner, who helped Hitler
build his V-2's. Ernst Zolling, the former head of the intelligence
branch of the Afrika Korps, and Captain Werner Kahl, a tank
specialist, joined the men helping the Egyptian army.

Not only Germans sought refuge in Egypt. Per Olaf Andersson,
who was a member of the Swedish Brownshirt Nazi Movement
and who worked as a photographer with the German army in
Finland, and then with the Quisling Red Horse League in
Norway, also turned up in Cairo.

It was hardly surprising that a spokesman for the West German
Trade Unions, Herr Rosenberg, commented: 'Egypt is a breed-
ing ground for new Nazis.'

Nasser relies heavily on the former Nazis of Hitler's Germany
and is influenced by their racialist and fascist theories. These
men, who operate quite openly under their own names or under

slightly disguised Islamic titles after embracing their new faith,
are in constant communication with fascist and Nazi groups in
Western Europe and Latin America.

Their ideology has not changed one iota from the 1930's and
their war-time days, and their allegiance to Nasser is based on
convenience and opportunism. Nasser is using them now, but
their objects are wider than a simple desire to serve Cairo.

The Egyptian ruler considers them useful tools, but should the
opportunity ever be presented for these Nazis to expand their
influence and activities in the Middle East and farther afield to
Europe, then they will surely grasp their chances with characteristic ruthlessness.

A striking parallel to the present situation occurred after the
First World War when the Bolsheviks provided for the Reichs-
wehr facilities which had been banned by the Versailles Treaty.
Today facilities are being provided by the Egyptians. Germans in
Egypt are dodging Allied restrictions on the development of
nuclear arms and missiles imposed on the Bonn Government.

The West Germans have made one or two half-hearted attempts
to try and halt the activities of these former Nazis or play down
their importance. But there is some evidence that there are men
in Bonn who are not too anxious that German scientists should
cease their illegal work in Egypt. For instance, Dr Gronau, who
for three years was in charge of the jet fighter production programme at Helwan, near Cairo, claims that the West German
Government approves and supports the activities of scientists
and technicians in Egypt.

Dr Gronau, who worked under Professor Messerschmitt,
returned to Germany after realizing his activities could result in a
Middle Eastern war. After changing his mind, Gronau made
repeated requests to the German Embassy in Cairo for documents
to enable him to return home, but he was encouraged to stay on
in Egypt and continue his work there. Gronau asserted that the
German Embassy military attaché told him: 'It is the wish of the
Bonn authorities and the Defence Minister (who at the time was
Herr Strauss) that the German technicians should stay on to
prevent the Russians from coming in to take their places.'

Whether this was an isolated instance or not, the fact of the
matter is that German scientists are helping Nasser's rocket
programme. This is in addition to the huge sums of economic

aid that the Bonn Government has handed over to the Egyptian leader. Taken in conjunction, these two factors have produced a situation full of danger.

During the past few years West German economic aid to Egypt has been larger than either American or Russian contributions, and since 1959 the Germans have established some eighty factories in the country—about the same number as the Russians and the Americans combined.

As a result of economic aid from both East and West, and with the help of Nazi scientists, Nasser is building up a massive military force armed with the latest equipment. So advanced is his rocket programme that Nasser's officials claim that they will soon have something like a thousand rocket missiles under their command.

These rockets include the Al Zafar (The Victor) which is capable of carrying a half-ton warhead with a range of 375 miles, and Al Raid (The Explorer) which when fully operational will have a range of over 600 miles.

The object of all this build-up is plain. Nasser is aiming at the total destruction of Israel, and he has never pretended otherwise. If he presses on with his objective, then the outcome will be another war in the Middle East, which could mean war for all mankind. It would be ironical indeed if the re-emergence of fascism—and that is exactly what is happening in Egypt—precipitated the end of Western civilization.

Index

Hoecherl, Hermann, 201, 208
Hofer, Hans, 285
Hoffmann, Wolfgang, 192
Hofman, B., 185
Hoggan, David, 207, 208
Holland, 23, 46, 173, 184–7; 197, 203
Holler, Alfons, 199
Holm, Eric, 302, 303
Holm, John 231
Honduras, 269
Hoover, Herbert, 132
House Committee on Un-American Activities, 132
Hudal, Alois, 9
Hugenberg, 208
Human Events, 132
Hungarian Centre for World-Wide Nazi Propaganda, 250
Hungarian Community Centre, 252
Hungarian Council, 250
Hungarian émigrés, 23, 72, 175, 206, 242–55; 279, 285
Hungarian Fortress, 246, 249
Hungarian Freedom Fighters, 242
Hungarian Institute for research on modern history and society, 251
Hungarian Life, 251
Hungarian Martyrs, The, 242
Hungarian National Youth, 251
Hungarian Nationalist Party, 249
Hungarian Unity, 251
Hungarian Veterans' Association, 252
Hungarian Voice of America, 249
Hungarist (*see* Arrow Cross), 250
Hungarista Mosgalom, 252
Hungary in Chains, 244
Hunt, Haroldson, 87, 106, 107
Hunt, John, 68
Husseinforder, Hans, 158
Huxley, 243

Ibero-American Institute, 266
Iceland, 231
Iglesia Catolica Espanola, 289
Ihlefeld, Per-Olof, 229
Ilia, Arturo, 294
Immigration Issue, 28–9; 33, 34, 35, 54–9; 62–4, 66, 67, 68](Great Britain); 200, 202 (Germany); 238–239 (Switzerland)
Imperial Fascist League, 45, 51
Independent American, 109

India, 304, 316
Informazione, 151
Integralist World Association, 61
Integrists, 258
Intelligence Survey, 70
International Commission of Jurists, 261, 309
International Nazi Fascist, 131
International Union of Resistance Fighters and Deportees, 18, 19
Intra, 315
Ipolyi, Geza, 250
Iraq, 276
Ireland (Eire), 17, 19, 27, 38, 39, 196, 203, 219, 254
Irish National Youth (INY), 27, 219
Irlov, Bengt, 233
Iron Guard, 206, 255
Israel, 42, 44, 61, 227, 230, 246, 251, 274, 277, 279, 284, 290, 304, 311, 314, 315, 316, 317, 318, 319, 321, 325
Israel, the Enemy of Africa, 319
Istria, 145, 146, 150
Italian elections, 142, 143, 146
Italian Social Movement (MSI), 22, 23, 24, 29, 40, 48, 140, 141, 142, 143, 145–52; 175
Italy, 15, 16, 22, 23, 28, 40, 46, 139, 140–53; 163, 165, 176, 254, 257, 262, 275

Jackson, Andrew, 110
Jackson, C. D., 104
Jaeckel, Otto C., 203
Janssens, Emil, 183
Japan, 30, 106
Jefimov, Alexai, 248
Jeune Europe, 41, 173, 174, 176, 219, 278
Jeune Légion Européenne, 174
Jeune Nation, 41, 155, 158, 159, 164, 166, 173
Jeune Révolution, 157
Jeunesse Nationale, 183
Jew, A Historical Tragedy, The, 288
Jewish People's Bank, 293
Jewish Ritual Murder, The, 109, 131
Jewish World Domination, 285
Jews Have Their Eye on You, The, 317
Jews and Their Lies, 109
Joentvedt, Einar, 235
Johansson, Allan, 224

12*